Stratospheric Ozone Damage and Legal Liability

While government enforcement of laws and regulations to control the production of chlorofluorocarbons in 1987 has been hailed as exemplifying the precautionary principle, for almost two decades US companies failed to take precautionary measures to prevent chemical emissions, despite the probable risk of stratospheric ozone loss. As a result, human harms in the form of skin cancer have reached epidemic proportions globally and in the United States where, today, one person dies every hour from skin cancer. This book reviews US laws, regulations, and policies, as well as case law regarding similar toxic tort cases to consider whether companies can and should be held legally liable under tort common law theories and related tort justice theories for having contributed to increased risks of skin cancer.

Lisa Elges is a leading climate and environmental governance policy analyst. As Head of Climate Policy at Transparency International, she has authored numerous articles on the integrity of climate and carbon finance. She holds an LL.M. in International Human Rights Law from the University of Essex, UK, and Doctorate in Political Science at the Freie Universität, Germany. She has three children and lives and works in Brussels and Berlin.

Routledge Research in International Environmental Law

Environmental Law and the Ecosystem Approach
Maintaining ecological integrity through consistency in law
Froukje Maria Platjouw

Ecological Integrity and Global Governance
Science, ethics and the law
Laura Westra

Stratospheric Ozone Damage and Legal Liability

US public policy and tort litigation to protect the ozone layer

Lisa Elges

Routledge
Taylor & Francis Group

LONDON AND NEW YORK

First published 2017
by Routledge

2 Park Square, Milton Park, Abingdon, Oxfordshire OX14 4RN
711 Third Avenue, New York, NY 10017

Routledge is an imprint of the Taylor & Francis Group, an informa business

First issued in paperback 2018

British Library Cataloguing in Publication Data
A catalogue record for this book is available from the British Library

Library of Congress Cataloging-in-Publication Data
Names: Elges, Lisa, author.
Title: Stratospheric ozone damage and legal liability : US public policy and
tort litigation to protect the ozone layer / Lisa Elges.
Description: New York : Routledge, 2016. | Series: Routledge research in
international environmental law | Includes bibliographical references and
index.
Identifiers: LCCN 2016000851| ISBN 978-1-138-64887-6 (hbk) |
ISBN 978-1-315-62616-1 (ebk)
Subjects: LCSH: Liability for environmental damages—United States. |
Ozone layer depletion—Law and legislation—United States. | Ozone layer
depletion—Government policy—United States. | Skin—Cancer—United
States. | Torts—United States.
Classification: LCC KF1299.O96 E44 2016 | DDC 344.7304/633—dc 3
LC record available at http://lccn.loc.gov/2016000851

ISBN: 978-1-138-64887-6 (hbk)
ISBN: 978-1-138-61429-1 (pbk)

Typeset in Baskerville
by FiSH Books Ltd, Enfield

To Reinhold, Malaya, Hillel and Nicolas

Contents

     10.1 Summary of conclusions to Part III   160

PART IV
Rationale, relevance and objectives of the ozone layer case   161

11 **The basis for assessing why the ozone layer case is relevant and**
     important   163
     11.1 Should tort law remedies be pursued in the ozone layer case?   166
     11.2 Are administrative remedies available, and if not, is a tort remedy
          warranted?   166
     11.3 Are other legal remedies available, and if not, is a tort remedy
          warranted?   170

12 **Tort law policy basis for the ozone layer case**   172
     12.1 Corrective justice   172
     12.2 Social justice   174
     12.3 Deterrence   180

13 **Lessons and benefits for climate change policy and litigation**   183

14 **Conclusion**   186

     Appendix: Annual production of ozone depleting substance
     globally and by US companies in the United States, 1931–2012   188

     Bibliography   193
     Index   215

Table of laws and regulations

US laws and regulations

Clean Air Act: 42 U.S.C. § 7401 et seq. (1970)
Consumer Product Safety Act: 15 U.S.C. § 2051 et seq. (1972)
Federal Food, Drug, and Cosmetic Act: 21 U.S.C. § 301 et seq. (1938)
Federal Hazardous Substances Act (FHSA): 15 U.S.C § 1261 et seq. (1960)
Toxic Substances Control Act: 15 U.S.C. § 2601 et seq. (1976)
Chlorofluorocarbon propellants (Federal Regulation): 21 C.F.R. §§ 700.23
Hazardous Substances, Administration and Enforcement (Federal Regulation): 16 C.F.R. § 1500
National Emission Standards for Hazardous Air Pollutants (Federal Regulation): 40 C.F.R § 61
Protection of Stratospheric Ozone (Federal Regulation): 40 C.F.R. § 82
Use of ozone-depleting substances in foods, drugs, devices, or cosmetics (Federal Regulation): 21 C.F.R. § 2.125

International laws and declarations

Convention for the Protection of the Ozone Layer: TIAS No. 11,097; 1513 UNTS 323; 26 ILM 1529 (1987)
Montreal Protocol on Substances that Deplete the Ozone Layer: 1522 UNTS 3; 26 ILM 1550 (1987)
Rio Declaration on Environment and Development: UN Doc. A/CONF.151/26 (vol. I); 31 ILM 874 (1992)

Table of cases

List of figures

List of tables

List of acronyms

AFEAS	Alternative Fluorocarbons Environmental Acceptability Study
CFC	Chlorofluorocarbon
CPSC	United States Consumer Product Safety Commission
EPA	United States Environmental Protection Agency
FDA	United States Food and Drug Administration
FHSA	United States Federal Hazardous Substances Act
GWP	Global Warming Potential
HCFC	Hydrochlorofluorocarbon
HFC	Hydrofluorocarbon
ICNIRP	International Commission on Non-Ionizing Radiation Protection
IMOS	United States Federal Task Force on Inadvertent Modification of the Stratosphere, Fluorocarbons and the Environment
MTBE	Methyl tertiary butyl ether
NAS	United States National Academy of Sciences
NASA	United States National Aeronautics and Space Administration
NOAA	United States National Oceanic and Atmospheric Administration
NRDC	National Resource Defence Council
ODC	Ozone Depleting Chemical
ODP	Ozone Depleting Potential
OECD	Organisation for Economic Co-operation and Development
OSHA	United States Occupational Safety and Health Administration
TSCA	United States Toxic Substances Control Act
UNEP	United Nations Environment Programme
WHO	World Health Organisation
WMO	World Metrological Organisation

Foreword and acknowledgements

This study confronts basic questions of justice and power in response to catastrophic risks. It is the story of stratospheric ozone destruction from the perspective of today's and future generations which face and will continue to endure damages over decades as a result of anthropogenic chemicals emitted into the atmosphere for over a century. This study questions the liability of corporate actors who produced and used the chemicals which have contributed to that damage. It is not, however, intended to malign those actors. To the contrary, the purpose is to explore reasonable arguments and solutions for dealing with factual injury and for devising future policies to cope with the long term impacts of commercial activities on the environment, human health and sustainable development.

This book touches on a number of complex legal and technical issues. It addresses a wide range of concerns in research areas including atmospheric science, meteorology, chemistry, physics, medicine, oncology, refrigeration and insulation technology, political science, economics and law. As such, the depth at which each of these disciplines could be studied is limited. Nevertheless, the study outlines questions where further research could be undertaken to shed light on the scientific, legal and philosophical questions raised.

Undertaking this study was a fascinating journey back in time to the political, environmental and economic struggles which were taking place during my childhood in the United States. It was a chance to reflect on how the same political debates over saving the ozone layer are dominating climate change negotiations.

I would like to express my appreciation to Durwood Zaelke, Miranda A. Schreurs and Robert V. Percival for their inspiration, supportive advice and kind criticisms to help me present and argue the more complex issues the book confronts. I must thank all my family for their patient and loving support – my parents Thomas and Ruth Prevenslik, my children, Malaya Takeda, Hillel Takeda and Nicolas Elges, and my husband, Reinhold Elges for among countless things, our balcony talks.

Part I

The ozone layer case

1 The case for stratospheric ozone damage and legal liability

1.1 Scientific evidence of ozone depletion

At the turn of the twentieth century, human beings discovered that the earth is protected by a thin layer of ozone in the stratosphere – 10–50 kilometres above the earth's surface.[1] The ozone layer prevents harmful solar ultraviolet radiation from reaching earth, making earth habitable.[2,3] It absorbs the shortest wavelengths of UV radiation known as UV-B and UV-C.[4] In the early 1970s, human beings also came to know that the ozone layer could be disappearing due to the emissions of special fluorinated chlorine and bromine chemicals.

Ozone depleting chemicals[5] most widely known as chlorofluorocarbons or CFCs were also discovered and developed during the last century.[6] The advent of these chemicals was claimed to be a miracle because they were not toxic or flammable, and could perform a range of highly useful commercial and industrial functions.[7] By the early 1970s, they were commonly used as fire suppressants, refrigerants, propelling agents, foam blowing agents and solvents.[8]

---

1   Sivasakthivel, T., K. K. Siva Kumar Reddy (2011, February). Ozone Layer Depletion and Its Effects: A Review. *International Journal of Environmental Science and Development,* 2(1).

2   National Aeronautics and Space Administration (2005). *Basics on Ozone.* Retrieved November 3, 2013, from National Aeronautics and Space Administration: www.nasa.gov/vision/earth/environment/ozone_hole101.html; US EPA (2010, August 19). *Ozone.* Retrieved November 4, 2013, from United States Environmental Protection Agency: www.epa.gov/ozone/.

3   NASA (n.d.). *The Ozone Resource Page.* nasa.gov/ozone.

4   NASA (2005, August 24). *Basics on Ozone.* It prevents UV-C entirely and 90% UV-B from reaching earth. nasa.gov/ozone

5   US EPA (2013, June 21). *Class I Ozone-depleting Substances.* www.epa.gov/ozone/science/ods/classone.html.

6   Morrisette, P. (1989).The Evolution of Policy Responses to Stratospheric Ozone. *Natural Resources Journal,* 29, 793–820. CFCs were first developed in 1928 by Thomas Midgley, a chemist working for General Motors.

7   *Ibid.*

8   *Ibid.*

In 1974, scientists Sherwood Rowland, Mario Molina and Paul Crutzen published their ozone depletion theory – concluding that damage was not only plausible but alarming given estimable amounts of the chemical emissions.[9] Their theory posited that airborne halogenated fluorocarbons travel to the stratosphere where they are broken down by the sun's ultraviolet radiation thereby freeing chlorine and bromine atoms. Those atoms then bond with ozone (O_3) to form oxygen (O_2) and chlorine monoxide (ClO) or bromine monoxide (BrO).[10] Through a three cycle process, liberated single chlorine or bromine atoms have the capacity to destroy "up to tens of thousands of ozone molecules during the total time of (their) stay in the stratosphere."[11]

In the United States, the ozone depletion theory caused wide public concern.[12] People feared serious impacts to the environment and human health, particularly in the form of skin cancer. Citizens and civil society groups called for the chemicals to be banned. They boycotted aerosol spray products and sales began to drop dramatically.[13]

The US government responded by investigating the chemical threat. In 1976 and 1977, Congress and three federal agencies declared that the chemicals posed a potentially unreasonable risk of harm to the environment and human health.[14] Regulations were passed requiring that warning labels be placed on aerosol products containing CFCs[15] and later banning the production and use of the chemicals for all such non-essential

---

9   Molina, M. J., and Rowland, F. S. (1974, June 28). Stratospheric Sink for Chlorofluoromethanes: Chlorine Atom-Catalysed Destruction of Ozone. *Nature*, 810–812. Stolarski, R. and Cicerone, R. J. (1974, January). Stratospheric Chlorine: A Possible Sink for Ozone. *Canadian Journal of Chemistry*, 52, 1610.(1) UNEP, Environmental Effects Assessment Panel 2010: *Questions and Answers about the Environmental Effects of the Ozone Layer Depletion and Climate Change: 2010 Update.*

10 Morrisette, P. (1989), *op. cit. supra* at n.6: Citing Johnston, Reduction of Stratospheric Ozone by Nitrogen Oxide Catalysts from Supersonic Transport Exhaust, 173 *Science* 517, 1971.

11 World Meteorological Organization (2011). What are the Chlorine and Bromine Reactions that Destroy Stratospheric Ozone? In *Scientific Assessment of Ozone Depletion: 2010, Global Ozone Research and Monitoring Project-Report* (Vol. 52), Geneva.

12 Harrington, W., Morgenstern, R. D., and Sterner, T. (eds) (2004). *Choosing Environmental Policy: Comparing Instruments and Outcomes in the United States and Europe.* Washington, D.C.: Resources for the Future, 160.

13 Cook, E. (1990). Global Environmental Advocacy: Citizen Activism in Protecting the Ozone Layer. *Ambio*, 19(6/7), 334–338.

14 42 U.S.C. § 7451 (repealed); Parson, E. A. (2003). Protecting the Ozone Layer: Science and Strategy. New York: Oxford University Press, 39; 43 *Fed. Reg.* 11301, 11312 (17 March 1978).

15 US Consumer Product Safety Commission. (April 1977). *FDA and CPSC Announce Fluorocarbon Labelling Plan* www.cpsc.gov/en/Newsroom/News-Releases/1977/FDA-And-CPSC-Announce-Fluorocarbon-Labeling-Plan; Reitze, A. W. (2001). *Air Pollution Control Law: Compliance and Enforcement.* Washington, D.C.: Environmental Law Institute, 388.

purposes.[16] This largely unilateral action made a successful dent in reducing ozone depleting chemical emissions from non-essential aerosol sprays.[17] However, while the Environmental Protection Agency was empowered to promulgate further regulations on the production, sale and use of CFCs and other ozone depleting chemicals for *non-aerosol* uses, such comprehensive rules did not emerge until after a global agreement, the Montreal Protocol on Substances that Deplete the Ozone Layer was reached in 1987 to control and phase out all production and consumption of the chemicals.[18]

Under the Montreal Protocol, governments initially agreed to start reducing CFC production in 1993 to achieve a 50 percent cut (based on 1986 production levels) by 1998.[19] Between 1990 and 1992, the Protocol was strengthened to prohibit the production of the most potent ozone depleting chemicals (ODCs) from 1996 in OECD countries. Developing country governments also agreed to end their reliance on most of the chemicals by 2010. In compliance, the American government imposed a CFC production freeze in 1989,[20] and adopted laws and regulations effective in 1993 to accomplish a complete ban on most ODC manufacture by the end of 1995.[21]

Today, such global resolve and precautionary actions are hailed as one of the most important achievements of the twentieth century for having avoided global catastrophe.[22] In the United States alone, an estimated 6.3

16 Federal Food, Drug and Cosmetic Act (FFDCA) 21 U.S.C. §§ 341, 342, 351, 352, 361, 362; Chlorofluorocarbon Propellants (Federal regulation regarding *Cosmetics* under *Food and Drugs*) 43 *Fed. Reg.* 11317, Mar. 17, 1978, 21 C.F.R. § 700.23; Use of ozone-depleting substances in foods, drugs, devices, or cosmetics (Federal regulation *Applicable to Specific Products Subject to the Federal Food, Drug, and Cosmetic Act*) 67 *Fed. Reg.* 48384, 21. C.F.R. 2.125; Toxic Substance Control Act (TSCA) 15 U.S.C. §§2601-2692 at §2605 (a) (1) (2) (3) (4); Fully Halogenated Chlorofluoroalkanes (Federal regulation) 40 C.F.R. §762.1 et seq. at § 762.45(a).

17 Cook, E. (ed.) (November 1996). *Ozone Protection in the United States: Elements of Success.* Washington, D.C.: World Resources Institute, 11; Morrisette, P. (1989), *op. cit. supra* at n.6 chapter 1.

18 Montreal Protocol on Substances that Deplete the Ozone Layer: 1522 UNTS 3; 26 ILM 1550 (1987).

19 *Ibid.*

20 53 *Fed. Reg.* 30566 (12 August 1988).

21 *Protection of Stratospheric Ozone* 40 C.F.R. 82.

22 Andersen, S., Halberstadt, M. L. and Borgford-Parnella, N. (2013). Stratospheric Ozone, Global Warming, and the Principle of Unintended Consequences—An Ongoing Science and Policy Success Story. *Journal of the Air & Waste Management Association*, 63(6), 607–647; Benedick, R. E. (1998). *Ozone Diplomacy: New Directions in Safeguarding the Planet.* Cambridge, Massachusetts: Harvard University Press; Kaniaru, D., Shende, R., Stone, S. and Durwood, Z. (2007). Strengthening the Montreal Protocol: Insurance against Abrupt Climate Change. *Sustainable Development Law & Policy*, 7(2), 3–9. Morrisette, P. (1989), *op. cit. supra* at n.6. Percival, R. V. (1997). Responding to Environmental Risk: A Pluralistic Perspective. *Pace Environmental Law Review*, 14(2), 513–529; Sunstein, C. R. (2007). *Worst-case Scenarios.* Cambridge: Harvard University Press; United National Environment Programme (2007). *A Success in the Making: The Montreal Protocol on Substances that Deplete*

million skin cancer deaths and 22 million cataract illnesses have been averted.[23]

While the successes achieved from the 1990s onwards are rightly praised, the problem remains that production, use and emissions of ozone depleting chemicals up until that point have nevertheless had serious impacts on the environment and human health. The ozone layer has been damaged. Stratospheric ozone over the Polar Regions and mid-latitudes continues to be broken down by ODCs.[24] In 2015, the "ozone hole" over Antarctica was the second largest observed over the past 36 years estimated at 28.2 million km². [25] As a result, skin cancer prevalence has increased globally.[26] In the United States, the disease has become a national health problem.[27] It is estimated that melanoma incidence rates have increased 300 percent since 1975.[28] Today, approximately five million adults are treated for skin cancer each year.[29] One person dies every hour.[30] Skin cancers can be prevented by avoiding mid-day sun exposure but this means that vulnerable people must curtail daytime outdoor recreational and employment activities. This

the Ozone Layer. Kenya, United National Environment Programme; Morone, J. G. *et al.* (1986). *Threats to the Ozone Layer* in *Averting Catastrophe: Strategies for Regulating Risky Technologies.* Berkley: University of California Press; Kauffman, J. (1997). A Case Study of the Montreal Protocol. In M. A. Schreurs and E. C. Economy (eds), *The Internationalization of Environmental Protection*, 74–96, Cambridge: Cambridge University Press.

23   United National Environment Programme (n.d.). *Key Achievements of the Montreal Protocol to date 1987–2012.*

24   Shepherd, T. G. *et al.* (2014). Reconciliation of Halogen-induced Ozone Loss with the Total-column Ozone Record. *Nature Geoscience.* See also Knibbe, J., van der A, R. and de Laat, A. (2014). Spatial Regression Analysis on 32 Years Total Column Ozone Data. *Atmospheric Chemistry and Physics Discussion*, (14), 5323–5373. Discussing other factors affecting ozone layer depletion such as volcanic eruptions and the solar cycle but determining chlorine loading as the most important factor attributable to stratospheric ozone loss, 5347; Butler, J., Montzka, S., Clarke, A., Lobert, J., & Elkins, J. (1998, January 20). Growth and Distribution of Halons in the Atmosphere. *Journal of Geophysical Research*, 103, 1503–1511.

25   International Commission on Non Ionizing Radiation Protection (2010). ICNIRP Statement on Protection of Workers against Ultraviolet Radiation. *Health Physics,* 99(1), 66–87, at 70–71.

26   World Health Organisation. (2014). *How Common is Skin Cancer?* Retrieved from Ultraviolet radiation and the INTERSUN Programme: www.who.int/uv/faq/skin-cancer/en/index1.html

27   US Department of Health and Human Services (2014). *The Surgeon General's Call to Action to Prevent Skin Cancer.* Washington, D.C.: US Dept of Health and Human Services, Office of the Surgeon General (hereinafter, Surgeon General's Report (2014).

28   American Cancer Society. (2013). *Cancer Facts and Figures 2013.* Atlanta, Georgia, USA, at 4; American Cancer Society. (2014). *Cancer Facts and Figures 2014.* Atlanta, Georgia: American Cancer Society Inc., at 4.

29   *Id.* at 4.

30   Surgeon General's Report (2014), *op. cit. supra* at n.27 chapter 1, at 1, 4–5: Young adults are in the age group 15–39.

includes children who are more sensitive to radiation exposure.[31]

Taking these issues into consideration, this book calls into question the liability of the US chemical companies for aggravating damages to US citizens and States by producing and marketing ODCs prior to regulatory controls which came into effect in 1993. This is the *ozone layer case*. The case is premised on the precautionary principle which asserts that: "Where there are threats of serious or irreversible damage, lack of full scientific certainty shall not be used as a reason for postponing cost-effective measures to prevent environmental degradation".[32]

The case concerns the conduct of US based companies with regard to injuries sustained by US citizens and States. This focus is adopted given the considerable share of global ODC production occupied by US chemical manufacturers and the availability of skin cancer data collected by US public agencies based on which damages and injuries can be assessed.

The case alleges that between 1976 and 1992, the former ODC manufacturers increased production and sales of the chemicals domestically and globally, directly emitted ODCs during manufacturing processes and prior to sale, and failed to warn their purchasers of the harms the chemicals could cause. It is proposed that liability may begin from 1976 when Congress and federal agencies asserted their endangerment findings i.e. that the chemicals posed an unreasonable risk of harm, based on which regulatory actions were initiated. The period would end in 1992, as from 1993 comprehensive regulations came into effect requiring that ODC production be curbed, that emissions control technologies be used and that warning labels be applied.[33]

As a hypothetical case, it argues the liability of the companies based on common law tort theories of negligence, strict product liability defective product and failure to warn, and public nuisance. With respect to each of these theories, the case proposes that the alleged conduct of the companies was a substantial factor in bringing about injuries endured today by US citizens and States and that such conduct was wrongful because the probable risk of unreasonable harm was of such great magnitude that it outweighed precautionary costs, i.e. the costs to prevent future damage from happening. The public nuisance theory further contends that the alleged conduct

---

31 World Health Organisation. (2003). *Climate Change and Human Health: Risks and Responses*. Geneva: WHO; Cercato, M., *et al.* (2013, March). Improving Sun-Safe Knowledge, Attitude and Behaviour in Parents of Primary School Children: A Pilot Study. *Journal of Cancer Education*, 28(1), 151–157; US Preventive Services Task Force. (2003, October). *Counselling to Prevent Skin Cancer*.

32 UN Doc. A/CONF.151/26 (vol. I); 31 ILM 874 (1992): Rio Declaration on Environment and Development, Principle 15.

33 *National Emission Standards for Hazardous Air Pollutant*s 40 C.F.R. §§ 61, 63; *Protection of Stratospheric Ozone* 40 C.F.R. §§ 82.5, 82.6, 82.106.

contributed to damaging a global public good[34] and that has created an interference with public rights to health and enjoyment of the environment.

Exploring the *ozone layer case*, or the broader issue of stratospheric ozone damage and legal liability is a valuable and novel undertaking[35] because it provides important findings to address current and future stratospheric ozone damage and climate change impacts. As a personal injury suit, the case has never been attempted or studied in depth.[36] Aside from a reference that Ozone Action and Greenpeace had prepared but abandoned to sue chemical manufacturers for skin cancer and other damages,[37] no litigation seems to have been proposed. This is remarkable considering that legal actions have been initiated to demand remedies in response to global warming. In contrast to climate change litigation where proving causation has been unmanageable,[38] the *ozone layer case* vies as a near prima facie case:

34   Barrett, S. (2007). *Why Cooperate?: The Incentive to Supply Global Public Goods.* Oxford University Press. Blackden, C. M. (2009). *Gender Equality and Global Public Goods: Some Reflections on Shared Priorities.* OECD. Choi, E. K., Hartigan, J. C. (2008). *Handbook of International Trade: Economic and Legal Analyses of Trade Policy.* John Wiley & Sons, 164. *Edwards v. Post Transportation Co.*, 228 Cal. App. 3d 980 (App. 4th D. Cal. 1991); Ferroni, M. and Mody, A. (2002). *International Public Goods: Incentives, Measurement, and Financing.* Washington, D.C. *Fischer v. Johns-Manville Corp.*, 512 A. 2d 466 (1986); Campbell, H. E. *et al.* (2012). Urban Environmental Policy Analysis. U.S.A: 28. Barkin, J. S., *et al.* (1999). *Anarchy and the Environment: The International Relations of Common Pool Resources.* SUNY Press, at 101–102; Jones, R. J. (2002). *Routledge Encyclopaedia of International Political Economy.* Routledge, 573. Pearce, D. W. (2002). *Capturing Global Environmental Value.* London: Earthscan Publ., 28–29.

35   An extensive review of case law and relevant literature conducted throughout this study has revealed that no tort litigation has been brought by citizens, interest groups or States against corporate producers or users of ODCs for injuries resulting from stratospheric ozone loss.

36   However, citizens' actions have been brought against local and federal government bodies to urge that federal regulations be enforced or be strengthened. See *Covington v. Jefferson County*, 358 F. 3d 626 (9th Cir. 2004); The Natural Resources Defense Council v. EPA, 440 F. 3d 476 (D.C. Cir., 2006). Natural Resources Defense Council v. EPA, 464 F.3d 1 (D.C. Cir., 2006); Doniger, D. and Quibell, M. (2007). *Back from the Brink: How NRDC Helped Save the Ozone Layer.* New York: Natural Resources Defense Council, at 4–5; Collins, C. (2010). *Toxic Loopholes: Failures and Future Prospects for Environmental Law.* New York: Cambridge University Press, at 166.

37   Andersen, S. O. and Sarma, K. M. (2002). *Protecting the Ozone Layer: The United Nations History.* UK, USA: Earth Scan, Ltd., United Nations Environmental Programme at 331 (Table 9.1).

38   Three well known cases include: *Conn. v. Am. Elec. Power Co.*, 582 F. 3d 309 (2nd Cir. 2009), reversed by *American Elec. Power Co., Inc. v. Connecticut*, 131 S.Ct. 2527 (S. Ct., 2011); *Kivalina v. Exxon Mobile*, No. 09-17490, 696 F.3d 849 (9th. Cir., 2012); *Comer v. Murphy Oil USA*, 585 F. 3d 855, 859–860 (5th Cir. 2009), dismissed on other grounds in *Comer v. Murphy Oil USA*, 607 F. 3d 1049, 1053–55 (5th Cir. 2010). In *Comer*, the plaintiffs who were victims of Hurricane Katarina claimed punitive and compensatory damages not only from heavy emitting fossil fuel corporations but from chemical companies including Du Pont, Dow Chemical, and Honeywell.

the limited number, names and market shares of former ODC producers (and their successors) world-wide are known and their past activities are scientifically linked with increased skin cancer prevalence. With a few exceptions, no intervening causes upset the causality chain.[39]

Further, although the story of stratospheric ozone protection has been studied extensively under various disciplines,[40] the liability question regarding the conduct of the ODC producers has received little attention. Some writers have suggested that the companies acted negligently[41] and also that the threat of tort litigation over skin cancer damages may have influenced American CFC producers to support regulatory controls to protect the ozone layer.[42] One 1990 Canadian law journal article discusses the limits of private law to influence market behaviour in the absence of regulatory controls.[43] The article analyses that it would be daunting to prove causation in *ozone layer case* type litigation for three reasons: (1) Legal bias in favour of the ozone depleting chemical industry and against the victims due to misinformation publicised by the industry which portrayed the ozone problem as inconsequential;[44] (2) Scientific uncertainty regarding the

---

39   See Chapter 4, Section 3 Proximate Cause *infra*.
40   Andersen (2002), *op. cit. supra* at n.37 chapter 1. Among others, this publication is one of the first comprehensive documentaries of US global policy development; Liftin, K. T. (1995). *Ozone Discourses: Science and Politics in Global Environmental Cooperation*. New York: Colombia University Press, Chapter 4 (hereinafter, Liftin (1995));. Benedick (1998), *op. cit. supra* at n.22, at 314; Parson (2003), *op. cit. supra* at n.14, at 174; Percival, R. V. (2005). *Who's Afraid of the Precautionary Principle, Legal Studies Research Paper No. 2005 – 62*. University of Maryland School of Law at 2, 53–54; Kauffman, J. M. (1997). Domestic and International Linkages in Global Environmental Politics: A Case Study of the Montreal Protocol in M. Schreurs (ed.), *The Internationalisation of Environmental Protection*. Cambridge: Cambridge University Press at 74–75, 95; Schreurs, M. (2004). *Environmental Politics in Japan, Germany, and the United States*. Cambridge University Press at 144; Grundmann, R. (1998). *The Protection of the Ozone Layer*. UN Vision Project on Global Policy Networks at 32–33; Farman, J. (2002). Halocarbons, the Ozone Layer and the Precautionary Principle. In Harremoes, D., Gee, M., MacGarvin, Stirling, A., Keys, J., Wynne, B. *et al.* (eds), *The Precautionary Principle in the 20th Century: Late Lessons for Early Warnings*. Earthscan; Megie, G. (2006). From Stratospheric Ozone to Climate Change: Historical Perspective on Precaution and Scientific Responsibility. *Science and Engineering Ethics*, 12(4), 596–606; Razman, M. R., Hadi, A., Jamaluddin, M., Shah, A., Sani, S. and Yusoff, G. (2009). Negotiations of the Montreal Protocol to Protect Global Ozone Layer (O3) from Chlorofluorocarbons (CFCS) by Using UNEP as Global Forum in Promoting the Precautionary Principle Based on Global Environmental Governance and Law Perspectives. *Research Journal of Biological Sciences*, 765–772.
41   Cagin, S. and Dray, (1993). *Between Earth and Sky: How CFCs Changed our World and Endangered the Ozone Layer*. New York: Pantheon Books at 354.
42   Roan, S. (1990). *Ozone Crisis: The 15-Year Evolution of a Sudden Global Emergency*. New York: Wiley, 193. See also, Rowlands, I. H. (1995). The Politics of Atmospheric Change. Manchester: Manchester University Press, at 113; Collins, C. (2010), at 197, *op. cit. supra* at n.36; Andersen (2002), *op. cit. supra* at n.37 chapter 1, at 205.
43   Elrifi, I. (1990). Protection of the Ozone Layer: A Comment on the Montreal Protocol. *McGill Law Journal*, 387–423 at 399–401, 422.

causal link between ozone depleting chemical releases and environmental and human damages;[45] (3) The lack of material damage to prove causation.[46] Regarding the latter, the "delay between (chemical) release and damage" would be critical because the damages were not yet visible enough and would not likely become manifest for decades.[47] Further, to the extent the injuries would be widespread, the legal standard of demonstrating special injury under nuisance law would present additional difficulties.[48]

This book essentially picks up where that article left off. It bares challenges and opportunities for the US common law of torts to provide a remedy for skin cancer maladies and to deter future injuries by establishing a precautionary duty of care policy with respect to activities that pose unreasonable risks to the environment and human well-being despite scientific uncertainties. It confronts issues of injustice with regard to future generations that bear uninsurable, long-term damages caused latently by corporate business activities predicated in the last century. The investigation reaffirms the importance of the precautionary principle by squarely addressing the direct consequences of delaying environmental regulation. As such, this analysis may serve as a litmus test for similar cases to be pursued in other jurisdictions and against former ODC producers based in other countries. Importantly, it provides a formidable basis to hasten corporate actions to address climate change by mitigating greenhouse gas emissions and thereby insuring against future damages.

1.2 Outline of the book

As introduced above, the main purpose of this book is to test the viability of the case for legal liability for stratospheric ozone damage. To that end, the study is divided into four main parts. The first part is the case description. It begins with outlining the main contours of the case. This is advanced in the next chapter which is focused on the case defendants. It explains which US chemicals companies would be joined as defendants and the basis for their selection. This is followed by a statement of alleged counts of liability under the theories of negligence, strict product liability and public nuisance. The ensuing section provides evidence based on publicly available information regarding the defendants' knowledge of unreasonable risks of harm, their failure to warn about their product dangers, their dissemination of information touting that their products were safe, their increased production and sales of the products, and their failure to prevent emissions by not employing emissions capture

---

44   *Id.* at 396–399.
45   *Id.* at 399.
46   *Id.* at 400
47   *Ibid.*
48   *Id.* at 400–401.

technologies during the chemical production phase and by delaying the commercialisation of safe chemical replacements.

Chapter 3 proceeds to describe who the plaintiffs in the *ozone layer case* could be suggesting that individuals or US States could potentially bring a claim. It then describes the injuries and damages which have resulted from emissions of ozone depleting chemicals. The discussion includes the current state of stratospheric ozone loss, the impact on climate change, and increased skin cancer incidence and death rates in the United States. Regarding the latter, an attempt is made to assess the economic and non-economic damages born by individuals and US States. Based on this and the market share information presented in Chapter 2, the next section suggests a model to assess and apportion the financial liability of the defendants.

Part II of the book tests the *ozone layer case* on common law tort theories of negligence, strict product liability and public nuisance. Therein, Chapter 4 discusses the application of negligence and strict product liability theories together given their close overlap. It begins by exploring the statutory and common law duties of care which would be applicable to the defendants. It delves into whether causation and proximate cause can be established. Finally, it assesses the existence of injuries and damages. Chapter 5 proceeds by examining the applicability of the public nuisance theory. It questions whether an unreasonable interference with public rights as well as particularised harms can be demonstrated.

Part III turns to the possible defences which the defendants could argue to limit their liability. It begins with Chapter 6 which discusses whether statutes of limitations and repose could bar the *ozone layer case*. Chapter 7 looks at whether the suit would be pre-empted under the Clean Air Act. The next three chapters assess the viability of defendants contending the regulatory compliance, sophisticated intermediary and open and obvious risk defences.

The aim of Part IV of the book is to revisit the relevance, purpose and objectives of the *ozone layer case* in the broader context of environmental protection policy and the goals of tort common law to advance social policies to prevent and remedy wrongful conduct. Chapter 11 calls into question whether a common law action should be pursued by the plaintiffs based on a review of what other remedies might be available to them. Chapter 12 turns to examine how and if the purposes of tort law would be achieved in trying the case. This focus on tort law aims to achieve corrective and social justice and deterrence, looking in particular at the legal and economic impacts of a plaintiff favourable judgement. Chapter 13 looks at similar questions through the lens of legal and policy challenges in addressing climate change. It attempts to pull from foregoing discussions specific lessons and recommendations in support of precautionary action to limit global warming. The final chapter summarises the key findings of the book and presents some issues for further study and reflection.

2 Case defendants and evidence

2.1 The defendants

The defendants in the *ozone layer case* would comprise the companies which formerly produced and sold ozone depleting chemicals during 1976–1992, and where relevant, their successor companies. In most cases, such companies can be identified by name, what chemicals they produced and what their production market share was. The only information gap exists with respect to the producers of Carbon tetrachloride. Thus, between 1976 and 1992, the 20 known producers were: Akzo Chemicals, Inc., Allied-Signal, Degussa Corporation, Ansul, Dow Chemical, DuPont, Elf Atochem North America, Inc., Ethyl Corporation, FMC Corporation, Great Lakes Chemical Corporation, Hanlin Chemicals, Inc., ICI Americas, Kaiser Aluminum and Chemicals, Laroche Chemicals, Occidental Chemical Corporation, Pennwalt, PPG Industries, Racon, Stauffer Chemicals, and Vulcan Materials.[1] Today, the corporate identify of most chemical producers has changed due to various mergers and acquisitions. Yet, it is possible to identify their successor companies most of which continue in the same line of business. To the extent that successor liability may be pursued,[2] the companies which would be named as defendants in the *ozone layer case* would include the following 11 companies: Airgas, AkzoNobel, Albemarle Corporation, Arkema, Chemtura, Dow Chemical, DuPont, Honeywell, OxyChem, PPG Industries and Solvay Solexis. The following Table 2.1 attempts to capture this changing landscape of ODC producers from the 1970s to present day.

---

1   See Table 2.1 which attempts to record the US companies which were active in producing ozone depleting chemicals.

2   *Ramirez v. Amsted Industries, Inc.*, 431 A. 2d 811 (N.J. 1981) at 358 (Liability of successor company remains intact if the successor company continues the same line of manufacturing as the predecessor); Beyer, J. (2005). Left Holding the Bag? Understanding the Successor Liability Defense. *In-House Defense Quaterly*, 20.

Table 2.1 Former ozone depleting chemical manufacturers and their successors (1976–2015)

Chlorofluorocarbons

Companies (1976–1980)	Market share 1980[1]	Companies (1980–1990)	Market share 1986[2]	Companies 1990 to present	Current business
DuPont	55%		57%	DuPont → Chemours Company (2015)[3]	Supplier of fluoroproducts and industrial chemicals
Allied-Signal Corporation	22%		28%	Allied Signal → Honeywell (1999)[4]	Honeywell continues to produce a wide range of chemical products including CFC replacement gases.[5]
Pennwalt Corporation	10%	Elf Atochem North America, Inc.[6]	18%	Elf Atochem → Solvay Solexis, Inc.[7] and Arkema, Inc. (now owned by Total).[8] Solvay sells	Both Arkema and Solvay continue to sell substitutes: Forane[9] and Solkane.[10]
Racon, Inc.	3%				
Kaiser Aluminum and Chemicals, Inc.	9%	Laroche Chemicals[11]	10%	Laroche → Airgas (2005)[12]	Airgas Specialty Products which now sells chlorofluorocarbon replacement gases for various uses.[13]

Halon gases

Companies (1976–1980)	Market share 1980[14]	Companies (1980–1990)	Market share 1986[15]	Companies 1990 to present	Current business
DuPont[16]		DuPont	55%	See above	See above
Ansul[16]		Ansul[17]	0%		

Table 2.1 continued

Companies (1976–1980)	Market share 1980[14]	Companies (1980–1990)	Market share 1986[15]	Companies 1990 to present	Current business
The Great Lakes Chemical Corporation[18]		The Great Lakes Chemical Corporation	34%	Great Lakes Chemical Corporation → Chemtura[19]	Chemtura continues the Great Lakes business in offering halon gas replacement products and technology in flame retardant and bromine solution areas.[20]
ICI Americas, Inc.[21]		ICI Americas, Inc.	11%	ICI Americas → AkzoNobel (2008)	Retains speciality chemical business

Carbon tetrachloride

Companies (1976–1980)	Market share 1980[22]	Companies (1980–1990)	Market share 1986[23]	Companies 1990 to present	Current business
Dow Chemical		Dow Chemical	37%	Dow Chemical[24]	All 3 corporations continue to produce and sell carbon tetrachloride but restrict buyers and use for feedstock purposes only.[25]
Vulcan materials		Vulcan materials	43%	Vulcan Chemicals → Occidental Chemical Corporation[26] (2005) → OxyChem[27]	
Stauffer Chemical		Stauffer Chemical → Akzo Chemicals, Inc.	15%	Akzo Chemicals, Inc. → AkzoNobel[28]	
Allied Chemical		ICI Americas, Inc.	2%		
FMC Corporation		unknown			

Companies (1976–1980)	Market share 1980[31]	Companies (1980–1990)	Market share 1986[32]	Companies 1990 to present	Current business
DuPont		DuPont	<1%	See above	
		Hanlin Chemicals-WV, Inc	<1%	unknown	
		Occidental Chemical Corp	2%	See above re Vulcan	
		Degussa Corporation	<1%	Degussa Corporation → Evonik Industries (2007)[29]	

Methyl chloroform[30]

Companies (1976–1980)	Market share 1980[31]	Companies (1980–1990)	Market share 1986[32]	Companies 1990 to present	Current business
Dow Chemical		Dow Chemical	63%	Dow Chemical	Dow Chemical
Vulcan Materials		See above	28%	See above	See above
PPG Industries		PPG Industries	9%	PPG Industries	PPG Industries

Methyl bromide

Companies (1976–1980)	Market share 1980[33]	Companies (1980–1990)	Market share 1986[34]	Companies 1990 to present	Current business
Dow Chemical		Dow Chemical → Ethyl Corporation (1986)		Dow Chemical	Dow Chemical
Ethyl Corporation		Ethyl Corporation	70%	Ethyl Corporation → Albemarle Corporation (1994)[35]	Albemarle continues same business[36] having been issued critical use allowance by the federal government.[37]
Great Lakes Chemical Corporation		See above	30%	See above	Chemtura

Notes:

1 Mooz, W. E., Wolf, K. A. and Camm, F. (1986). *Potential Constraints on Cumulative Global production of Chlorofluorocarbons.* Santa Monica, California: Rand Corporation at 10, Table 3.

2 See production allowance data based on 1986 production levels in the United States in *Protection of Stratospheric Ozone* 40 C.F.R. §82.5.

3 The set-up of the DuPont subsidiary took place on February 1, 2015. www.fluorogistx.com/chemours-company-dupont-to-spin-off-fluoropolymer-division/

4 Deutsch, C. H. (1999, June 7). Allied Signal and Honeywell to Announce Merger Today. *New York Times.*

5 Honeywell International Inc. (2014). *Chemicals, Specialty Materials and Fertilizers.* Retrieved January 29, 2014, from Honeywell: http://honeywell.com/Products-Services/Pages/chemicals.aspx#Solvents, Reagents and Aerosols.

6 *Ibid.:* Pennwalt's fluorocarbon business and Racon, Inc. were bought by Elf Atochem, N.A.

7 Bloomberg BusinessWeek. (2014, January 29). *Chemicals: Company Overview of Solvay Solexis, Inc.* Retrieved from http://investing.businessweek.com/research/stocks/private/snapshot.asp?privcapId=4319716; Solvay (2014, January 15). *History.* Retrieved from About Solvay: www.solvay.com/en/about-solvay/history/index.html: Solvay was one of the main global CFC producers in Europe.

8 Akema (n.d.). *The Creation and Growth of the Arkema Group.* Retrieved January 2, 2014, from Arkema History: www.arkema.com/en/arkema-group/history/index.html.

9 Arkema (2014). *Forane.* Retrieved from Products: www.arkema-americas.com/en/products/product-portal/range-viewer/Forane/?back=true.

10 Solvay (2013, October 12). *Welcome to SOLKANE® – A brand by Solvay Fluor.* Retrieved from Solvay Products: www.solvaychemicals.com/EN/products/Fluor/solkane.aspx.

11 Airgas. (2005, July 1). *Airgas Completes Acquisition of LaRoche Industries Ammonia Distribution Business.* Retrieved from Airgas Press Releases: www.airgas.com/content/pressReleases.aspx?PressRelease_ID=1164: Kaiser Aluminum and Chemical Corporation's CFC works seems to have been sold to LaRoche Chemicals, another chemical giant engaged traditionally in fertilizer, chlorine and ammonia refrigerant markets.

12 *Ibid.*

13 Airgas (2013). *Refrigerant Gases.* Retrieved from Airgas Products: www.airgas.com/browse/product_list.aspx?catID=316&WT.svl=316.

14 Mooz, *et al.* (1986). *op. cit. supra* at n.1, at 10, Table 3.

15 See production allowance data based on 1986 production levels in the United States in *Protection of Stratospheric Ozone* 40 C.F.R. §82.5.

16 Ford, C. L. (1975). An Overview of Halon 1301 Systems. *American Chemical Society Symposium Series.* Washington, D.C.: American Chemical Society: DuPont and the Ansul Company made Halon 1301 and Halon 1211 commercially available from the 1960s and 1970s, respectively.

17 By 1986, Ansul had dropped out of the market, see Ansul Incorporated (2004). *Ansulex R-102 material safety data sheet:* www.wellsbloomfield.com/oldsite/new-bloomfield-ind/~WELLS/WELLS%20LIBRARY/WELLS%20Agency%20Docs/Ansulex%20R-102%20MSDS.pdf; Tyco. (2013). *ANSUL History.:* www.ansul.com/en/us/Pages/OurHistory.aspx?value=Our History

18 Chemtura. (2014) *About Chemtura: Historical Timeline.* Retrieved from Chemtura: www.chemtura.com/corporatev2/v/index.jsp?vgnextoid=cfa9708b7507d210VgnVCM10000007538l0aRCRD&vgnextchannel=cfa9708b7507d210VgnVCM10000007538l0aRCRD&vgnextfmt=default.

19 *Ibid.*

20 *Ibid.*

21 Although not much is known about ICI Americas, Inc., the company also entered the market at some point after it was established in the US as a part of the British Imperial Chemical Industries (ICI) in 1970, see Syngenta (2013). *Company History.* Retrieved May 2014, from Syngenta:

www.syngenta.com/global/corporate/en/about-syngenta/Pages/company-history.aspx.

22 Mooz, *et al.* (1986), *op. cit. supra* at n.1, at 10, Table 3.

23 See production allowance data based on 1986 production levels in the United States in *Protection of Stratospheric Ozone* 40 C.F.R. §82.5.

24 The Dow Chemical Company (1995–2014) (n.d.). *Dow Chlorinated Organics.* Retrieved May 12, 2014, from Dow: www.dow.com/gco/prod/c_tetra.htm.

25 Akzo Nobel N.V. (2014). *Carbon Tetrachloride.* Retrieved May 12, 2014, from AkzoNobel Industrial Chemicals: www.akzonobel.com/ic/products/carbon_tetrachloride/; The Dow Chemical Company (1995–2014) (n.d.). *Dow Chlorinated Organics.* Retrieved May 12, 2014, from Dow: www.dow.com/gco/prod/c_tetra.htm; Occidental Chemical Corporation (2010, July 13). *Carbon Tetrachloride Safety Data Sheet.* Retrieved May 12, 2014, from OxyChem: http://sds.oxy.com/private/document.aspx?prd=M47013~~PDF~~MTR~~ANSI~~EN~~2010-12-17%2011:35:15.0~~Carbon%20 Tetrachloride,%20Technical%20Grade; Occidental Petroleum Corporation (n.d.). *Chlorine and Derivatives.* Retrieved May 12, 2014, from Our Business: www.oxy.com/ourbusinesses/chemicals/products/pages/chlorineandderivatives.aspx.

26 Vulcan Materials Company (2013). *Company History.* Retrieved May 2, 2014, from About Vulcan: www.vulcanmaterials.com/about-vulcan/history.

27 OxyChem is owned by the Occidental Petroleum Corporation: Occidental Petroleum Corporation (n.d.). *Historical Highlights.* Retrieved May 12, 2014, from Oxy: www.oxy.com/AboutOxy/WhoWeAre/Pages/HistoricalHighlights.aspx.

28 Akzo Nobel N.V. (2014), *op. cit. supra* at n.2.

29 See http://history.evonik.com/sites/geschichte/en/predecessor-companies/degussa/pages/default.aspx

30 Morrison, R., Murphy, B. L. and Mudge, S. (2013). *Chlorinated Solvents: A Forensic Evaluation.* Cambridge: Royal Society of Chemistry at 187–188.

31 Mooz, *et al.* (1986), *op. cit. supra* at n.1, at 10, Table 3.

32 See production allowance data based on 1986 production levels in the United States in *Protection of Stratospheric Ozone* 40 C.F.R. §82.5.

33 Mooz, *et al.* (1986), *op. cit. supra* at n.1, at 10, Table 3.

34 See production allowance data based on 1986 production levels in the United States in *Protection of Stratospheric Ozone* 40 C.F.R. §82.5.

35 *Albemarle Corporation* (1997, March 31). Retrieved May 2, 2014, from Corpwatch: www.corpwatch.org/article.php?id=901; Albemarle Corporation (2011, April 7). *History.* Retrieved May 2, 2014, from Albemarle: www.albemarle.com/about/history-10.html.

36 Albemarle Corporation (2014, April 16). *Agricultural Actives and Intermediates.* Retrieved May 2, 2014, from Albemarle: www.albemarle.com/products—markets/performance-chemicals/fine-chemistry-services/agricultural-actives—intermediates-673.html.

37 *Protection of Stratospheric Ozone* 40 C.F.R. §82.8.

2.2 Liability allegations

The *ozone layer case* alleges that the defendants are liable under tort law theories of negligence, strict product liability regarding defective products and failure to warn, and public nuisance. The specific counts of liability include:

- **Negligence and strict product liability for marketing defective products:** The defendants could be liable for not exercising their duty of care in introducing into the stream of commerce products which were defective in design. Ozone depleting chemicals may have been defective in design because:
  - The chemicals posed potential unreasonable risks of harm to the environment and human health.
  - The companies could have introduced safe alternative technology into the stream of commerce much earlier than they did because such technology was available and feasible.
  - The companies failed to attach warning labels to their products informing of their potential harms and rather promoted information that the products were safe.
- **Negligence for increased production and sale of ozone depleting chemicals:** The defendants could be liable for having increased their domestic and global production and sales of ODCs despite their awareness of unreasonable risks of potentially great magnitude and irreversibility.
- **Negligence for not preventing emissions.** The defendants could be liable for failing to prevent ODC emissions by:
  - directly emitting the chemicals into the environment during production and pre-sale stages in the absence of employing emissions capture technologies;
  - delaying the availability and feasibility of safe alternative technologies and their introduction into the stream of commerce.
- **Public nuisance:** As a consequence of the defendants' activities, they may have created an environmental condition in which vulnerable individuals face increased risks of skin cancer. This interferes with the public rights to health, safety, employment and enjoyment of the environment.

The evidence base on which these theories are pursued is discussed next.

2.3 Evidence

Based on the above allegations, this section provides evidence based on publicly available information as a basis for assessing liability in Chapters 4 and 5. The evidence regarding public nuisance liability is discussed in Chapter 3 as it is more associated with the damage caused as a result of the alleged behaviours.

2.3.1 Evidence that the producers could have known an unreasonable risk of harm existed

As stated in the introduction to this book, the liability period explored is 1976 to 1992. This section reviews how the risks of unreasonable harm were perceived by the mid-1970s and what information was and was not known by the government and industry within the United States at that point in history. It also looks at what was reportedly known in science, how public policy understood the risks, and how industry interpreted both science and politics.

In the 1960s and 1970s, in tandem with developments in space and high speed flight travel, scientists hypothesised and conducted research to assess the impacts certain chemicals could have on the earth's protective radiation shield. Beginning in the 1950s, British meteorologists began taking physical measurements of stratospheric ozone at the Halley Bay Observatory in Antarctica, using a Dobson Spectrophotometer.[3] That research observed a thinning of the ozone layer beginning around 1965.[4] Around that time, the United States government also conducted a number of satellite missions to further investigate the ozone layer in relation to UV radiation.[5] These initial research efforts gave way to scientific postulations that the ozone layer was being depleted as a result of man-made industrial gases.[6]

Early 1970s research in the United States examined the impacts of emissions from Super Sonic Transport (SST),[7] space shuttles,[8] nuclear tests and fertilisers[9] on the ozone layer. Emerging from the research was that both nitrogen (from SSTs)[10] and chlorine (from space shuttles)[11] compounds

---

3 NASA (2013, September). *History of the Ozone Hole.*

4 *Ibid.*

5 NASA (2013, May). *Missions.*

6 Morone, J. G. *et al.* (1986), *op. cit. supra* at n.22 chapter 1. Citing Boeing Scientist Alters SST View, *The New York Times*, August 27, 1970, 19; Molina and Rowland (1974). Stratospheric Sink for Chlorofluoromethanes: Chlorine Atom-Catalysed Destruction of Ozone, *Nature*, 249, 810; Also Stolarski and Cicerone (1974). Stratospheric Chlorine: A Possible Sink for Ozone, *Can. J. Chemistry*, 52, 1610.

7 Morone, J. G. *et al.* (1986), *op. cit. supra* at n.22 chapter 1, at 78, citing Boeing Scientist Alters SST View, *The New York Times*, August 27, 1970, 19; 3. *Ibid.* Also Halstead Harrison (1970). Stratospheric Ozone with Added Water Vapor: Influence of High-Altitude Aircraft, *Science* 170, 734–36; 4. Study of Critical Environmental Problems (SCEP) (1970). *Man's Impact on the Global Environment: Assessment and Recommendations for Action.* Cambridge: MIT Press, 16; *The New York Times*, May 18, 1971, 78; Johnston, H.S. (1971). Reduction of Stratospheric Ozone by Nitrogen Oxide Catalysts from Supersonic Transport Exhaust, *Science* 173, 517–22.

8 Kowalok, M. E. (1993). Common Threads: Research Lessons from Acid Rain, Ozone Depletion, and Global Warming. *Environment, 35* (6), 12–20, 35–38, at 17.

9 Rowlands, I. H. (1995), *op. cit. supra* at n.42 chapter 1, at 47.

10 Morrisette (1989), *op. cit. supra* at n.6 chapter 1, citing Grobecker (1974). Research Program for Assessment of Stratospheric Pollution, 1 Acta Astronautica 179; Grobecker, A., Coroniti, S. and Cannon, R. The Report of Findings: The Effects of Stratospheric Pollution by Aircraft 1974 DOT-TST-75-50; and National Academy of Sciences, Environmental Impact of Stratospheric Flight, 1975. Rowlands (1995), *op. cit. supra* at n.42 chapter 1, at 46.

could induce a breakdown of ozone in the stratosphere. With the SST programme coming to a close, attention was focused on chlorine, specifically chlorofluorocarbons.[12] The move was bolstered by British scientist James Lovelock's studies in 1972, in conjunction with the US NOAA and DuPont, which showed that chlorofluorocarbons were accumulating and persisting in the atmosphere for decades.[13] This development alerted chemical producers to the possible atmospheric and environmental consequences of CFC emissions.[14]

In July 1972, DuPont convened a meeting of CFC chemical producers based in North America, Europe, Japan and Australia to explore such risks. DuPont inspired the call for meeting attendance, stating:

> Fluorocarbons are intentionally or accidentally vented to the atmosphere world-wide at a rate approaching one billion pounds per year. These compounds may be either accumulating in the atmosphere or returning to the surface, land or sea, in the pure form or as decomposition products. Under any of these alternatives, it is prudent that we investigate any affects which the compounds may produce on plants or animals in the future.[15]

As one of the meeting's outcomes, the Chemical Manufacturers Association formed a Fluorocarbon Program Panel composed of participating chemical producers.[16] The Panel's aim was to further research regarding the environmental impacts of CFCs which it began funding in 1972.[17]

11   Kowalok, M. E. (1993), *op. cit. supra* at n.8, at 17.
12   Rowlands (1995), *op. cit. supra* at n.42 chapter 1, at 46–47, Parson (2003), *op. cit. supra* at n.14 chapter 1, at 31.
13   Lovelock, J. (1971, April). Atmospheric Fluorine Compounds as Indicators of Air Movements. *Nature,* 230 (5293). Parson (2003), *op. cit. supra* at n.14 chapter 1, at 23, citing Lotto and Schirff (1978). Kowalok, M. E. (1993), *op. cit. supra* at n.8, at 18.
14   Andersen (2002), at 197, *op. cit. supra* at n.37 chapter 1. The authors refer to the 1972 International Conference on the Ecology and Toxicology of Flurocarbons discussed *Infra.*
15   Glas, J. (1989). Protecting the Ozone Layer: A Perspective from Industry. In H. E. Sladovich (ed.), *Technology and Environment.* National Academy of Engineering; DuPont De Nemours & Company (Inc.) (1981, January 5). *Comments on the Advanced Notice of Proposed Rulemaking of the Environmental Protection Agency* (hereinafter, The DuPont Report), Volume 3 at K-2.
16   Parson (2003), *op. cit. supra* at n.14 chapter 1, at 23.
17   *Id.* Smith, B. (1998, April). Ethics of DuPont's CFC strategy 1975–1995. *Journal of Business Ethics* at 560. This is also referenced in the Written Statement of Dr Mack McFarland on behalf of the Fluorocarbon Program Panel of the Chemical Manufacturers Association to the Environmental Protection and Hazardous Wastes and Toxic Substances Subcommittees of the Committee on Environment and Public Works United States Senate, October 27, 1987.

Meanwhile, studies by Richard Stolarski, Ralph Cicerone,[18] Michael Mc Elroy and Steven Wofsy[19] supported the ozone depleting potential of chlorine compounds. Then, in 1973 (officially June 1974),[20] scientists Sherwood Rowland, Mario Molina and Paul Crutzen published their ozone depletion theory.[21] The theory postulated that CFCs were breaking down ozone at an exponential rate in the stratosphere and that such environmental damage would threaten human and terrestrial life on the planet.[22]

The chemical industry was hesitant to embrace the theory. The industry viewed the theory as speculative, lacking concrete supporting evidence and being riddled with scientific uncertainties.[23] DuPont's initial, well quoted reaction was that it would stop producing chlorofluorocarbons if "credible scientific data" showed that they could not be used without threatening human health.[24] Still, from 1974 onward, DuPont among others began researching possible chemicals and technologies which could replace CFCs.[25]

On the political front, the ozone controversy spurred Congressional hearings on the impact of fluorocarbons on health and the environment beginning in December 1974.[26] This was followed by other Congressional meetings in 1975 when the Federal Task Force on Inadvertent Modification of the Stratosphere, Fluorocarbons and the Environment (IMOS) was formed to assess the feasibility of regulating CFCs. It recommended that *aerosol* uses of CFCs be regulated under three agencies: the Environmental Protection Agency (EPA), the Food and Drug Administration (FDA) and the Consumer Product Safety Commission (CPSC). The Task Force did not recommend that other non-aerosols uses of CFCs be regulated immediately on the assumption that the chemicals were contained in equipment or

---

18 Kowalok, M. E. (1993), *op. cit. supra* at n.8, at 18; Lambright, W. H. (2005). *NASA and the Environment: The Case of Ozone Layer Depletion.* Washington, D.C.: National Aeronautics and Space Administration, at 5.

19 Kowalok, M. E. (1993), *op. cit. supra* at n.8, at 18.

20 Molina, M. J. and Rowland, F. S. (1974, June 28), *op. cit. supra* at n.9 chapter 1.

21 World Meteorological Organization (2011), *op. cit. supra* at n.11 chapter 1.

22 Molina, M. J. and Rowland, F. S. (1974, June 28), *op. cit. supra* at n.9 chapter 1.

23 Andersen (2002), *op. cit. supra* at n.37 chapter 1, at 197. E. I. DuPont Nemours & Company (Inc.) (1981). *Ozone Depleting Chloroflurocarbons: Proposed Production Restriction* (Volume 2). Wlimington, Delware: United States Environmental Protection Agency; Maxwell, J. and Briscoe, F. (1997). There's Money in the Air: The CFC Ban and DuPont's Regulatory Strategy. *Business Strategy and the Environment*, 6, 276–286.

24 Parson (2003), *op. cit. supra* at n.14 chapter 1, at 33; Meadows, D. H., Meadows, D. L. and Randers, J. (1992). *Beyond The Limits: Confronting Global Collapse, Envisioning a Sustainable Future.* Chelsea Green Pub., at 150.

25 See Section 2.3.4, n.230 *infra*.

26 Morone, J. G. *et al.* (1986), *op. cit. supra* at n.22 chapter 1, citing US Congress, House of Representatives, *Fluorocarbons: Impact on Health and Environment, Hearings Before the Subcommittee on Public Health and Foreign Commerce on H.R. 17577 and 17545*, 93rd Cong., 2d sess., 1974; Parson (2003), *op. cit. supra* at n.14 chapter 1, at 32.

systems and would not be released into the environment. If necessary, future regulations on non-aerosol uses should be pursued by the EPA under the Toxic Substances Control Act.[27]

In 1975 also, the National Academy of Sciences (NAS) came to similar conclusions.[28] Although indecisive regarding the urgency of precautionary action needed,[29] the Academy's conclusions confirmed the probability that CFCs negatively impact the ozone layer and that human injuries would follow,[30] stating "all the evidence that we examined indicates that the long-term releases of CFC-11 and CFC-12 at present rates will cause an appreciable reduction in the amount of stratospheric ozone."[31]

As federal agencies were developing regulatory controls in 1976, credible evidence validating the ozone depletion theory began emerging. High altitude air samples showed that predicted quantities of chlorofluorocarbons existed in the mid-stratosphere where they were being broken down by sunlight. Such data was collected by using weather balloons and U-2 flights which revealed abnormal concentrations of hydrochloric acid in the upper atmosphere.[32] The physical data was backed up by laboratory tests demonstrating the molecular disassociation of chlorofluorocarbons when exposed to ultraviolet radiation.[33]

In Congress, policy makers made clear the inherent dangers incumbent with the risks of chlorofluorocarbons and their release into the atmosphere. They "recognised that the adverse effects of CFC emissions could fall more upon future generations than upon those presently living and were unwilling to await a 'body count' to prove the reality of the dangers".[34] In 1976, Congress passed the Toxic Substances Control Act (TSCA) which first gave the EPA the authority to regulate CFCs.[35] A year later, a Clean Air

27 Parson (2003), *op. cit. supra* at n.14 chapter 1, at 35: Task Force also recommended that the Toxic Substance Control Act – which had not yer been passed then – be enacted by Congress for this purpose.
28 *Ibid.*
29 *Id.* at 39–40, 77.
30 National Academy of Sciences (1976). Halocarbons: Effects on Stratospheric Ozone; National Academy of Sciences (1976). Halocarbons: Environmental Effects of Evolution of Policy Responses to Stratospheric Ozone Depletion and Chlorofluoromethane Release.
31 Andersen (2002), *op. cit. supra* at n.37 chapter 1, at 11.
32 National Center for Atmospheric Research (1975, August 18). NCAR Scientists add Support to Ozone Destruction Theory. Yorktown Saskatchewan; *Id.* (1975, June 11). Two Records Set at the Scientific Balloon Facility. *Information release.* Palestine, Texas; Parson (2003), *op. cit. supra* at n.14 chapter 1, at 34.
33 Morone, J. G. *et al.* (1986), *op. cit. supra* at n.22 chapter 1. at 80–81, citing Making a Case: Theory That Aerosols Deplete Ozone Shield is Attracting Support, *Wall Street Journal,* December 3, 1975, 1, 27.
34 Thomas, H. (1979). *Some Non-Essential Aerosol Propellant Uses Finally Banned.* Retrieved June 3, 2012, from University of New Mexico School of Law Library: http://lawlibrary.unm.edu/nrj/19/1/16_thomas_some.pdf, at 218, note 4.
35 Toxic Substances Control Act, 15 U.S.C. §§.2601–2629 (1982).

Act Amendment was passed. The Amendment which also empowered the EPA to regulate CFCs was based on a presumption of foreseeable risks to human health and the environment posed by the release of the chemicals into the atmosphere. The Amendments' preamble states that:

> ...Congress finds, on the basis of presently available information, that (1) halocarbon compounds introduced into the environment potentially threaten to reduce the concentration of ozone in the stratosphere; (2) ozone reduction will lead to increased incidence of solar ultraviolet radiation at the surface of the Earth; (3) increased incidence of solar ultraviolet radiation is likely to cause increased rates of disease in humans (including increased rates of skin cancer), threaten food crops, and otherwise damage the natural environment....[36]

In step with Congress and based on their endangerment findings, the EPA, FDA and CPSC initiated rule-making processes to control CFCs.[37] In 1976–77, the FDA and CPSC promoted labelling rules requiring that CFC containing aerosol products carry the marker: "Warning: Contains a chlorofluorocarbon that may harm the public health and environment by reducing ozone in the upper stratosphere".[38] Together the labelling rules imposed by both agencies were aimed to affect "almost half of the 2.4 billion pressurized containers sold in the United States each year" thereby encouraging "voluntary consumer action" to reduce use.[39] From hair sprays to pesticides, the intent was to reduce consumption at least one third and at best by half.[40]

The CPSC's label warning rule applied broadly to *all* CFC-containing imported or manufactured aerosol products under its jurisdiction.[41] The FDA imposed the same warning label requirement on aerosol products under its control including hair sprays, perfumes and deodorants which constituted an estimated 85 percent of all aerosol products on the US market, and 50 percent of the total domestic production of CFCs was for aerosol spray applications.[42] In addition, the FDA also banned the *use of*

---

36 Clean Air Act, Ozone Protection 42 U.S.C. § 7452(1) (repealed). The 1977 Amendments defined 'halocarbon' as "chemical compounds CFCI3 and CF2CI2 and such other halogenated compounds as the Administrator determines may reasonably be anticipated to contribute to reductions in the concentration of ozone in the stratosphere."

37 Parson (2003), *op. cit. supra* at n.14 chapter 1, at 39.

38 US Consumer Product Safety Commission (1977, April 26). *FDA and CPSC Announce Fluorocarbon Labelling Plan* www.cpsc.gov/en/Newsroom/News-Releases/1977/FDA-And-CPSC-Announce-Fluorocarbon-Labeling-Plan/.

39 *Ibid.*

40 *CPSC/FDA/EPA Announce Phase Out of Chlorofluorocarbons* (1977, May 11). Retrieved from US Consumer Product Safety Commission.

41 *Ibid.*

42 Reitze, A. W. (2001). *Air Pollution Control Law: Compliance and Enforcement.* Washington, D.C.: Environmental Law Institute, at 388.

CFCs "in cosmetics as propellants in self-pressurised containers" as well as the sale of such products[43] by declaring such products misbranded or adulterated.[44] Likewise, the EPA enacted precautionary regulations under the Toxic Substances Control Act (TSCA) banning the production, import and sale of chlorofluorocarbons for use as propellants in aerosol products such as pesticides and cleaning solvents.[45] The Agency's aim was "to reduce emissions of chlorofluorocarbons to the atmosphere, thereby reducing the health and environmental risk caused by depletion of the ozone layer."[46] The EPA reasoned that restricting the sale for processing purposes would suffice to achieve its objective in reducing CFC emissions.[47]

In proposing and enacting these rules, each agency applied regulatory impact assessments to conclude that the unreasonable risk of harm posed by the chemicals warranted legal controls.[48] The CPSC clearly stated:

> The stratospheric ozone shield is of great importance in protecting life on earth from shortwave ultra-violet rays of the sun. Ozone depletion allows more of these rays to reach the earth, and the consequences include *a possibility of a significant increase in human skin cancer and other effects of unknown magnitude on man, animals, and plants.* Chlorofluorocarbon release may also cause climatic change, both by reducing stratospheric ozone and by increasing infrared absorption in the atmosphere. The Commission believes that the requirements ... *will enable consumers to make a conscious choice of whether to use products that contain chlorofluorocarbon propellants.* The Commission also believes that these requirements are necessary in order to carry out the purposes of the Consumer Product Safety Act of (a) helping to protect the public against unreasonable risks of injury associated with consumer products and (b) assisting consumers in evaluating the comparative safety of consumer products.[49]

The FDA concluded that the release of CFCs from spray products posed a serious risk of injury to the public. Available information – although inconclusive – was sufficient enough to substantiate the causal link between the

---

43 Use of ozone-depleting substances in foods, drugs, devices, or cosmetics (Federal Regulation): 21 C.F.R. § 2.125; Chlorofluorocarbon propellants (Federal Regulation): 21 C.F.R. §700.23.

44 Federal Food, Drug, and Cosmetic Act (FFDCA): 21 U.S.C. §§ 341, 342, 351, 352, 361, 362.

45 Toxic Substance Control Act (TSCA): 15 U.S.C. § 2605(a) (1) (2) (3) (4); 40 C.F.R. § 762.45(a).

46 43 *Fed. Reg.* 11319 (1978, March 17).

47 *Ibid.*

48 *Id.* at 11301; 15 U.S.C §§ 2605, 2058 (f) (1)(2).

49 Hazardous Substances, Administration and Enforcement (Federal Regulation): 16 C.F.R. §1401.2.

release of the chemicals from spray devices, the ozone layer depletion, the increase of ultraviolet radiation and the threat of skin cancers. In early 1977, the FDA's Commissioner David Kennedy stated that stratospheric ozone loss "could increase the incidence of skin cancer worldwide, cause changes in the climate and have other undesirable effects."[50] While studies on the effect of ultraviolet radiation on melanoma were just emerging, the risk of non-melanoma skin cancers alone constituted a justifiable basis to restrict the production and sale of such products.[51]

In its risk analysis, the FDA also rejected postponing the ban. Delaying regulatory action on the basis of "scientific uncertainty" would not be reasonable because considerable time might be needed to verify all facts whilst the threat of injury would be increasing. Complete certainty would not alter – in any event – the risk.[52] The unavailability of safe substitutes was also not a sufficient reason to defer action. Eschewing the argument that regulation be delayed on the basis that safe alternative chemicals were not available or had not yet been full tested, the FDA stated that it could not justify "the possibility of further chlorofluorocarbon-induced alterations in stratospheric ozone while waiting for the development of alternative propellants for nonessential aerosol uses."[53] Further, even if some financial losses could be anticipated for the chemical industry, overall such losses were passable in light of the potential risks of harm to people.[54] Also, in view of the need to enlist world-wide efforts to tackle the urgent problem, the FDA also held that the US government should demonstrate its commitment and leadership by initiating regulatory action without delay.[55]

Considering these factors, the EPA first recognised the human and environmental risks posed by CFC emissions, the most immediate one being skin cancer and the potentially serious problem of climate change.[56] Given that the aerosol industry used half of all CFCs produced in 1975, it deemed that reducing emissions from that sector would be a prudent and effective

---

50   Andersen (2002), *op. cit. supra* at n.37 chapter 1, at 297.
51   43 *Fed. Reg.* 11301, 11307 (17 March 1978). The FDA also argued that the climate change impacts of CFCs were "potentially serious" so as to warrant regulatory action.
52   *Id.* at 11303.
53   *Id.* at 11309.
54   *Id.* at 11311.
55   *Ibid.*
56   *Id.* at 11301, 11312. In the Agency's words: "Effects of chlorofluorocarbons on health and the environment: Chlorofluorocarbons produce a risk to human health and the environment by causing depletion of the ozone layer. ... The ozone layer helps shield the Earth's surface from ultraviolet (UV) radiation. As the layer is depleted, the Earth's surface is bombarded with more UV radiation. Current estimates are that if chlorofluorocarbon emissions continue at the 1975 rate, the ozone layer would be depleted ultimately by 11 to 16%. While the effects of ozone depletion are very difficult to quantify, they are quite serious. The major immediate concern is that increased UV radiation leads to a statistically significant increase in skin cancer...."

first effort to tackle the problem. Like the FDA, the EPA also recognised some financial losses would be sustained by chemical producers and some small enterprises operating as fillers. However, the Agency reasoned that the magnitude of the risk and the effectiveness of the ban required those businesses bear the disadvantage.[57] The Agency also assessed that substitute propellants such as hydrocarbons and carbon dioxide were available.

In addition, under the 1977 Clean Air Act amendments, the EPA was empowered to regulate ODCs more broadly but on the proviso that the Agency confirm that such chemicals would "reasonably be anticipated to cause or contribute to the endangerment of public health or welfare." [58] This gave the Agency the authority to propose further controls on CFC production, use, imports, exports and sales, beyond what federal rules were already in place.[59] At the time, it was envisioned that the EPA would enact and enforce a regulatory programme affecting the whole chlorofluorocarbon industry.[60]

While the Agency did propose a set of regulations to control the CFC production, use and emissions, the rules were not promulgated.[61] Numerous historians, economists, political scientists and others have analysed why they were not passed and what factors caused the regulatory delay of almost a decade until comprehensive laws and regulations were enacted and enforced in the 1990s. Of these, the chemical industry's opposition[62] to new regulations deserves special consideration as it may relate to what the companies knew or believed in 1976 and beyond. As indicated above, the chemical producers, most vocally DuPont, made a strong case for scientific uncertainty. They asserted that computer modelling of ozone layer depletion, for example, was not only inaccurate but was also based on "uncertain assumptions".[63] However, the value and credibility of their scientific uncertainty arguments needs to also be understood with some objectivity: were they genuine or doctored reasons to dispute the ozone layer depletion theory and probable risks to human health?[64]

57   *Ibid.*
58   Clean Air Act 42 U.S.C. § 7450 (*repealed*).
59   *Id.* at § 7453, 7454, 7455 (*repealed*).
60   40 C.F.R. §§ 762.45(a), 762.50 as of 15 December 1978, *Federal Register* 17 March 1978, 43(53). This would include spray and non-spray applications for refrigeration, air-conditioning, fire retardation, and foam blowing agents.
61   EPA (1982). *Report of the Progress of Regulations to Protect the Stratospheric Ozone Layer: Report to Congress.* Washington, D.C.: EPA, at p. 2.
62   Parson (2003), *op. cit. supra* at n.14 chapter 1, at 39.
63   Diamond, J. Lessons from Environmental Collapses of Past Societies. Fourth Annual John H. Chafee Memorial Lecture on Science and the Environment. Washington, D.C.: National Council for Science and the Environment, 2004: Quoting Sherwood Rowland, Nobel Laureate at his presentation at the 2001 inaugural John Chafee lecture.
64   Maxwell, J. and Briscoe, F. (1997), *op. cit. supra* at n.23.

To address uncertainty issues, the Fluorocarbon Program Panel reportedly spent US$1 million annually from 1972 until 1982[65] (increasing thereafter) on this research and by 1987 had funded projects in total of US$18 million. However, despite that investment and the high scientific research standards applied, evidence conclusively disproving the ozone depletion theory never emerged. The Panel's work was suspected by some to buy scientific opinion which would "vindicate CFCs" and thus support regulatory delays.[66] For example, in DuPont's 1981 report to the EPA,[67] without disproving the ozone theory, the company concluded that because no ozone loss had been detected and because scientists disagreed on aspects of the theory, there was "no scientific justification for any further regulation of CFCs...."[68] Yet other reports suggested that other chemicals as well as volcanic eruptions caused stratospheric ozone loss and the impact of CFCs on the ozone column would not be significant.[69]

Industry also funded research to investigate whether ozone loss would lead to escalated skin cancer harms. While the research findings refuted cause for alarm, the conclusions did not rule out potential increased injuries and deaths. For example, based on a 1981 study (presumably) commissioned by DuPont, the company argued that no appreciable increase of skin cancer would accrue if regulations were delayed for a *five* year period.[70] That conclusion is however misleading on two accounts: (1) The study on which DuPont's conclusion was based recognised that skin cancers are caused by solar UV radiation exposure and only disputes that genetic factors may also influence melanomas; (2) The study also acknowledged that CFC emissions would lead to increased but negligible human skin cancers. While what "negligible" means in terms of numbers of incidences and deaths is not qualified, DuPont assumes the "negligible" increase factor by estimating emissions of CFC-11 and CFC-12 alone and by predicting that the US production, use and emissions would *decrease* based on 1978–1979 emission levels and that world-wide emissions would remain constant.[71] In those years, national and global emissions were *the lowest* observed between 1972 and 1990. Because the company knew that

65   Smith, B. (1998, April). Ethics of DuPont's CFC strategy 1975–1995. *Journal of Business Ethics* at 560; The DuPont Report, *op. cit. supra* at n.15, Volume 3 at K1 – K77; DuPont reports that US$9.5 million had been spent on research by the end of 1980 and that a total of US$11 million would have been spent by the end of calendar year 1981.

66   Parson (2003), *op.cit supra* at n.14 chapter 1, at 125.

67   The DuPont Report, *op. cit. supra* at n.15.

68   Ibid., Volume I, ES-9.

69   Chemical Manufacturers Association (1986, February 24–28). Recent Research Results and Ongoing and Planned Research Programmes. *Coordinating Committee on the Ozone Layer, Eighth Session, UNEP/CCOL/8/3.*

70   The DuPont Report, *op. cit. supra* at n.15, Vol. 2, App. F: Effects of Ozone Depletion, S. F-1 (Human Skin Cancer Review by Professor Federick Urbach, M.D.) pp. 1–199.

71   *Ibid.*

domestic and overseas production and sales of CFCs as well as other ODCs were increasing dramatically, they equally must have been aware that their own initial negligible impact finding was no longer valid.

Further, what underscores that the chemical producers appreciated that risks of unreasonable harm could exist is their argument that even if the ozone layer depletion theory were true, emissions rates at the time would have a small impact and therefore regulations could be delayed.[72] The contention thus recognised the possibility of harm but attempted to demote its severity. Should the emissions rate increase, which it did and which the chemical producers were well aware, logically the possibility of harm would increase not decrease. Still, DuPont and others proposed that not regulation but "continuing assessment of the science and surveillance of the ozone layer is the only sensible option open to the world's governments".[73] Again, this proposal to keep monitoring the situation is not likely one which chemical producers would have proposed had they had strong evidence to support that the risk was entirely bogus.

In terms of science, more conclusive evidence that CFCs were the primary cause of stratospheric ozone destruction did come in 1985 when British scientists revealed recordings of stratospheric ozone loss over Antarctica and in 1987 when NASA disclosed satellite pictures of the "ozone hole" over Antarctica.[74] This information afforded a reasonable basis to form global scientific consensus on the ozone layer depletion theory, to displace numerous scientific uncertainties, and to support policy actions to control the ODCs.[75] That consensus was reflected in the second assessment of the Ozone Trends Panel, which recognised "both evidence of ozone layer depletion *and* substantial proof of its cause"[76] and which moved policy makers and some chemical industry members to see the environmental harm as a concrete problem and no longer a probable risk. Inspired by the report, DuPont formally announced that it would phase out CFC production in 1988.[77]

Even so, it seems fairly clear from the facts outlined above that US chemical producers were well aware that risks of unreasonable harm existed well before conclusive evidence appeared in 1987. Importantly, they knew of the endangerment findings reached by Congress and three federal agencies in 1976–1977. They also knew that those findings that CFCs and other

72   *Id.*; at Volume I, ES-9.

73   *Ibid.*

74   Farman, J., Gardiner, B. G. and Shanklin, J. D. (1985). Large Losses of Total Ozone in Antarctica Reveal Seasonal ClOx/NOx Interaction. *Nature,* 315, 207–10; Lambright, W. H. (2005), *op. cit. supra* at n.18, at 15, 20; Parson (2003), *op. cit. supra* at n.14 chapter 1, at 154; Collins, C. (2010), *op. cit. supra* at n.36 chapter 1, at 167.

75   Lambright, W. H. (2005) at 15, 20, *op. cit. supra* at n.18.

76   Rowlands, I. H. (1995)*, op. cit. supra* at n.42 chapter 1, at 110.

77   Parson (2003), *op. cit. supra* at n.14 chapter 1, at 147, 157.

halogenated compounds posed a potential unreasonable risk of harm to the environment and human health were never revoked throughout the 1970s and 1980s. As discussed above, this is because no substantial evidence disproving such risks was ever submitted and because most of the various uncertainties have since been resolved.

2.3.2 Evidence that chemical producers failed to warn of product dangers and rather promoted that ozone depleting chemicals were safe

Notwithstanding the unreasonable risk of harm posed by ODCs, evidence suggests that the chemical producers not only failed to warn about the potential of such risks but also promoted that such risks were unfounded i.e. that the chemicals were not harmful to human health and the environment. Regarding warning labels, as discussed above, the FDA and CPSC did require that aerosol products containing CFCs as propellants be labelled to inform consumers of the products' potential harm to the environment and human health by depleting the ozone layer from 1977 onwards. However, the same requirement did not apply to the sale of chemicals themselves such as a label requirement on containers of CFCs sold to downstream product manufacturers.[78] The label requirement also did not apply to non-aerosol or essential products. Warning labels on both were only required from 1993 in accordance with the 1990 stratospheric ozone protection regulations.[79] Although further research is required to confirm that no such warning labels were used by chemical producers, no evidence could be found which demonstrates that this practice was followed other than what was required by regulations. That civil society led campaigns continued to demand the use of warning labels throughout the 1980s suggests that such labels were in fact absent.[80]

Corporate behaviour throughout the 1970s and 1980s showed more reluctance to recognise the chemical risk and rather a proactive effort to promote that the chemicals were not harmful. From 1974, chemical producers, notably DuPont, publicly declared that regulations on CFC production and use could be delayed as continued emissions would not amount to a "significant risk to the health and welfare of the population."[81] It is said that DuPont wanted to change public perceptions fuelled by environmentalists and insufficient scientific fact that stood behind the call for regulatory action.[82]

---

78   *Ibid.*; US Consumer Product Safety Commission (1977, April 26). *FDA and CPSC Announce Fluorocarbon Labelling Plan*. Retrieved January 15, 2014, from US Consumer Product Safety Commission: www.cpsc.gov/en/Newsroom/News-Releases/1977/FDA-And-CPSC-Announce-Fluorocarbon-Labeling-Plan/.
79   40 C.F.R. § 156.
80   Andersen (2002), *op. cit. supra* at n.37 chapter 1, at 343.
81   The DuPont Report, *op. cit. supra* at n.15, Volume 3 at K-2.
82   Maxwell, J. and Briscoe, F. (1997), *op. cit. supra* at n.23.

In 1980, a coalition of some 400 chlorofluorocarbon producers and users based mainly in the United States formed the Alliance for a Responsible CFC Policy.[83] At its inception, the Alliance's executive committee included representatives from Dow Chemical, the Great Lakes Chemical Corporation, Pennwalt, Kaiser Aluminum & Chemical, Racon Inc., Allied Chemical and DuPont.[84] The purpose of the Alliance was to delay the federal government from passing regulations banning CFCs "based on unproven and unverified theory".[85] According to its Charter, the Alliance promoted that:

> According to most of the world's scientific community, there is no unreasonable risk to health and environment in awaiting scientific verification of the extent and impact, if any, of ozone depletion. The CFC users and manufacturers are committed to make certain that the adverse economic and social consequences of any further regulation are widely understood.[86]

The Alliance's initial 18 month budget was estimated between US$650 thousand and US$1 million of which approximately one-third was meant to be allocated for research and half on "counsel and advocacy" costs.[87] This supported a campaign to oppose the additional CFC regulations proposed by the EPA in 1980. The alliance organised the sending of some 2,300 opposition letters to the Agency[88] and arranged that some of its members representing small and medium-sized enterprises testify before Congressional committees that the proposed regulations would be deleterious for their businesses and livelihoods.[89] Alliance members publicly asserted that that ozone science was flawed and that further research would be needed to confirm the truth necessary to justify regulator action.[90]

This stance remained consistent throughout the 1980s. In 1986, despite the Alliance's chairman's statement that "on the basis of current information, we believe that large increases in fully halogenated CFCs…would be unacceptable to future generations",[91] the organisation's newsletter continued to profess that "no significant modification of the ozone layer

83 The Alliance has since been renamed as the Alliance for Responsible Atmospheric Policy. *See* The Alliance for Responsible Atmospheric Policy. (n.d.). *Alliance Fact Sheet.* Retrieved from The Alliance for Responsible Atmospheric Policy: www.alliancepolicy.org/downloads/documents/Alliance_Fact_Sheet.pdf.

84 Alliance for Responsible CFC Policy (1980, September). Alliance for Responsible CFC Policy Charter. *Alliance for Responsible CFC Policy News* at 6.

85 Liftin (1995), *op. cit. supra* at n.40 chapter 1.

86 Alliance for Responsible CFC Policy (1980), *op. cit. supra* at n.84.

87 *Ibid.*

88 Cagin, S. and Dray, P. (1993), *op. cit. supra* at n.41 chapter 1, at 224.

89 *Ibid.*

90 *Id.* at 247.

91 Parson (2003), *op. cit. supra* at n.14 chapter 1, at 126.

is expected during the next few decades" and that "therefore, there is no imminent threat to human health and the environment from current CFC use or emission".[92] That view persisted in 1987 when the Alliance praised the adoption of the Montreal Protocol as "an unprecedented step to protect the global environment" while maintaining that "current use of the compounds presents no significant risks to health or the environment".[93]

Some historians recount that the Alliance waged an aggressive campaign both nationally and at the State level purporting these views.[94] Authors Cronin and Kennedy vividly tell how this movement made use of public relations companies to inspire notions that the ozone depletion theory was full of holes even up until 1995.[95] Reportedly also, the Alliance made substantial political campaign contributions to support its cause.[96]

In the 1990s, the Alliance was renamed as the Alliance for Responsible Atmospheric Policy. As such, its focus moved to "encourage responsible, reasonable, and cost-effective ozone protection and climate change policies to be determined at the international level and to oppose the development of a patchwork of different policies at the lower levels of government".[97] It now has a membership of "about 100 manufacturers and businesses which rely on HCFCs and HFCs".[98]

2.3.3 Evidence that ozone depleting chemical production increased between 1976 and 1992

Numerous historical and analytical sources on the ozone layer depletion problem confirm that production, use and emissions of chlorofluorocarbons increased dramatically in the 1980s. Although overall chemical emissions declined sharply in the mid-1970s around the imposition of the aerosol bans,[99] production increased incrementally, surpassed 1974 levels

---

92 Alliance for a Responsible CFC Policy (1986, October). Policy Statement. *CFC Alliance Newsletter* at 2.
93 Liftin (1995), Chapter 5, *op. cit. supra* at n.40 chapter 1.
94 *Ibid.*
95 Cronin, J. and Kennedy, R. J. (1999). *The Riverkeepers.* New York: Touchstone.
96 Collins, C. (2010), *op. cit. supra* at n.36 chapter 1, at 164.
97 The Alliance for Responsible Atmospheric Policy (n.d.), *op. cit. supra* at n.83.
98 Alliance for Responsible Atmospheric Policy (n.d.). *The Alliance is an Industry Coalition.* Retrieved from Alliance for Responsible Atmospheric Policy: www.alliancepolicy.org/about.php: The Alliance's Board members and corporate members can be accessed at this website.
99 Parson (2003), *op. cit. supra* at n.14 chapter 1, at 80, 113: Parson states that "US use of CFCs in aerosols fell 95% from its 1974 peak to about 10,000 tonnes in 1980. Other uses grew strongly and were vigorously promoted, particularly foams and auto air conditioning, but could only slightly offset the collapse of the largest market. Consequently, total US production of CFC-11 and CFC-12 fell 45% from 1974 to 1980, declining from about 50 to 30% of world production.

in 1983 and kept growing. Production of other ODCs such as CFC-113 methyl chloroform and methyl bromide also experienced steady increases in the 1970s and the more rapid production rates in the 1980s.[100] In fact, despite the aerosol bans, chlorofluorocarbon use continued to expand and sales of CFC-11 and CFC-12 surged: "On average, CFC sales increased by 13 percent annually between 1958 and 1983. More specifically, the sale of CFC-11 and CFC-12 grew by 5 percent between 1982 and 1984 alone."[101] This growth pattern is evidenced by different data sources which are explained below.

These assessments are supported in review of reported production volumes prior to and after 1976. For this book case study, three major and three minor data sets were used although each have their respective limitations.

Source 1: The United Nations Environment Programme's Ozone Secretariat

This source provides data regarding the production and consumption of ozone depleting chemicals which are controlled under the Montreal Protocol and subsequent amendments thereto.[102] The data's accuracy relies on reports submitted every four years by State Parties for the years 1986, and 1989 to present. Production information is compiled according to country and by groups of ozone depleting substances. However, the data is not disaggregated according to specific chemicals e.g. CFC-11, CFC-12 and not according to corporate producers e.g. the production amounts for say Mexico do not reflect what percentage of Mexico's domestic production is attributable to Mexican companies or foreign-based companies operating in the country. Finally, the United Nations information does not include emissions data.[103]

Source 2: The Chemical Manufacturers Association

Based on surveys of chemical companies based in the United States, Europe and Japan, this source provides data on production, sales and

---

100 *Id.* at 80.
101 Elrifi, I. (1990). Protection of the Ozone Layer: A Comment on the Montreal Protocol. *McGill Law Journal*, 387-423 at 393, citing Stoel, T., Miller, A. S. and Milroy, B. (1980). *Fluorocarbon Regulation: An International Comparison.* Lexington, Massachusetts: Lexington Books, at 9.
102 UNEP Ozone Secretariat (2012). *Data Access Centre.* Retrieved from Publications: http://ozone.unep.org/new_site/en/ozone_data_tools_access.php.
103 *Ibid.*

releases[104] of CFC-11 and CFC-12 for the time frame: 1931 to 1980.[105] Its authenticity has been certified by a public auditor in the United States.[106] The data is limited in that it does not discriminate between national and corporate production data and it omits production information from China and the then Soviet Union.

Source 3: The Alternative Fluorocarbon Environmental Acceptability Study[107]

This data set is compiled from voluntary reports of the study's member companies.[108] It records production volumes of CFCs 11 and 12 between 1931 and 2004, of CFCs 113, 114 and 115 between 1979 and 2003 and on HCFC-22 between 1970 and 2007.[109] The source is limited in representing only member company information.[110] Its accuracy is questionable given it has not been verified.[111]

Source 4: EPA

The EPA provides data on combined CFC-11 and CFC-12 production which it draws from other sources and the US International Trade Commission. This data does specify the amount of production attributed to the United States in relation to the rest of the world although it is not clear if it includes production by US companies outside the United States.[112]

104 In 1977, DuPont staff at the company's Organic Chemicals, and Central Research and Development Departments published a formula to calculate the amount of CFC releases in relation to production and sales data. Essentially that report concluded that between 1950 and 1975, of the total amount of CFC-11 produced (3,430 million kg), 2,930 million kg were released and of the total amount of CFC-12 produced (5,080 million kg), 4,400 million kg were released. See McCarthy, R., Bower, F. A. and Jesson, J. (1977). The Fluorocarbon-ozone Theory—I. Production and Release—World Production and Release of CCl_3F and CCl_2F_2 (fluorocarbons 11 and 12) through 1975. *Atmospheric Environment*, 11(6), 491–497.
105 Chemical Manufacturers Association (1980). *UNEP/CCOL1/5/9: 1980 World Production and Sales of Fluorocarbons.* Copenhagen: UNEP.
106 *Ibid.*
107 Alternative Fluorocarbons Environmental Acceptability Study (hereinafter, AFEAS) (2006). *AFEAS Research and Assessment Program:* www.afeas.org/about.html.
108 AFEAS (1993). *Production, Sales and Atmospheric Release of Fluorocarbons through 1992:* www.ciesin.columbia.edu/docs/011-423/011-423.html.
109 AFEAS (2009). *Annual Fluorocarbon Production Reported (metric tons):* www.afeas.org/data.php?page=prod_table.
110 AFEAS (2007). *Production and Sales of Fluorocarbons:* www.afeas.org/overview.php.
111 Parson (2003), *op. cit. supra* at n.14 chapter 1, at 79.
112 US EPA (2010). *Environmental Indicators: Ozone Depletion.* Retrieved from Ozone Layer Protection – Science: www.epa.gov/Ozone/science/indicat/.

Source 5: The European Economic Community

An EEC study details production and sales data of CFC-11 and -12 in Europe, the United States and elsewhere between 1976 and 1979.[113]

Source 6: DuPont

DuPont submitted a report to the EPA in 1981 in which it estimated US and global production of CFCs 11, 12, 113 and 114 as well as HCFC-22 between 1976 and 1979.[114]

Regarding other ozone depleting substances, some resources provide production data for halon gases 1211 and 1301 for years 1963 to 1996,[115] for methyl chloroform from 1971 until 2000[116] and for methyl bromide between 1984 and 1996 world-wide and in the United States.[117] Historical production data regarding carbon tetrachloride however seems to be wanting prior to 1989 when, as discussed above, countries were required to report their production amounts as a part of their obligations under the Montreal Protocol. Given this missing information, the following calculations exclude all data regarding the substance. Inevitably, the discount of carbon tetrachloride will paint a false picture of the actual contributions to emissions globally and in the United States. This is significant because the ozone depleting potential of the chemical is 1.1, higher than CFC-11 and because it had been produced and used for over a hundred years prior to its phase-out in 1996.[118]

Accordingly, based on all available data as illustrated in the Appendix, Figure 2.1 is composed to illustrate both global and US production trends over the 80 year period between 1931 and 2012. Throughout the entire period 1931 to 2012, US production peaked in 1985 at close to 500 thousand ozone depleting potential (ODP) tonnes.[119]

113 Metra Consulting Group Ltd (1981). *Aspects of Effecting Further: Reductions in Chlorofluorocarbon Usage in the EEC: Final Report.* Commission of the European Communities, Environment and Consumer Protection Service. London: European Economic Community.

114 E. I. DuPont Nemours and Company (Inc.) (1981). *Ozone Depleting Chlorofluorocarbons: Proposed Production Restrictions.* Wilmington, Delaware: US EPA

115 Fabian and Onkar, S. N. (1999). *Reactive Halogen Compounds in the Atmosphere.* Germany: Springer-Verlag Berlin Heidelberg, at 175.

116 McCulloch, A. and Midgley, P. M. (2001). The History of Methyl Chloroform Emissions: 1951–2000. *Atmospheric Environment*, 5311–5319.

117 *Historical US Methyl Bromide Sales* (n.d.). Retrieved from Methyl Bromide Alternatives Outreach: http://mbao.org/methyl_back/sales.pdf; Methyl Bromide Technical Options Committee (1998). *Report of the Methyl Bromide Technical Options Committee.* UNEP/Earthprint, at 22.

118 Walker, S. J., Weiss, R. and Salameh, (2000). Reconstructed Histories of the Annual Mean Atmospheric Mole Fractions for the Halocarbons CFC-11, CFC-12, CFC-113, and Carbon Tetrachloride. *Journal of Geophysical Research*, 14285-14296.

119 See Appendix, *infra*.

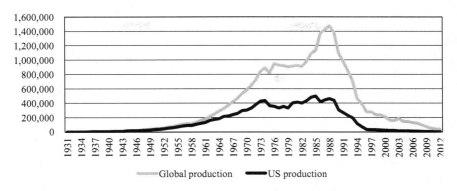

Figure 2.1 Ozone depleting substance production trends 1931–2012

A closer look at CFC production rates between 1970 and 1990 in Figure 2.1 shows that production levels begin to drop from 1974 onwards but then sharply increase after 1979 overtaking 1974 production level from 1982 onwards. The production decrease witnessed during 1974–1979 is attributable to decreased consumer demand for CFC laden aerosol products and the imposition of federal regulations banning the sale of such products from 1979 onwards. The availability of hydrocarbon replacement gases as well as pump spray technology enabled the market production to decline even prior to the ban.[120] However, at the same time, one of the policy rationales behind the 1970s aerosol ban was to reduce production of CFC by 60 percent.[121] As illustrated in Figure 2.2, that target was never actually achieved until 1990. This suggests that CFC production for non-aerosol uses was already increasing in the mid-1970s. Clearly, from 1979 onwards, production increases annually with some regressions between 15 percent and 35 percent until 1990.

Meanwhile, the production of other ozone depleting substances[122] unaffected by the aerosol ban grew steadily between 1970 and 1990. This can be observed in Figure 2.3 which displays production trends of halon gases, methyl chloroform, methyl bromine and hydrochlorofluorocarbons (HCFCs). For these substances, production peaks in 1988 and then begins to decline.

120 Parson (2003), *op. cit. supra* at n.14 chapter 1, at 80, 113; Maxwell, J. and Briscoe, F. (1997), *op. cit. supra* at n.23.
121 *CPSC/FDA/EPA Announce Phase Out of Chlorofluorocarbons* (1977, May 11). Retrieved from US Consumer Product Safety Commission: www.cpsc.gov/en/Newsroom/News-Releases/1977/CPSCFDAEPA-Announce-Phase-Out-Of-Chlorofluorocarbons/.
122 See *supra* on Data sources. This excludes carbon tetrachloride for which reliable data appears to be unavailable.

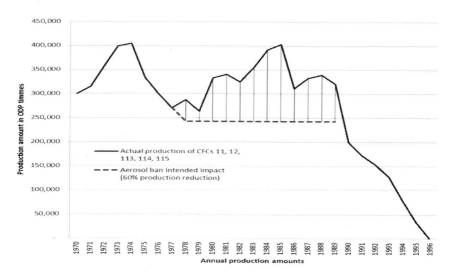

Figure 2.2 Chlorofluorocarbon production 1970–1996

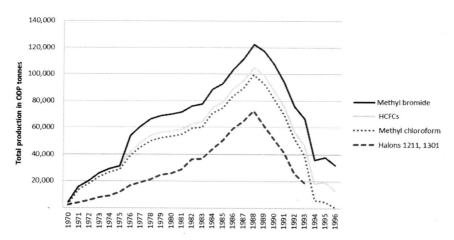

Figure 2.3 US corporate production of non-CFC ozone depleting chemicals from 1970–1996

Global production of ODCs also amassed in the 1980s, peaking in 1988 as shown in Figure 2.3 above. European, Japanese and US companies were responsible for the bulk of this production in developed and developing countries. Table 2.2 below attempts to show which multinational companies had home-based business and overseas subsidiaries engaged in

Table 2.2 Global production by reporting parent and subsidiary companies, 1931–2007

Reported production and emissions (1931–1980)[1]				Reported production volumes in 1993 survey[2]				Reported production volumes in 2005–2007 survey[3]			
Parent Co.	Country	Subsidiary	Country	Parent Co.	Country	Subsidiary	Country	Parent Co.	Country	Subsidiary	Country
Allied Chemical Corporation	US	Allied Chemical Canada Ltd	Canada	Allied-Signal, Inc.	US	Allied Canada, Inc.	Canada	Honeywell	US	Honeywell Canada	Canada
										Honeywell Fluoro-chemicals Europe BV	Netherlands
E.I. du Pont de Nemours & Company, Inc.	US	Du Pont de Nemours, NV	Netherlands	E.I. du Pont de Nemours & Company, Inc.	US			E.I. du Pont de Nemours & Company, Inc.	US	Du Pont de Nemours, NV	Netherlands
		Ducilo SA	Argentina			Ducilo SA	Argentina			Ducilo S.A.	Argentina
		Du Pont do Brasil SA	Brazil			Du Pont do Brasil SA	Brazil			Du Pont do Brasil SA	Brazil
		Halo-carburos SA	Mexico			Halocarburos S.A.	Mexico			Halo-carburos SA	Mexico
		Du Pont Canada, Inc.	Canada			Du Pont Canada, Inc.	Canada			Du Pont Canada, Inc.	Canada
										DuPont Europe SA	
Essex Chemical (Racon)	US										

Table 2.2 continued

Reported production and emissions (1931–1980)[1]				Reported production volumes in 1993 survey[2]				Reported production volumes in 2005–2007 survey[3]			
Parent Co.	Country	Subsidiary	Country	Parent Co.	Country	Subsidiary	Country	Parent Co.	Country	Subsidiary	Country
Kaiser Aluminum & Chemical	US			LaRoche Chemicals, Inc.	US						
Pennwalt	US										
Union Carbide	US										
Rhone Poulenc Industries	France			Rhone Poulenc Industries	France	Rhône-Poulenc Chemicals, Ltd	UK			Rhodia Organique Fine, Ltd (formerly Rhône-Poulenc) Chemicals, Ltd	UK
						Societe des Industries Chimiques du Nord de la Grece, SA	Greece				
Pechiney Ugine Kuhlmann, Produits Chimiques	France	Ugimica SA	Spain	Elf, Atochem S.A.	France	Pacific Chemical Industries Pty. Ltd	Australia	Arkema SA	France		
						Elf Atochem Espana	Spain			Arkema Espana	Spain
						Elf Atochem North America	US			Arkema North America	US

Table 2.2 continued

Reported production and emissions (1931–1980)[1]				Reported production volumes in 1993 survey[2]				Reported production volumes in 2005–2007 survey[3]			
Parent Co.	Country	Subsidiary	Country	Parent Co.	Country	Subsidiary	Country	Parent Co.	Country	Subsidiary	Country
Hoechst AG	Germany	Hoechst Iberica	Spain	Hoechst AG	Germany	Hoechst Iberica	Spain				
		Hoechst do Brasil Quimica e Farmaceutica SA	Brazil			Hoechst do Brasil Quimica e Farmaceutica SA	Brazil				
Kali Chemie Aktiengesellschaft i	Germany	Kali Chemie Iberia SA	Spain			Kali-Chemie Iberia SA	Spain				
Solvay, SA	Belgium	Chemiewerk Nünchritz GmbH	Germany	Solvay, SA	Belgium	Solvay Fluor und Derivate (Kalie Chemie)	Germany	Solvay, SA	Belgium	Solvay Fluor GMBH	Germany
						Solvay SA France	France			Solvay SA France	France
										Solvay Fluor Iberica SA	Spain
										Solvay Solexis SA	Italy

Table 2.2 continued

Reported production and emissions (1931–1980)[1]				Reported production volumes in 1993 survey[2]				Reported production volumes in 2005–2007 survey[3]			
Parent Co.	Country	Subsidiary	Country	Parent Co.	Country	Subsidiary	Country	Parent Co.	Country	Subsidiary	Country
Imperial Chemical Industries Limited	UK	African Explosives & Chemical Industries, Ltd	South Africa	Imperial Chemical Industries Limited	UK	African Explosives & Chemical Industries, Ltd	South Africa	Ineos Fluor Limited	UK	Ineos Fluor America	US
										Ineos Fluor Japan	Japan
ISC Chemicals Ltd	UK										
Asahi Glass Co., Ltd	Japan			Asahi Glass Co., Ltd	Japan			Asahi Glass Co., Ltd	Japan	Asahi Glass Chemicals America, Inc	US
Daikin Kogyo Co., Ltd	Japan			Daikin Kogyo Co., Ltd	Japan			Daikin Kogyo Co., Ltd	Japan	Daikin Chemical International Trading (Shanghai) Co. Ltd	China
Mitsui Fluoro-chemicals Ltd,	Japan			Mitsui Fluoro-chemicals Ltd,	Japan			Mitsui-DuPont Fluoro-chemicals Co., Ltd	Japan		

Table 2.2 continued

Reported production and emissions (1931–1980)[1]			Reported production volumes in 1993 survey[2]				Reported production volumes in 2005–2007 survey[3]			
Parent Co.	Subsidiary	Country	Parent Co.	Country	Subsidiary	Country	Parent Co.	Country	Subsidiary	Country
Showa-Denko, KK		Japan	Showa-Denko, KK	Japan						
			Japan Flon Gas Association	Japan		(Japan), Daikin Industries, Ltd (Japan)	Central Glass Co., Ltd		Japan	
Montedison Intermedi e Ausiliarich-imiei per l'Industria (formerly Montedison SPA)		Italy	Ausimont SPA (formerly Montefluos, owned by Montedison)		Ausimont, US	US				
Quimo-basicos, SA		Mexico	Quimo-basicos, SA	Mexico						
Australian Fluorine Chemical Pty. Ltd		Australia								
Produven		Venezuela	Produven	Venezuela						

Notes:
1 Chemical Manufacturers Association (1980). *UNEP/CCOL/5/9: 1980 World Production and Sales of Fluorocarbons*. Copenhagen: UNEP.
2 AFEAS (1993), *op. cit. supra* at n.108 chapter 2.
3 AFEAS (2007), *op. cit. supra* at n.110 chapter 2.

production to feed local demands. In the 1980s, ODC production in developing countries increased substantially: between 1986 and 1995, chlorofluorocarbon production shot up by almost 2.5 times meanwhile the use of the chemicals increased nearly 40 percent.[123] In India and Thailand, for example, CFC consumption swelled 300 percent between 1985 and 1991.[124] Meanwhile, as predicted,[125] chemical use also multiplied in other countries such as China, India, Brazil, Saudi Arabia, Algeria, South Korea, Indonesia, Nigeria, Mexico, Turkey, Venezuela and Iran.[126] In China, CFC consumption grew by 20 percent in the 1980s[127] and halon gas production also escalated from 4,000 to 10,000 metric tons between 1991 and 1995.[128] In addition, the use of replacement gas HCFC-22 in developing countries increased dramatically over the past 20 years. One writer tells how in Mauritius, chemical use increased 100 fold due to hotel construction and the need for refrigeration to support the country's fishing industry.[129] Such amplified chemical production and use was and remains problematic since limited or no emissions controls and product maintenance in many of those countries has predicated long term chemical emissions.[130]

The question in the *ozone layer case* is from where the chemicals came: were they produced and used locally by domestic companies? Were they imported from other countries? Were they produced by multinational chemical companies in developing countries? One assumption is that US-based chemical companies globalised and grew their business overseas largely in developing country markets substantially and precisely during the time period 1977–1990. Still, in most literature and corporate resources reviewed, factual information regarding such overseas businesses activities is scant and would require extensive research to unearth. Still, there are indicators that US companies indeed propagated their enterprises

123 World Resources Institute (n.d.). *Black market CFCs.* Retrieved from World Resources Institute: http://d5.wri-main.atendesigngroup.com/publication/content/8360 citing Oberth, S. (1997). *Production and Consumption of Ozone-Depleting Substances, 1986–1995.* Bonn, Germany: Deutsche Gesellschaft for Technische Zusammenarbeit.

124 Anand, R. (2004). *International Environmental Justice: A North-South Dimension.* Ashgate Publishing Ltd., at 93.

125 *Ibid.*

126 Ozone Secretariat (1987, September 16). *The Montreal Protocol on Substances that Deplete the Ozone Layer.* Retrieved June 10, 2014, from UNEP: Ozone Secretariat: http://ozone.unep.org/new_site/en/Treaties/treaties_decisions-hb.php?art_id=64.

127 Collins, C. (2010), *op. cit. supra* at n.36 chapter 1, at 207.

128 World Resources Institute (n.d.), *op. cit. supra* at n.123, citing UNEP (1996). *Plan for Halon Phase-out in China, Working paper submitted to the Executive Committee of the Multilateral Fund for the Implementation of the Montreal Protocol 20th meeting.* Montreal, Canada: UNEP.

129 Johansen, B. E. (2009). *The Encyclopaedia of Global Warming Science and Technology.* Santa Barbara, CCA: Greenwood Press at 16.

130 Dauvergne, P. (2008). *The Shadows of Consumption: Consequences for the Global Environment.* Cambridge, MA: Massachusetts Institute of Technology, at 110.

abroad.[131] Allied Chemical, for example, had been producing CFCs in India prior to 1988, when the company sold its production facility to the government that year.[132] Similarly, in 1986, DuPont planned to produce CFC-113 in Japan and CFC-11 and CFC-12 in China.[133] Until 1994 or 1995, DuPont was selling and producing CFCs for non-essential aerosol uses also in developed countries.[134] In developing countries, that business continued until 1999 when the company divested or shut down its Fluorochemical and Fluorspar businesses in Brazil[135] which was its last chlorofluorocarbon production facility.[136]

Again, despite these indications, the extent to which subsidiaries of US companies expanded the ODC market cannot be sufficiently understood and requires further research. Nevertheless, the overseas activity of such companies begs to be considered in relation to the liability questions raised in this study.

2.3.4 Evidence the defendants failed to prevent unreasonable risks of harm by preventing emissions

The proposition that the defendant chemical producers failed to prevent emissions is based on two considerations: (1) their direct efforts to prevent chemical releases into the environment at the point of production and prior to sale, and (2) their efforts to develop and market safe alternative chemicals and technologies.

Regarding the first issue, it is highly likely that chemical emissions during manufacturing processes were not prevented. As with many other informational issues regarding the companies' behaviour and knowledge, publicly available documentation explaining what emissions controls were available and employed throughout the last century is wanting. As such, further investigation would be needed to verify this allegation. Some literature suggests that technology to recover the chemicals during use and in manufacturing processes as well as from existing banks was available

131 Benedick, R. (1998), *op. cit. supra* at n.22 chapter 1, 1–5, 148; Rosencranz, A. and Milligan, R. CFC Abatement: The Needs of Developing Countries, *Ambio* 19 (6/7), CFCs and stratospheric Ozone (1990, Oct.), 312–316.

132 Kumar, K. K. (n.d.). *Montreal Protocol*. Retrieved June 16, 2013, from www.mse.ac.in/trade/pdf/Compendium%20Part%20B/4.%20Kavi-MP.pdf at 103.

133 Parson (2003), *op. cit. supra* at n.14 chapter 1, at 124.

134 DuPont Dymel, Aerosol Propellants: United States Environmental Fact Sheet. E-64725-3 08/07 (2007); E. I. DuPont de Nemours and Company (20 April 2011) *Position statement: 20 Years of Progress: Implementing the Montreal Protocol.* www2.dupont.com/Media_Center/en_US/position_statements/montreal_protocol.html?src=position_statements_index.

135 E. I. DuPont de Nemours and Company (April 2001). *DuPont DATABOOK 2000*, at 33.

136 DuPont (2011), *op. cit. supra* at n.134.

throughout the 1970s and 1980s.[137] However, little information exists regarding what was used, when and by whom. Only DuPont reported to have successfully adopted and used such know-how at some point after 1992.[138]

In many ways, evidence confirming that the chemical producers could have introduced safe alternative chemicals earlier than they did and purposefully did not do so is inconclusive, although studied extensively.[139] During the liability period, 1976–1992, the defendant producers argued that alternative chemicals were too expensive or unsafe and that it would require several years before they could become commercially available.[140] The doubt arises partly because industry had the requisite know how[141] and had invested heavily in research to develop chemical alternatives during 1974–1981,[142] which should have produced some useful results. Further, some suspicion also prevails given the speed at which replacement chemicals and technologies became available when the 1990 regulations came into effect.[143]

---

137 Mooz, W., Dole, S., Jaquette, D., Krase, W., Morrison, Salem, S. *et al.* (1982, March). *Technical Options of Reducing Chlorofluorocarbon Emissions*: www.rand.org/content/dam/ rand/pubs/reports/2008/R2879.pdf: The 1982 study suggests, *inter alia*, that service techniques for mobile airconditoners be improved and that solvent use "improve equipment and operating practices, use carbon absorption recovery for pure CFC-113 and use extrenal waste reclamation"; Knopeck, G., Zwolinski, L. and Selznick, R. (1989). An Evaluation of Carbon Absorption for Emissions Control and CFC-11 Recovery in Polyurethane Foam Processes. *Journal of Cellular Plastics*, 164–172. Farmer, R. and Nelson, T. (1988, March). *Control Technology Overview Report: CFC-11 Emissions from Flexible Polyurethane Foam Manufacturing*. Research Triangle Park, NC: US EPA. Bishop, F. S. (1979). *Report on the Progress of Regulations to Protect Stratospheric Ozone: Report to Congress*. US EPA, Office of Toxic Substances. Also See Wijmans, J. and Hans, G. (1993). *Treatment of CFC and HCFC Emissions*: http://cfpub.epa.gov/ncer_abstracts/index.cfm/fuseaction/display.abstractDetail/abstract/1675/report/0.

138 DuPont asserts that by 2011 "Dramatic engineering improvements in containment have led to a 99.98% recovery rate of all processing agent". DuPont (2011), *op. cit. supra* at n.134 chapter 2.

139 See e.g. Parson (2003), *op. cit. supra* at n.14 chapter 1; Doniger, D. and Quibell, M. (2007), *op. cit. supra* at n.36 chapter 1; Liftin (1995), *op. cit. supra* at n.40 chapter 1.

140 The DuPont Report, *op. cit. supra* at n.15; Parson (2003), *op. cit. supra* at n.14 chapter 1, at 193.

141 See e.g. DuPont's website illustrating the high level of personnel that drove innovation: www.dupont.com/corporate-functions/our-company/dupont-history.html.

142 Maxwell, J. and Briscoe, F. (1997), *op. cit. supra* at n.23 chapter 1; But also see Parson (2003), *op. cit. supra* at n.14 chapter 1, at 54–55, 175–177 recounting that DuPont spent US$10 million by 1979 and US$15 million by the mid-1980s; Andersen (2002), at 199, *op. cit. supra* at n.37 chapter 1. The DuPont Report, *op. cit. supra* at n.15, Vol. 1 at II-6. It is unclear when exactly what research was resumed or initiated by whom. DuPont is said to have restarted its alternative chemical research in 1988.

143 Maxwell, J. and Briscoe, F. (1997), *Ibid.*; Miller, A. (1990, October). The Development of Substitutes for Chlorofluorocarbons: Public–Private Cooperation and Environmental Policy, *Ambio* 19(6/7), CFCs and Stratospheric Ozone, 338–340; Parson (2003), *op. cit. supra* at n.14 chapter 1, at 54.

Parson (2003) contends that technology could have been commercially available and the fact that it was not "represented a serious lost opportunity". In his view, what drove rapid innovation in the late 1980s and early 1990s was not some kind of miraculous technological breakthrough but rather "the power of regulation and institutions to influence the rate and character of technological change".[144] In fact, in 1986, DuPont apparently announced that the absence of regulatory signals (which the company had been opposing)[145] and public incentives impeded its development of chemical alternatives.[146]

Still, the question remains whether such precautionary measures were possible or not. Again, while publicly available information is deficient in this area, two sources of evidence may be submitted: (1) information regarding technologies used prior to the advent of CFCs and information regarding what of those technologies were adopted as substitutes in and after the 1990s, and (2) similar information which was published during the 1970s and early 1980s by industry, the government and other technical evaluators.

As illustrated in the tables below, largely before and after the era of ozone CFCs and other ozone depleting substances, a variety of chemicals were and are currently used for refrigerant, fire retardant and foam blowing uses. While the tables serve as a snap shot of selected chemical uses and lack sophisticated technical analysis, they do provide a basis to probe whether such chemicals could not have been introduced as replacements earlier. For example, the tables show that the technology to produce some HCFCs and HFCs existed decades before such chemicals were produced and used from the 1990s as core substitutes in the US.[147] They also show that Ammonia, CO_2, water and hydrocarbons were used prior to the advent of CFCs and today are now being promoted as preferred replacements for HFCs and HCFCs.[148] Given their high global warming potentials and in light of global efforts to combat climate change, the US and other countries have resolved in recent years to transition away from using HFCs and

144 Parson (2003), *Id.* at 193.
145 Notably, DuPont claimed that unilateral regulations would have negative economic impacts and be ineffective in achieving environmental goals, and that if regulation were adopted, it should not hamper production but emissions. See The DuPont Report, *op. cit. supra* at n.15, Volume I, ES 10–11.
146 Andersen (2002), *op. cit. supra* at n.37 chapter 1, at 199; Parson (2003), *op. cit. supra* at n.14 chapter 1, at 126; Rowlands, I. H. (1995), *op. cit. supra* at n.42 chapter 1, at 114.
147 Falkner, R. (2005). The Business of Ozone Layer Protection: Corporate Power in Regime Evolution. In D. L. Levy and Newell, *The Business of Global Environmental Governance.* Cambridge: MIT Press at 126–127.
148 See e.g. US EPA (2010, October). *Transitioning to Low-GWP Alternatives in Commercial Refrigeration.* Retrieved from www3.epa.gov/ozone/downloads/EPA_HFC_ComRef.pdf

Table 2.3 Fire retardant chemical and technology development pre-1940 to present

Pre-1940	1940–1995	1995–present
US: 1911: **CO_2**[1]; 1924: Walter Kiddie Company introduces **CO_2** fire extinguisher[2]	Halon gases 1211 and 1301;	1990s: FM-100 (HCFC 22B1; FM-200 (HFC 227ea)[4]
	Mid-1950s: **Water mist** fire suppressions systems[3]	Today: Dry chemicals, **CO_2**, **water** and foams[5] approved by EPA[6]

Notes:
1   *Randolph Laboratories Inc. v. Specialties Development Corporation,* (1949) 178 F. 2d 477.
2   Worcester Polytechnic Institute, Eastern Kentucky University. (2012). *Ordinary People and Effective Operation of Fire.* Fire Equipment Manufacturers' Association.
3   Spadafora, R. R. (n.d.). *Halon Replacement: Water Mist Fire Extinguishing Systems.* Retrieved January 3, 2014, from Fire Engineering University: www.fireengineeringuniversity.com/courses/7/PDF/Spadafora-Jan08.pdf.
4   Robin, M. L. (n.d.). *Halon Alternatives: Recent Technical Progress.* Retrieved March 22, 2014, from National Institute of Standards Safety: www.nist.gov/el/fire_research/upload/R9400569.pdf.
5   Andersen, S. O., Sarma, K. M. and Taddonio, K. N. (2007). *Technology transfer for the Ozone Layer: Lessons for Climate Change.* London: Earthscan at 176–177.
6   US EPA (2012). Halon Substitutes Under SNAP as of December 14, 2012: www2.epa.gov/sites/production/files/2014-11/documents/halons_as_of_12-14-12-final.pdf

HCFCs.[149] This has catalysed new growth in the use of hydrocarbons by US manufacturers.[150]

149   The White House Office of the Press Secretary (2013). *United States, China, and Leaders of G-20 Countries Announce Historic Progress Toward a Global Phase Down of HFCs*: www.epa.gov/ozone/intpol/mpagreement.html, *United States and China Agree to Work Together on Phase Down of HFCs:* www.epa.gov/ozone/intpol/mpagreement.html; US EPA (2014). *2014 North American Amendment Proposal to Address HFCs under the Montreal Protocol:* www.epa.gov/ozone/intpol/mpagreement.html.
150   Galyen, J. (2009, September 9). *Hydrocarbons Charge Up Refrigeration Innovations: Industry Likely to See Propane and Isobutane Products.* Retrieved from Danfoss North America: www.danfoss.com/North_America/EnVisioneering/EnVisioneering/Hydrocarbons+charge+up+refrigeration+innovations.htm; Honeywell International, Inc. (2012, August 15). *Whirlpool Corporation and Honeywell Introduce Most Environmentally Responsible and Energy Efficient Insulation Available into US Made Refrigerators.* Retrieved from Honeywell: Press releases: http://honeywell.com/News/Pages/Whirlpool-Corp-and-Honeywell-Introduce-Most-Environmentally-Responsible-and-Energy-Efficient-Insulation-Available-Refridge.aspx; Underwriters Laboratories (2011). *White Paper: Revisiting Flammable Refrigerants.* Retrieved from http://ul.com/global/documents/library/white_papers/UL_WhitePaper_FlammableRefrigerants.pdf; Unilever (2014). *Climate Friendly Refrigeration.* Retrieved from www.unilever.com/sustainable-living-2014/reducing-environmental-impact/greenhouse-gases/climate-friendly-refrigeration.

Table 2.4 Refrigerant chemical and technology development[1]

Chemical	Pre-1940	1940–1995	1995–present
Ammonia	1860: Ferdinand Carré (France) develops ice-making machine using ammonia making home/commercial refrigeration possible.[2] 1876: Karl von Linde (Germany) introduces ammonia system for brewery cooling, later to be modified for smaller household uses: By 1891, more than 12,000 home units were produced in Germany.[3] 1925: Ammonia is being used as refrigerant by companies in Germany (2) and US (2).[4] 1931: Considered for use by DuPont.[5]		Ammonia, although toxic, has been and continues to be widely used as a natural refrigerant in combination with the use of safe containment and leakage detection equipment in commercial, retail refrigeration.[6] However, initially, its toxic and explosive potential has made it unsuitable for household refrigeration. in US.[7] 1995–96: EPA approved as replacement.[8] As of 2013: approved for various replacement used in US.[9]
Aqua Ammonia	1925: Aqua Ammonia is being used as refrigerant by companies in Germany (2), France (2), Canada (1) and in the US (8).[10] 1931: Considered for use by DuPont.[11]		

Table 2.4 continued

Chemical	Pre-1940	1940–1995	1995–present
Sulphur dioxide	1876: Developed by British industrialists for indoor skating rinks 1925: Used by 8 US refrigerator companies.[12] 1931: Considered for use by DuPont[13] 1930s: Sulphur dioxide while poisonous was considered a safer choice.[14]	Post 1945: used as refrigerant[15] but development incl. leakage control technology due to CFCs.[16]	
Dimethyl ether	1930s: is used as refrigerant.[17]		As of 2012: approved by EPA as for aerosol use.[18]
CO_2	1880s: CO_2 is developed as more efficient and safe refrigerant (Germany, UK). 1890: CO_2 is widely used for British ship refrigeration and as coolant in US.[19] Early 1900s: CO_2 plus numerous chemicals are used and developed as refrigerants and propellants for various commercial and non-commercial uses[20] (US).[21] 1925: used by Carbone, Inc. (US and Switzerland). 1931: Considered for use by DuPont.	Developed as CFC replacement	1990s: Development and use increase especially in Europe.[22] 1994: EPA approved for "tobacco expansion" use.[23] As of 2013–4: EPA approved for various refrigerant,[24] foam[25] uses in US.

Table 2.4 continued

Chemical	Pre-1940	1940–1995	1995–present
Air	1925: Air is being used by 2 US companies.[26]		
Methyl chloride	1920s: used as refrigerant. 1929: refrigerant leakage causing death of children heightens consumer fears.[27]	Post 1945: used as refrigerant.[28]	As of 2014: EPA approved for some foam[29] uses in US.
Chloroethane	1913: (US) home refrigeration model is introduced using Chloroethane. 1925: used by 7 US companies.[30]		
Chloromethane	1925: used by 3 US companies.[31]		
Butane/ Propane	1925: Butane and Pentane are used by the Copeland Co. (US).[32]		1994: EPA approved for "tobacco expansion" use.[33] As of 2013: EPA approved for various refrigerant uses.[34]
Isobutane	1930s: used by 11 of 60 US refrigerator manufactures.[35]		1992: developed as Greenfreeze in Germany.[36] Late 1990s: Outside US, 12+ million hydrocarbon refrigerators are sold world-wide (with over 100 models available).[37] As of 2012–14: EPA approved for various refrigerant,[38] foams[39] and aerosol uses.[40]

Table 2.4 continued

Chemical	Pre-1940	1940–1995	1995–present
HFC 134a	1936: is first synthesised.[41]	1987: US, UK and Japanese companies exclusively hold patents for HFC 134a.[42]	1990s: choice replacement for CFC-12 in US.[43]
HCFC-22		1950s: commercial use begins for air conditioning and foam blowing.[44] 1970s: produced and used for some applications. 1988: approved by FDA for packaging use. 1986–1992: Production doubles.	1990s: choice replacement for CFC-11.

Notes:

1 Stevenson, A. (1925). *Report on Domestic Refrigerating Machines 1923–1925*; Liberman, S. (2011). *American Food by the Decades*. Santa Barbara, CA: Greenwood at 32: By 1922, some 600 refrigerants were known. By 1929, more than one million refrigerators had been manufactured. See also, www.ashrae.org/File%20Library/docLib/.../20061121545_347.pdf
2 Clark, R. P. (2000). *Global Life Systems: Population, Food and Disease in the Process of Globalization*. Rowman & Littlefield at 198.
3 Carlisle, R. (2005). *Scientific American Inventions and Discoveries: All the Milestones in Ingenuity-From the Discovery of Fire to the Invention of the Microwave Oven.* Hoboken, USA: John Wiley and Sons.
4 Stevenson, A. (1925), *op. cit. supra* at n.1.
5 Soman, K. (2011). *Thermal Engineering*. New Delhi: PHI Learning, at 601.
6 *Ibid.*
7 Rees, J. (2013). *Refrigeration Nation: A History of Ice, Appliances and Enterprise in America*. Baltimore: The Johns Hopkins University Press, at 159: Ammonia was used in industrial refrigeration and was known to leak but not necessarily lead to explosions. Rees suggests that media reports concerning ammonia being explosive was faulty. This misguided public opinion regarding the chemical's safety.
8 60 *Fed. Reg.* 38792; 61 *Fed. Reg.* 47012.
9 US EPA (2013). Substitute Refrigerants Under SNAP as of May 17, 2013: www2.epa.gov/sites/production/files/2014-11/documents/reflist.pdf.
10 Stevenson, A. (1925), *op. cit. supra* at n.1.
11 Soman, K. (2011), *op. cit. supra* at n.5.
12 Stevenson, A. (1925), *op. cit. supra* at n.1.
13 Soman, K. (2011), *op. cit. supra* at n.5.

14 Rees, J. (2013), *op. cit. supra* at n.7, at 160: Methyl chloride was manufactured in Europe from 1875is odourless, consumers cannot detect its leakage, making the chemical dangerous.

15 Contracting Business. (January 2009). *The 1940s: War and Amazing Prosperity.* Retrieved from Contracting Business.com: http://contractingbusiness.com/feature/1940s_war_prosperity.

16 Rees, J. (2013), *op. cit. supra* at n.7, at 161. Frigidaire was awarded the patent for CFC-12 in 1931.

17 American Society of Refrigerating Engineers. (1945). *Index to Refrigerating Engineering, Five Year Index 1941–1945.* Retrieved from American Society of Heating, Refrigerating and Air-Conditioning Engineers: www.ashrae.org/.../docLib/.../ASRE_Indexes_1941-1945.pdf; American Society of Refrigerating Engineers. (1934). *Index to Refrigerating Engineering 1905–1934.* Retrieved from American Society of Heating, Refrigerating and Air-Conditioning Engineers: www.ashrae.org/.../docLib/.../ASRE-Index_1905-1934.pdf; American Society of Refrigerating Engineers. (1940). *Index to Refrigerating Engineering 1935–1940.* Retrieved from American Society of Heating, Refrigerating and Air-Conditioning Engineers: www.ashrae.org/.../docLib/.../ASRE_Indexes_1935-1940.pdf.

18 US EPA (2012). Substitute Aerosol Solvents and Propellants Under SNAP as of August 10, 2012 www2.epa.gov/sites/production/files/2014-11/documents/aerosol.pdf.

19 Bodinus, W. S. (1999, April). The Rise and Fall of Carbon Dioxide Systems. *ASHRAE Journal*, 37–42, at 37.

20 American Society of Refrigerating Engineers. (1945). *op. cit. supra* at n.17: Between 1905 and 1945, a substantial body of knowledge supported refrigeration mechanical and chemical know-how in using various refrigerants.

21 See Rees, J. (2013), *op. cit. supra* at n.7.

22 Maroto-Valer, M. M. (2010). *Developments and Innovation in Carbon Dioxide (CO2) Capture and Storage Technology.* Cambridge, UK: Woodhead Publishing, at 382–383.

23 US EPA (2015). Substitutes in Tobacco Expansion: www2.epa.gov/snap/substitutes-tobacco-expansion.

24 US EPA (2013). Substitute Refrigerants Under SNAP as of May 17, 2013; www2.epa.gov/sites/production/files/2014-11/documents/reflist.pdf

25 US EPA (2014) Foam Sector Substitutes under SNAP as of October 21, 2014: www2.epa.gov/sites/production/files/2014-11/documents/foams.pdf

26 Stevenson, A. (1925), *op. cit. supra* at n.1.

27 *Ibid.*

28 Contracting Business. (2009), *op. cit. supra* at n.15.

29 US EPA (2014), at n.25.

30 Stevenson, A. (1925), *op. cit. supra* at n.1.

31 *Ibid.*

32 *Ibid.*

33 US EPA (2015), *op. cit. supra* at n.23.

34 US EPA (2013), *op. cit. supra* at n.24.

35 Andersen, S. O., Sarma, K. M., & Taddonio, K. N. (2007), *op. cit. supra* at n.5 table 2.3, at 288.

36 *Ibid.*

37 Van der Linde, C. (1994). Competitive Implications of Environmental Regulation in the Refrigerator Industry. Management Institute for Environment and Business: This study provides a good overview of the competitive concerns of European and US industries; Falkner, R. (2005), *op. cit. supra* at n.147 chapter 2, at 118–119; Vanner, R. (June 2006). *Ex-post estimates of costs to business of EU environmental policies: A case study looking at Ozone Depleting Substances.*

Policy Studies Institute citing: Stockholm Environment Institute (1999). *Costs and Strategies presented by Industry during the Negotiation of Environmental Regulations*. Stockholm, Sweden: Stockholm Environment Institute; UNEP (April 1997). *Montreal Protocol* XE "Montreal Protocol" *on Substances that Deplete the Ozone Layer: Technology and Economic Assessment Panel, Volume II,*. UNEP. See also, Parson (2003), *op. cit. supra* at n.14 chapter 1, at 187.

38 US EPA (2013), *op. cit. supra* at n.24.

39 US EPA (2014), *op. cit. supra* at n.25.

40 US EPA (2012), *op. cit. supra* at n.18.

41 Nagengast, B. A. (2006, May). *Air Conditioning and Refrigeration Chronology*. Retrieved from American Society of Heating, from US EPA: www.epa.gov/ozone/snap/refrigerants/hc12apet3.pdf.

42 Andersen (2002), at 231, *op. cit. supra* at n.37 chapter 1.

43 *Id.* at 180.

44 The DuPont Report, *op. cit. supra* at n.15 chapter 2, Volume 1 at II-8; Pool, R. (1989). The elusive replacements for CFCs. *Science, 242,* 666–68.

From an atmospheric integrity perspective, it may be equally relevant to ask why that transition could not have occurred much earlier as well.[151] This may very well be an issue which climate change litigation could potentially address, as reflected in Chapter 13.

2.3.4.1 Technical assessments of available CFC alternatives: 1976–1982

Fore and hindsight considerations aside, what actually was known and communicated regarding the feasibility of alternative technologies during the 1970s and 1980s deserves reflection. From the government's side, the EPA commissioned two known studies in 1976 and 1982 which aimed to assess the availability and feasibility of CFC alternative technologies. The first identified a number of potential substitutes and highlighted technical, cost and efficiency barriers for each one. However, it also underscored the capacity to overcome many of those obstacles using both traditional and new chemicals as well as innovative human and environmentally safe technologies.[152] The second study conducted by the Rand Corporation assessed close to 100 available alternatives. While concluding that high cost intensive replacement technologies should be avoided, the study proposes nine feasible options estimated to reduce emissions by 33 percent. These included using methylene chloride and pentane as alternative foam blowing agents and using R-502 as a substitute for CFC-12 in retail food

---

151 Some explanations include: (1) The energy saving potentials of HCFCs and HFCs (Fischer, S. K., Hughes and Fairchild, (1991, December). *Energy and Global Warming Impacts of CFC Alternative Technologies*:www.ciesin.org/docs/011-459/011-459.html); (2) Lower technology change/transition costs (See DuPont (2011), *op. cit. supra* at n.134 chapter 2; (3) Consumer safety reasons and potential over consumer injuries caused by using other toxic or flammable chemicals (Maclaine-Cross, I. L. (2003). Usage and Risk of Hydrocarbon Refrigerants in Motor Cars for Australia and the United States. *International Journal of Refrigeration,* 12; Parson (2003), *op. cit. supra* at n.14 chapter 1, at 187). Additionally, it is argued that the chemical industry lobby influenced government decisions regarding HCFCs and HFCs enabling a handful of US companies to monopolise the replacement chemical market. Falkner, R. (2005), *op. cit. supra* at n.147, at 118–119; Ziegler, O. (2013). EU Regulatory Decision Making and the Role of the United States: Transatlantic Regulatory Cooperation as a Gateway for US Economic Interests? Wiesbaden: Springer at 146. Corporate Europe Observatory (2012). *Climate Bombs Called HFCs How the Industry Lobby is trying to block a phase-out of Super Greenhouse Gases in Europe's Refrigeration and Air Conditioning Systems*; Greenpeace International (n.d.). *HFCs and other F-gases:The Worst Greenhouse Gases You've Never Heard Of.* Amsterdam; Parson (2003), *op. cit. supra* at n.14 chapter 1, at 182. Notably, DuPont had secured no less than "565 patents worldwide to help meet the phase-out schedules of the Montreal Protocol", See DuPont (2011), *op. cit. supra* at n.134 chapter 2.

152 Gruntfest, I. (1976, February). *Chemical Technology and Economics in Environmental Perspectives, Task 1 – Technical Alternatives to selected Chlorofluorocarbons uses.* Midwest Research Institute. Washington, D.C.: US EPA.

refrigeration.[153] While it is unsure the impact these studies had, they are nevertheless informative regarding what was available and what could be feasible early on.

Regarding what the chemical industry knew, only a 1981 DuPont report could be found. In that comprehensive study, the company stated that it had identified a number of CFC replacements. It assessed that none of these would be suitable for various reasons such as their flammability, toxicity, low purpose performance, energy efficiency and costs, as summarised in the Table 2.5.[154] However, in the assessment, what stands out is that most alternative chemicals were already available, some already in use, and that performance and cost evaluations lacked sufficient clarity or rationale to render proposed alternatives "unsuitable".

Still, while this information helps shed light on what substitute chemicals and technologies may have been feasible in the 1970s and 1980s, it remains inconclusive as to whether safe alternatives were genuinely available. During that time, such information was solely in the hands of the producers and was not disclosed.[155] As Parson (2003) has reflected,

> (b)efore (ozone layer) regime formation, authoritative technical knowledge about alternatives was narrowly controlled within firms, principally by the CFC manufacturers, who had no interest in sharing it with environmental activists or regulators who wished to use it to compel the firms to change their technologies. Attempts to conduct assessments of technical options were unable to breach this narrow control of knowledge, so it was widely believed that significant cuts in ozone-depleting chemicals would be extremely costly, and likely dangerous as well. Although activists believed this view to be mistaken, they could never make the case persuasively in policy debates.[156]

In light of this, in the *ozone layer case*, such evidence would likely only come from the producers themselves at trial.

153 Mooz, W., Dole, S., Jaquette, D., Krase, W., Morrison, Salem, S. *et al.* (1982, March). *Technical Options of Reducing Chlorofluorocarbon Emissions.* Retrieved from Rand Corporation: www.rand.org/content/dam/rand/pubs/reports/2008/R2879.pdf.

154 The DuPont Report, *op. cit. supra* at n.15 chapter 2, Volume 1 at II-9, 12, 16, 20. 23, 24, 26, 27, 31.

155 Parson (2003), *op. cit. supra* at n.14 chapter 1, at 54, suggesting DuPont did not disclose because of "commercial confidentiality or out of fear of embarrassing comparisons with their expenditures on research and public-relations to attack charges against CFCs."

156 *Id.* at 9.

Table 2.5 Industry assessment of the availability of CFC replacement technology in 1980

ODS	Use	Alternative	Performance constraints	Safety	Costs	Availability
CFC-12	Refrigeration	Not identified but various	Not identified	Flammable toxic	Not identified	Immediate
CFC-12	Motor vehicle air-conditioning	HCFC-22	None	Not identified	New compression technology; higher fuel costs (due to added weight in MVs)	5–7 years
		Air		none		Immediate
CFC-113	Solvents (cleaning)	Hydrocarbons; chlorocarbons	Corrosive	Flammable, toxic	Use; technology changes	Immediate
		Water	Residue/contamination	None	Clean-up costs	Immediate
CFC-11	Rigid polyurethane foams (thermal insulation)	Fibreglass, wood pulp	Less effective insulation, different weight/structural integrity	None	Material costs, energy inefficiency	Immediate
CFC-11	Flexible polyurethane foams (furniture, seat, bed padding, sound absorption, packaging)	Water	Less Foam flexibility	None	None	Immediate
		Methylene chloride	Insufficient for supersoft foams in furniture manufacturing	Toxic	Additional ventilation costs for safety	Immediate
	Polystyrene foams (e.g. fast food + industrial containers, disposable dinner ware, pipe insulation, flower packaging)	Pentane	Inability to eliminate property and worker hazards	Flammable	Explosion prevention technology est. @US$ 500,000/plant + 25% increase in energy costs	In use

Table 2.5 continued

ODS	Use	Alternative	Performance constraints	Safety	Costs	Availability
		Chinaware	Less sanitary	None	Labour and energy costs for cleaning	In use
	Low-density polyethylene foam and phenolic foams (packaging)	Chemical blowing agents	Limited use	None	More expensive, non-competitive	Not specified
		Wood pulp		None		Immediate
CFC-12?	Food freezing	Air blast	Reduced food quality	None		Immediate
		Cryogenics	None	None	Lower energy efficiency	Immediate
CFC + ethylene oxide	Medical equipment sterilisation	CO_2	Possible "inconsistent sterilisation"			Immediate
		Cold chemical; radiation	None	none	Higher cost, lower energy efficiency	Immediate
CFC?	Fluoropolymers (surface coating)	none				Not available

3 The plaintiffs, damages and liabilities

3.1 The plaintiffs

The plaintiffs in the *ozone layer case* would be those persons who have or will develop skin cancer as a result of exposure to increased levels of solar ultra-violet radiation during their lifetimes. Such plaintiffs may be treated as third parties or bystanders,[1] and therefore should be able to claim economic and non-economic damages in so far as they are able to prove liability of the defendants.[2]

The plaintiffs may also be US States or local governments.[3] They could bring civil actions representing state citizens and public interests under the *parens patriae* doctrine[4] and/or statutory authorities.[5] The former doctrine empowers States to protect their quasi-sovereign interests including the

---

1   American Law Institute (1965). *Restatement (Second) of Torts,* Comment (o).
2   Gifford, D. G. (2013). *Suing the Tobacco and Lead Pigment Industries: Government Litigation as Public Health Prescription.* Ann Arbor: The University of Michigan Press, at 50.
3   Some examples include *City of Bloomington v. Westinghouse Electric Corporation,* 891 F. 2d 611, 616 (7th Cir. 1989); *City of Chicago v. Beretta USA Corp.,* 785 NE 2d 16, 1st Div. (Ill. Appellate Court, 1st Dist. 2002); *City of Cincinnati v. Beretta USA Corp.,* 95 Ohio St. 3d 416 (Ohio 2002); *City of Gary ex rel. King v. Smith & Wesson Corp.,* 801 NE 2d 1222 (Ind. 2003); *In Re MTBE Prods. Liability Litig.,* 725 F. 3d 65 (2d. Cir. 2013); *People v. Atlantic Richfield Co.,* No. 1-00-CV-788657 (Cal. A 2014).
4   The *Parens Patriae* doctrine has evolved from the US Supreme Court ruling in *Georgia v. Tennessee Copper Co.,* 206 US 230 (1907) in which the state was allowed to bring a tort claim on behalf of state interests to protect its residents and property from the defendant company's noxious gas emissions. See also Kanner, A. (2005). The Public Trust Doctrine, Parens Patriae, and the Attorney General as the Guardian of the State's Natural Resources. *Duke Environmental Law & Policy Forum,* 16, 57–115 at 102–109; Gifford, D. G. (2013), *op. cit. supra* at n.2, at 123.
5   *People v. Atlantic Richfield Co.,* No. 1-00-CV-788657 (Cal. A 2014). See also Metz, B. E. (n.d.). *Reconstitutionalizing Parens Patriae: How Federal Parens Patriae Doctrine Appropriately Permits State Damages Suits Aggregating Private Tort Claims,* at 8: Metz provides examples of some state statutes authorising the Attorney General as parens patriae to represent the interests of citizens.

health and welfare of its residents.[6] Such actions are often brought under public nuisance theories and involve claims related to past[7] or future injuries.[8,9] They normally involve damage claims for recovery of environmental abatement costs in the interests of public health and welfare but may also include other economic losses[10] including public health care treatment and disease prevention costs.[11] It has been most recently invoked by States in climate change, tobacco and lead paint litigation.[12] Key to States or local governments representing the citizens and public interests is their capacity to demonstrate special injury under public nuisance law and *parens patria* requirements.[13]

3.2 Injuries: material damages and interferences with public rights

In the *ozone layer case*, multiple injuries to the environment, human health and public rights may be claimed. Predominantly, discussed here are stratospheric ozone loss, increased levels of tropospheric solar UV radiation, climate change and human skin cancers. The following sections review and update on the status of these maladies owing to the production, sale and emissions of ODCs.

3.2.1 The ozone layer and increased solar UV radiation

The ozone layer has been depleted. Global ozone loss is gauged by the volume of depreciation in stratospheric ozone in the Polar Regions. According to the table below, the first biggest loss recorded by NASA and

---

6   *Snapp v. Puerto Rico ex. Rel. Barez,* 458 US 592, 603, 607 (1982). Under the parens patriae doctrine a state must "articulate an interest apart from the interests of particular private parties i.e. the state must be more than a nominal party", show "alleged injury to a sufficiently substantial segment of its population", and defend that individuals whose injuries are represented by the State "could not obtain complete relief through a private suit". (*People of the State of New York by Abrams v. Cornwell Co.,* 695 F. 2d 34 (2d Cir. 1982) at 40. See also Gifford (2013), *op. cit. supra* at n.2, at 123.

7   *In Re MTBE Prods. Liability Litig.,* 725 F. 3d 65 (2d. Cir. 2013).

8   *People v. Atlantic Richfield Co.,* No. 1-00-CV-788657 (Cal. A 2014). (Claims were for future not past abatement costs); *Massachusetts v. EPA* (2007), 127 S. Ct. 1438; *Connecticut v. American Electric Power Co.,* 582 F. 3d 309, 346–47 (2d. 2009), reversed on other grounds in *American Electric Power Co. v. Connecticut,* 131 S.Ct. 2527 (2011).

9   *Davis v. Blige,* 505 F. 3d 90, 103 (2d Cir. 2007).

10   *Minnesota v. Ri-Mel, Inc.,* 417 NW 2d 102, 112 (Minn. Ct. A 1987).

11   *Texas v. American Tobacco Co.* 14 F. Supp. 2d 956, 962; See also Gifford, D. G. (2013), *op. cit. supra* at n.2, at 131–132, 138–168, 176–186.

12   *Connecticut v. American Electric Power Company* (2009), *op. cit. supra* at n.8, at 352; *Massachusetts v. EPA* (2007), 127 S. Ct. 1438; *Texas v. American Tobacco Co* (1997), *op. cit. supra* at n.11; Gifford, D. G. (2013), *op. cit. supra* at n.2.

13   Kanner, A. (2005), *op. cit. supra* at n.4; see also e.g. *In Re MTBE Prods. Liability Litig.,* 725 F. 3d 65 (2d Cir. 2013).

Table 3.1 Size of the "ozone hole": million km²

Year	1979	1980	1982	1985	1986	1993	1998	2003	2006	2013	2014	2015
Peak value	1.1	3.3	10.8	18.8	14.4	25.8	27.9	28.4	29.6	24.01	24.06	28.2

Source: National Aeronautics and Space Administration[1]

Note:
1   See National Aeronautics and Space Administration (2016). Goddard Space Flight Center, Ozone Hole Watch website: http://ozonewatch.gsfc.nasa.gov/meteorology/SH.html.

the NOAA occurred between 1979 and 1985. Thereafter, depletion increases.[14] The peak appears in 2006 at a size of close to 30 million km². After ebbing for some years, the "ozone hole" expanded to around 24 million km² in 2013 and 2014. By 2015, it amassed a size of 28.2 million km², larger than continental North America.[15] In the Arctic region, stratospheric ozone loss was measured at 30 percent in 1996 and 45 percent in 2005 based on 1970s levels.[16] The largest loss was witnessed in 2011 when scientists confirmed the existence of a second ozone hole[17] but were uncertain as to how severe the thinning would become.[18]

The Unites States Environmental Protection Agency confirms that:

> Worldwide monitoring has shown that stratospheric ozone has been decreasing for the past two decades or more. The average loss across the globe totalled about 3 percent at northern middle latitudes and 6 percent at southern middle latitudes since the mid-1960s, with cumulative losses of about 10 percent in the winter and spring and a cumulative 8 percent loss in the summer and autumn over North America, Europe, and Australia.[19]

14   Annual Records (2013, May 31). Retrieved from Ozone Hole Watch: http://ozonewatch.gsfc.nasa.gov/meteorology/annual_data.html.
15   International Commission on Non Ionizing Radiation Protection (2010), *op. cit. supra* at n.25 chapter 1, at 70–71.
16   Fergusson, A. (2010). *The Arctic Ozone Layer: How the Arctic Ozone Layer is Responding to Ozone-Depleting Chemicals and Climate Change*. Toronto: Canadian Ministry of the Environment at 13.
17   Manney, G. L. *et al.* (2011). Unprecedented Arctic Ozone Loss in 2011. *Nature.*
18   Dell'Amore, C. (2011, March 22). First North Pole Ozone Hole Forming? "Put On Your Sunscreen"—Damaging Air Mass Could Drift Far South. *National Geographic News.*
19   US EPA (2010, August 19). *Environmental Indicators: Ozone Depletion*. Retrieved May 15, 2014, from Ozone Layer Protection: Science: www.epa.gov/Ozone/science/indicat/; See also Carlowicz, M. (n.d.). *New Simulation Shows Consequences of a World Without Earth's Natural Sunscreen*. Retrieved May 15, 2014, from National Aeronautics and Space Administration Goddard Space Flight Center: www.nasa.gov/topics/earth/features/world_avoided.html.

Recent studies have demonstrated that the ozone layer has begun to self-repair although total ozone loss is anticipated to peak by 2020.[20] At best, by 2060–75 or later and 2050, respectively are ozone concentrations expected to return to pre-1980 levels over Antarctic and Arctic Polar Regions.[21] Restoration to 1960 levels will likely not be achieved until the end of this century.[22] While this prediction is hopeful, it is also stark notice of the impacts and damages that the next several generations will face.

One of the most serious consequences is that solar UV radiation has increased in the earth's troposphere. This is evidenced most clearly at the South Pole where the direct correlation to stratospheric ozone loss is detected.[23] Elsewhere, cloud cover, pollution and climate change influence where and how much radiation reaches the earth.[24] However, the high- to mid-latitude regions are most affected. In the United States, solar UV radiation intensified between 1979 and 2008[25] and is assessed to have increased 10 percent at mid-to-high latitudes over the past two decades.[26] Globally, a similar increase is expected around 2020 based on 1980 levels.[27]

3.2.2 Climate change

While climate change damages are not addressed in the *ozone layer case*, there is a reasonable basis that they could be pursued in tandem with ongoing and future climate change litigation.[28] For this reason and because of the symbiotic relationships between the atmospheric disturbances, the emissions of ozone depleting substances have also contributed to climate change. Given the extremely high global warming potential (GWP) of many of the chemicals (some being up to 20,000 times more potent than

---

20 International Commission on Non Ionizing Radiation Protection. (2010). ICNIRP Statement on Protection of Workers against Ultraviolet Radiation. *Health Physics*, 9(19), 66–87, at 70–71.

21 World Meteorological Organization (2007). *Scientific Assessment of Ozone Depletion: 2006, Global Ozone Research and Monitoring Project – Report No. 50*. Geneva: World Meteorological Organization at xxiv; World Meteorological Organization. (2010). *Scientific Assessment of Ozone Depletion: 2010, Global Ozone Research and Monitoring Project-Report* at E-4.

22 World Meteorological Organization. (2010). *Scientific Assessment of Ozone Depletion: 2010, Global Ozone Research and Monitoring Project-Report*, at xxiii.

23 *Id.* Chapter 2.

24 *Ibid.* See also Fitzka, M., Simic, S. and Hadzimustafic, J. (2012, December). Trends in Spectral UV Radiation from Long-term Measurements at Hoher Sonnblick, Austria. *Theoretical and Applied Climatology*, 110(4), 585–593.

25 Herman, J. R. (2010, February). Global Increase in UV Irradiance During the Past 30 Years (1979–2008) Estimated from Satellite Data. *Journal of geophysical Research: Atmospheres (1984 – 2012)*, 115.

26 World Health Organisation (2003), *op. cit.. supra* at n.31 chapter 1, at 13.

27 *Ibid.*

28 See e.g. Tol, R. S. (2002). Estimates of the Damage Costs of Climate Change. Part 1: Benchmark Estimates. *Environmental and Resource Economics*, 47–73.

that of their carbon dioxide equivalent), the reduction of ODCs has also been deemed as critical to averting serious climate change.[29] From the mid-1980s, they were reported to cause 15–20 percent of global warming with a possible impact of increasing global average temperature by 1.5C–4.5C by 2030–2050.[30] In 2005, further studies showed that the substances and their common replacement gases accounted for about 5 percent of total global GHG emissions.[31]

Scientific studies suggest further that climate change and stratospheric ozone loss in Polar Regions are interactive atmospheric alterations which impact both on ozone layer recovery and global warming aptitudes.[32] A 2014 study conducted by researchers at the University of California, Irvine and NASA's Jet Propulsion Laboratory has concluded that the West Antarctic ice sheet is melting irreversibly on account of global warming and ozone layer depletion over the South Pole. The glaciers which contain enough ice to raise the global sea level by 1.2 metres are bound to have serious impacts world-wide as they dissolve into the sea over time. Polar ozone loss has contributed to this problem by its impact on changing wind patterns and increasing warmer airflows in the region.[33]

Further, tropospheric temperature increases and wind changes due to greenhouse gas emissions have and are predicted to make stratospheric temperatures much colder which in turn increase ozone depletion and delay stratospheric ozone recovery by 15–20 years.[34] Also, as introduced

29   Morrisette, P. (1989), *op. cit. supra* at n.6 chapter 1, citing Ramanathan, Cicerone, Singh and Kiehl (1985). *Trace Gas Trends and Their Potential Role in Climate Change*, 90 *J. Geophysical Res.* 5547; Report of the International Conference on the Assessment of the Role of Carbon Dioxide and of Other Greenhouse Gases in Climate Variations and Associated Impacts (1986), World Meteorological Organization Pub. No. 661; Dickinson and Cicerone (1986). Future Global Warming from Atmospheric Trace Gases, 319 *Nature* 109; Volle, Seiler and Bolin (1986). *Other Greenhouse Gases and Aerosols: Assessing Their Role for Atmospheric Radiative Transfer, in The Greenhouse Effect, Climatic Change, and Ecosystems* 157.
30   *Id.*
31   Harvey, F. (2005, April 12). Ozone-friendly Gases "Cause Global Warming". *Financial Times.*
32   Previdi, M. and Polvani, L. M. (2014). Climate System Response to Stratospheric Ozone Depletion and Recovery. *Quarterly Journal of the Royal Meteorological Society;* Barnes, E. A., Barnes, N. W. and Polvani, L. M. (2014, January). Delayed Southern Hemisphere Climate Change Induced by Stratospheric Ozone Recovery, as Projected by the CMIP5 Models. *Journal of Climate,* 27(2), 852–867. Bekki, S., Rap, A., Poulain, V., Dhomse, S., Marchand, M., Lefevre, F. *et al.* (2013, June). Climate Impact of Stratospheric Ozone Recovery. *Geophysical Research Letters,* 40(11), 2796–2800.
33   West Antarctic Glacier Loss Appears Unstoppable. (2014, May 12). Retrieved May 22, 2014, from NASA Jet Propulsion Laboratory: www.jpl.nasa.gov/news/news.php?release= 2014-148; Voiland, A. (2009). *What's Holding Antarctic Sea Ice Back From Melting?* Retrieved May 22, 2014, from NASA: www.nasa-usa.de/topics/earth/features/antarctic_ melting.html.
34   Shindell, D. T., Rind, D. and Lonergan, (1998, April). Increased polar stratospheric ozone losses and delayed eventual recovery owing to increasing greenhouse gas concentrations. *Nature, 392,* 589–592.

above, climate change also impacts on the amount of solar UV radiation reaching the earth through changing cloud cover patterns. This affects human and environmental responses both positively and negatively.[35]

3.2.3 Skin cancer damages

Stratospheric ozone loss has aggravated human and environmental damages: skin cancers,[36] eye impairments such as cataracts,[37] and reduced immunities as well as aberrations in plant life, agriculture and ecosystems[38] with sensitive life forms being the most vulnerable.[39] Of these skin cancer has been the most widely studied. It is estimated that 80–90 percent of all skin cancers are caused by solar UV radiation exposure.[40] This includes melanoma which can be fatal[41] and non-melanomas: basal cell carcinoma[42]

35 World Meteorological Organization. (2010), *op. cit. supra* at n.22 chapter 2.
36 Kerr, J. and McElroy, C. (1993). Evidence for Large Upward Trends of Ultraviolet-B Radiation Linked to Ozone Depletion, *Science*, 262, 1032. Seckmeyer, G., Mayer, B., Erb, R. and Bernhard, G. (1994). UV-B in Germany higher in 1993 than in 1992, *Geophys. Res. Lett.*, 21, 577–580. Zerefos, C. S., A. F. Bais, C. Meleti and I. C. Ziomas (1995). A Note on the Recent Increase of Solar UV-B Radiation Over Northern Middle Latitudes, *Geophys. Res. Lett.*, 22, 1245–1247. International Commission on Non Ionizing Radiation Protection (2010). ICNIRP Statement on Protection of Workers against Ultraviolet Radiation. *Health Physics*, 99(1), 66–87, at 70–71; World Health Organisation (1990). *Environmental Health Criteria for Fully Halogenated Chlorofluorocarbons.* Geneva: World Health Organisation at § 10.1.2 at 67.
37 Emmett, E. A. (1986). *Health Effects of Ultraviolet Radiation.* In Effects of Changes in Stratospheric Ozone and Global Climate, Vol. 1 (Titus J. G., Ed.) Environmental Protection Agency, Washington, 129–45.
38 See e.g. Worrest (1986). *The Effect of Solar UV-B Radiation on Aquatic Systems: An Overview.* In Stratospheric Ozone and Climate, 175. Teramura, A. (1986). *Overview of Our Current State of Knowledge of UV Effects on Plants.* In Stratospheric Ozone and Climate, at 165; Caldwell, M., Ballare, C., Bornman, Flint, L., Broern, L., Teramura, A., *et al.* (2003). Terrestrial ecosystems, increased solar ultraviolet radiation and interactions with other climatic change factors. *Photochemical and Photobiological Science*, 2(1), 29–38.
39 Fergusson, A. (2010). *The Arctic Ozone Layer: How the Arctic Ozone Layer is Responding to Ozone-Depleting Chemicals and Climate Change.* Toronto: Canadian Ministry of the Environment at v.
40 Surgeon General's Report (2014), *op. cit. supra* at n.27 chapter 1, at 2; Young, C. (2009). Solar Ultraviolet Radiation and Skin Cancer. *Occupational Medicine*, 59, 82–89.
41 *Id.*; at 3–4; The Skin Cancer Foundation (2014). *Melanoma*: www.skincancer.org/skin-cancer-information/melanoma: Melanomas can occur when skin cell DNA is damaged by UV radiation and cannot repair itself. The process activates cells to multiply and form tumours. While melanoma can be treated if detected early on, chances of recovery are reduced in later stages once the cancer becomes invasive and spreads throughout the body.
42 *Id.*; The Skin Cancel Foundation. (2014). Basal Cell Carcinoma (BCC). Retrieved May 3, 2014, from Skin Cancer Foundation: www.skincancer.org/skin-cancer-information/basal-cell-carcinoma: Basal cell carcinoma is the most common type of skin cancer which forms tumours in the skin's basal cells at the deepest skin layer. Both long term and intense UV radiation exposure lead to these growths which often appear as open sores on the head and upper torso. If left untreated they can cause physical disfiguration and, in some cases, can spread throughout the body similar to melanomas.

and squamous cell carcinoma.[43] The disease usually develops in people over age 40 but is largely due to solar UV radiation exposure and sunburn during childhood. Between 50–80 percent of one's total exposure is concentrated between birth and 20 years of age.[44]

Skin cancer incidence rates have increased globally, largely amongst Caucasians but also darker skinned populations.[45] In 1998, UNEP estimated that more than two million non-melanoma skin cancers and 200,000 malignant melanomas were occurring annually and predicted with a 10 percent ozone layer depletion, an additional 300,000 non-melanoma and 4,500 melanoma cases would occur.[46] In Europe,[47] the UK,[48] South Africa,[49]

43 *Id.* The Skin Cancer Foundation. (2014). Squamous Cell Carcinoma (SCC). Retrieved May 2, 2014, from The Skin Cancer Foundation: www.skincancer.org/skin-cancer-information/squamous-cell-carcinoma: SCC forms in the skin's epidermis becoming visible as abnormal growths as a result of a person's cumulative UV radiation exposure. If not cured it can become invasive and result in death.

44 Committee on Environmental Health. (1999). Ultraviolet Light: A Hazard to Children. *Pediatrics*, 328–333 at childhood sunscreen use. Stern, R., Weinstein, M. and Baker, S. (1986). Risk Reduction for Nonmelanoma Skin Cancer with Childhood Sunscreen Use. *Arch Dermatol*, 537–545; Oliveria, S., Saraiya, M., Geller, A. C., Heneghan, M. K. and Jorgensen, C. (2006, February). Sun Exposure and Risk of Melanoma. *Archives of Disease in Childhood, 91*(2), 131–138; English, D., Armstrong, B. K., Kricker, A. and Fleming, C. (1997). Sunlight and Cancer. *Cancer Causes Control*, 8, 271–283; Martens, (1998). *Health and Climate Change: Modeling the Impacts of Global Warming and Ozone Depletion.* Earthscan.

45 See e.g. Martens, W. (1998, February). Health Impacts of Climate Change and Ozone Depletion: An Ecoepidemiologic Modeling Approach. *Environmental Health Perspectives, 106*(Supplement 1); Surgeon General's Report (2014), *op. cit. supra* at n.27 chapter 1, at 12; Pennello, G., Devesa, S. and Gail, M. (2000, March). Association of Surface Ultraviolet B Radiation Levels with Melanoma and Nonmelanoma Skin Cancer in United States Blacks. *Cancer Epidemiology, Biomarkers & Prevention*, 9, 291.

46 World Health Organisation (1998). Global Solar UV Index: Fact Sheet No. 133. 1; Godar, D., Urbach, F., Gasparro, F. and Van der Leun, J. (2003). UV Doses of Young Adults. *Photochem Photobiol*, 77(4), 453–457.

47 Between 2000 – 2012, newly diagnosed cases of melanoma increased from 35,000 to 82,100 while annual death tolls rose from 9,000 to 15,700. The Nordic countries face the highest incidence and mortality rates: In Denmark, skin cancer is increasing by 3.5–5% annually with 11,000 new cases diagnosed in 2007, a fourfold increase since 1978. See Boyle, Dore, J. F., Autier and Ringborg, U. (2004). Cancer of the Skin: A Forgotten Problem in Europe. *Annals of Oncology*, 15(1), 5–6; Ferlay, J., Steliarova-Foucher, E., Lortet-Tieulent, J., Rosso, S., Coebergh, J. W., Comber, H. *et al.* (2013). *European Journal of Cancer,* 49, 1374–1403; The Copenhagen Post. (2010, June 10). Skin Cancer Rate Highest in Europe.

48 Morris, S., Cox, B. and Bosanquet, N. (2008). Cost of Skin Cancer in England. *European Journal of Health and Economics.* The annual total skin cancer costs amounted to £240 million of which 42% were covered by the National Health Service. Per annum, more than 70,000 new cases are diagnosed and 2,000 persons die of skin cancers while Melanoma has doubled since the early 1970s. See also Cancer Research UK (2014). *Skin Cancer Incidence Statistics.*

49 See Balic, V. and Human, S. (2002). Contribution to Skin Cancer Prevention in South Africa: Modeling the UV Index Utilizing Imprecise Data. *Austrian Journal of Statistics, 31*, 169–175. South Africa bears the second highest incidence of skin cancer after Australia. In 2002, it was estimated that out of every 100,000 Caucasians 21.5 males and 17.8 females, respectively, had melanoma and approximately 197 aggregate had non-melanoma skin cancers.

Australia[50] and New Zealand,[51] new cancer rates are extremely high as are the costs to individuals and public health care systems.

In the United States, skin cancer is "the most commonly diagnosed cancer"[52] and incidence rates have increased dramatically over the last century. In 1935, one in every 1500 Americans were said to contract skin cancer during their lifetimes.[53] In 2012, the number escalated to *one in every 50 persons*.[54] Data from the National Cancer Institute Surveillance, Epidemiology, and End Results Program shows that melanoma incidence on average has tripled across all races and almost quadrupled in the case of white males in certain areas of the United States between 1975 and 2011.[55] Meanwhile, skin cancer incidences amongst older populations grew eight fold during the same time period.[56] Today, nationwide, one person dies every hour from melanoma.[57] In 2013 and 2014, according to the American Cancer Society, those figures increased to an estimated 76,690 and 76,100 new cases, respectively and a total of 18,650 deaths were reported for both years.[58] Statistically, men are more susceptible to the

50 *What is Skin Cancer?* (n.d.). Cancer Council SA: www.cancersa.org.au/information/a-z-index/what-is-skin-cancer#How common is skin cancer. "Australia has the highest rate of UV radiation induced skin cancer in the world. Skin cancer now accounts for over 80% of all cancer diagnosed. Two in every three Australians develops skin cancer at some time during their life. Each year, more than 750,000 new cases of non-melanomas are treated each year and 11,500 melanomas are diagnosed. Skin cancer costs the health system around $300 million each year".

51 In New Zealand, skin cancer costs in 2006 were estimated at NZ$ 57 million for treatment expenses while approximately NZ$ 66 million accounted for productivity/earning losses in cases of death. In 2005, 18,610 new cancer registrations were made. Of these, 2,107 were melanomas. See O'Dea, D. (2009). *The Costs of Skin Cancer to New Zealand*. Retrieved January 22, 2014, from Cancer Society of New Zealand: www.cancernz.org.nz/: www.cancernz.org.nz/assets/files/info/SunSmart/CostsofSkinCancer_NZ_22October2009.pdf.

52 Surgeon General's Report (2014) at 1, *op. cit. supra* at n.27 chapter 1.

53 Rigel, D. S. (2010). Epidemiology of Melanoma. *Seminars in Cutaneous Medicine and Surgery*, 29, 204–209.

54 The Skin Cancer Foundation (2014). *Skin Cancer Facts*. Retrieved from www.skincancer.org/skin-cancer-information/skin-cancer-facts, citing 11. Howlader, N., Noone, A. M., Krapcho, M., *et al.* (eds) SEER Cancer Statistics Review, 1975–2009 (Vintage 2009 Populations). Bethesda, MD: National Cancer Institute.

55 National Cancer Institute. (2014). *SEER Cancer Statistics Review 1975–2011*. http://seer.cancer.gov/csr/1975_2011/browse_csr.php?sectionSEL=16&pageSEL=sect_16_table.01.html.The data is modelled from nine SEER areas studied – San Francisco, Connecticut, Detroit, Hawaii, Iowa, New Mexico, Seattle, Utah and Atlanta.Rates are per 100,000 and are age-adjusted to the United States Population over 19 age groups.

56 Lowe, G. C., *et al.* (2014). Increasing Incidence of Melanoma among Middle-Aged Adults: An Epidemiologic Study in Olmsted County, Minnesota. *Mayo Clinic Proceedings*, 89(1), 52.

57 *Id.* at 1, 4–5. Young adults are in the age group 15–39.

58 American Cancer Society (2013), *op. cit. supra* at n.28 chapter 1, at 4. American Cancer Society (2014), *op. cit. supra* at n.28 chapter 1.

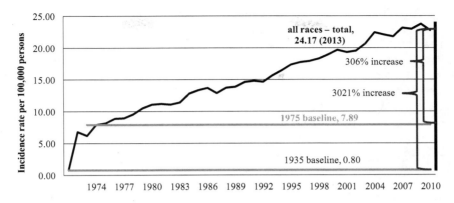

Figure 3.1 Melanoma incidence rates in the United States, 1935–2013

deadly skin cancer than women. Between 2008 and 2010, it was estimated that one in every 34 male and one in every 53 female white US inhabitants had the probability of developing melanoma during their lifetimes.[59] Statistics show further that melanoma fatalities in white males increased 50 percent between 1973 and 1988 and 21 percent in white females during that same time period.[60]

At the State level in 2014, new melanoma cases were estimated. The highest were California (8,530), Florida (5,330), New York (4,200), Texas (3,930), and Pennsylvania (3,890). States estimated to have between 2,000 and 3,000 new cases included Georgia, Illinois, Michigan, New Jersey, Ohio, Virginia and Washington.[61] In assessing factors such as race, latitude, and solar UV radiation levels across the nation, a study conducted by the US Surgeon General's office concluded that melanoma incidence rates varied: In Alaska 14.8 out of 100,000 persons (non-Hispanic whites) had contracted melanoma compared with Utah[62] and Hawaii where the ratio was significantly higher at 31.9 and 66.7 persons per 100,000, respectively.[63] Over all, States in southern latitudes have the highest death rates for melanoma among non-Hispanic white populations."[64]

59   *Id.* at 14.
60   Centers for Disease Control and Prevention (1992, January 17). *Death Rates of Malignant Melanoma Among White Men — United States, 1973–1988.* Retrieved January 17, 2014, from Morbidity and Mortality Weekly Report: www.cdc.gov/mmwr/preview/mmwrhtml/ 00015916.htm.
61   American Cancer Society (2013), *op. cit. supra* at n.28 chapter 1, at 8.
62   Surgeon General's Report (2014), *op. cit. supra* at n.27 chapter 1, at 8–9.
63   *Ibid.*
64   *Ibid.*

Mortality numbers and rates across the entire US population which are maintained by the US Centers for Disease Control and Prevention for the years 1968 to 2010 indicate a steady increase in death rates over the period. The Centers' data also suggests that based on 1974–5 baseline values, to-date a cumulative 76.7 thousand melanoma deaths have been additional and that current death rates show a 300 percent increase in relation to that year.[65] Table 3.2 attempts to demonstrate these increases based on the Centers' data and other nationally collected statistics.

Regarding non-melanoma skin cancers, the same level and detail of information is not available as such cases often go unreported and data is not systematically collected in the United States.[66] However, in 1992, 1,158,298 persons were reported to have been treated for non-melanoma skin cancers.[67] By 2006, it was estimated that 3.5 million persons had developed the disease of which around 2.15 million had received treatments.[68] Recent surveys estimate that today 4.3 million adults are treated for non-melanoma skin cancers annually. This represents 1.9 percent of the total US adult population today.[69] Further and specifically, 2.8 million cases of basal cell carcinoma were diagnosed in 2013[70]: those cases are expected to increase by 2 percent annually.[71] This constitutes 70–80 percent of all non-melanoma skin cancers.[72] As for squamous cell carcinomas, each year, approximately 700,000 new cases are diagnosed.[73] The disease claims the lives of 2,500[74] to 4,000 persons annually.[75]

---

65   Centers for Disease Control and Prevention, National Center for Health Statistics. Compressed Mortality File (1) 1999–2010 on CDC WONDER Online Database, released January 2013. Data are compiled from Compressed Mortality File 1999–2010, Series 20 No. 2P, 2013, (2) 1979–1998. CDC WONDER On-line Database, compiled from Compressed Mortality File CMF 1968–1988, Series 20, No. 2A, 2000 and CMF; 1989–1998, Series 20, No. 2E, 2003, (3) 1968–1978. CDC WONDER Online Database, compiled from Compressed Mortality File CMF 1968–1988, Series 20, No. 2A, 2000. Accessed at http://wonder.cdc.gov/cmf-icd8.html on May 22, 2014.
66   Surgeon General's Report (2014), *op. cit. supra* at n.27 chapter 1, at 4.
67   According to the US census, the total population in United States in 1992 was 254,994,517 persons which increased 14% by 2006 to 298,593,212. Taking that into account, the overall skin cancer growth rate from 1,158,298 cases in 1992 to 2,048,517 is calculated at 35%.
68   Rogers, H. W., Weinstock, M. A., Harris, A. R., Hinkley, M. R., Feldman, S. R., Fleischer, A. B. *et al.* (2010). Incidence Estimate of Nonmelanoma Skin Cancer in the United States, 2006. *Archives of Dermatology*, 146(3), 283–287.
69   *Ibid.*
70   American Cancer Society (2013), *op. cit. supra* at n.28 chapter 1, at 4; American Cancer Society. (2014), *op. cit. supra* at n.28 chapter 1, at 4.
71   Surgeon General's Report (2014) at 4, *op. cit. supra* at n.27 chapter 1, at 4.
72   *Ibid.*
73   American Cancer Society (2013), *op. cit. supra* at n.28 chapter 1, at 4; American Cancer Society (2014), *op. cit. supra* at n.28 chapter 1, at 4.
74   *Ibid.*
75   Surgeon General's Report (2014), *op. cit. supra* at n.27 chapter 1, at 4.

Table 3.2 Increased melanoma incidence rates 1973–2014 in the United States

Year	US population[1]	Incidence rate per 100,000 persons, all races – total[2]	Estimated number of new cases reported annually[3]	Increased incidence rate change based on 1975 baseline[4]	Increased number of cases based on 1975 incidence rate[5]	Percentage of additional cases reported annually 1975 base line rate[6]
1935		(0.80–1.10)[7]				
1973	211,908,788	6.80	14,410			
1974	213,853,928	6.20	13,259			
1975	215,973,199	7.89	17,040			
1976	218,035,164	8.15	17,770	0.26	566.89	3%
1977	220,239,425	8.86	19,513	0.97	2,136.32	11%
1978	222,584,545	8.95	19,921	1.06	2,359.40	12%
1979	225,055,487	9.55	21,493	1.66	3,735.92	17%
1980	227,224,681	10.51	23,881	2.62	5,953.29	25%
1981	229,465,714	11.09	25,448	3.20	7,342.90	29%
1982	231,664,458	11.19	25,923	3.30	7,644.93	29%
1983	233,791,994	11.09	25,928	3.20	7,481.34	29%
1984	235,824,902	11.40	26,884	3.51	8,277.45	31%
1985	237,923,795	12.78	30,407	4.89	11,634.47	38%
1986	240,132,887	13.31	31,962	5.42	13,015.20	41%
1987	242,288,918	13.67	33,121	5.78	14,004.30	42%
1988	244,498,982	12.88	31,491	4.99	12,200.50	39%
1989	246,819,230	13.73	33,888	5.84	14,414.24	43%
1990	249,438,712	13.86	34,572	5.97	14,891.49	43%
1991	252,127,402	14.63	36,886	6.74	16,993.39	46%
1992	254,994,517	14.78	37,688	6.89	17,569.12	47%
1993	257,746,103	14.64	37,734	6.75	17,397.86	46%
1994	260,289,237	15.66	40,761	7.77	20,224.47	50%
1995	262,764,948	16.47	43,277	8.58	22,545.23	52%
1996	265,189,794	17.36	46,037	9.47	25,113.47	55%
1997	267,743,595	17.74	47,498	9.85	26,372.74	56%
1998	270,298,524	17.94	48,491	10.05	27,165.00	56%
1999	272,690,813	18.31	49,929	10.42	28,414.38	57%
2000	282,171,957	18.96	53,499	11.07	31,236.44	58%
2001	285,081,556	19.69	56,132	11.80	33,639.62	60%
2002	287,803,914	19.32	55,603	11.43	32,895.99	59%
2003	290,326,418	19.54	56,729	11.65	33,823.03	60%
2004	293,045,739	20.68	60,601	12.79	37,480.55	62%
2005	295,753,151	22.45	66,396	14.56	43,061.66	72%
2006	298,593,212	22.09	65,959	14.20	42,400.24	68%
2007	301,579,895	21.78	65,684	13.89	41,889.45	70%
2008	304,374,846	23.14	70,432	15.25	46,417.16	74%
2009	307,006,550	22.96	70,488	15.07	46,265.89	67%
2010	310,232,863	23.77	73,742	15.88	49,264.98	81%
2011	312,818,676	22.74	71,135	14.85	46,453.57	66%
2012	315,091,138	24.20	76,250	16.31	51,389.31	67%
2013	317,297,938	24.17	76,690	16.28	51,655.19	67%
Totals			1,670,214		915,327.00	55%

Table 3.2 continued

Notes:
1   Population Estimates Program, Population Division, US Census Bureau (2000). *Historical National Population Estimates: July 1, 1900 to July 1, 1999.* Retrieved from Census.gov: www.census.gov/popest/data/national/totals/pre-1980/tables/popclockest.txt
2   National Cancer Institute (2014). *SEER Cancer Statistics Review 1975–2011, op. cit. supra* at n.55 in chapter 3 text, (710).
3   The estimated new cases are calculated by the population and rate per 100,000 persons.
4   This is the change based on the incidence rate of 1975 assessed at 7.89 per 100,000 persons. The change is the subtraction of 1975 rate from the annual rate assessed for each year.
5   This is the portion of cases attributable to the rate change factor.
6   This is the percentage of all new cases reported for each year which would be considered additional with respect to the 1975 baseline.
7   Rigel, D. S. (2010), *op. cit. supra* at n.53 in chapter 3 text, at 204–209. Rigel's study states that the lifetime probability of one developing skin cancer in America in 1935 was 1 in 1500. Today, it is estimated than one in every 5 persons will be diagnosed with melanoma during their lifetime. While specific annual incidence rates for 1935 could not be found, applying these figures relatively, an annual incidence rate of 0.805 may be assumed for 1935. That is assuming that in 1935, 666 out of 100,000 persons would develop melanoma and in 2012, 20,000 out of 100,000 persons would develop melanoma over a life time. Then the ratio of 1935 to 2012 multiplied to 2012 incidence rates at 24.2 per 100,000 would be calculated at 0.805 persons per 100,000 in 1935. This is an assumed number for the purpose of attempting to understanding melanoma increases in the United States. This also assumes that the 1935 data is correct.

Here, two other factors influencing this dramatic surge in skin cancer incidences and death rates should be addressed. The first is the change in American lifestyles i.e. preferences to dress lightly in hot weather.[76] However, there is no evidence to support this conjecture.[77] The second is the proliferated use of indoor tanning facilities[78] particularly amongst

76   Patel, R. V. and Goldenberg, F. A. (2011). An Update on Nonmelanoma Skin Cancer. *J Clin Aesthet Dermatol,* 4(2), 29–27. American Hospital of Paris (n.d.). *The Sun and Skin Cancer: Interview with Dr Louis Zylberberg:* www.american-hospital.org/en/health-information/diseases-et-conditions/the-sun-and-skin-cancer.html; Iliades, C. (2010). *Skin Cancer Diagnosis on the Rise:* www.everydayhealth.com/skin-cancer/diagnosis-on-the-rise.aspx; World Health Organisation (n.d.). *Sun Protection:* www.who.int/uv/sun_protection/en/
77   Hunt, Y., Augustson, E., Rutten, L., Moser, R. and Yaroch, A. (2012). History and Culture of Tanning in the United States. In C. J. Heckman, and S. L. Manne, *Shedding Light on Indoor Tanning.* Dordrecht, New York: Springer, at chapter 2(all); Boyd, J. E. (n.d.). *Thanks to Chemicstry: A Burning Desire:* Chemical Heritage Foundation at www.chemheritage.org/discover/online-resources/thanks-to-chemistry/ttc-health-suntan_lotion.aspx; *The History of the Suntan* (2014). Retrieved from suntan.com: www.suntan.com/?factshistory; Bosserhoff, A.-K. (ed.) (2011). *Melanoma Development: Molecular Biology, Genetics and Clinical Application.* Vienna: Springer, at 44.
78   Heckman, C. J. and Manne, S. L. (eds) (2012). *Shedding Light on Indoor Tanning.* Dordrecht, New York: Springer; Whiteman, D. and Green, A. (2011). Epidemiology of Malignant Melanoma. In R. D. al. (ed.), *Skin Cancer – A World-Wide Perspective.* Springer-Verlag Berlin Heidelberg; Pennello, G., Devesa, S. and Gail, M. (2000, March). Association of Surface Ultraviolet B Radiation Levels with Melanoma and Nonmelanoma Skin Cancer

young adults.[79] This variable should be taken into consideration in assessing the overall damage costs in question. However, more research would be needed to ensure an accurate accounting.

It is beyond the scope of this study to give a thorough and accurate assessment of damage costs. However, some ball park figures provide a sense of what is involved. In 2014, it was assessed that all skin cancer treatments amounted to US\$ 8.1 billion of which US\$ 3.3 billion was attributed to melanoma treatment costs.[80] These costs are presumably covered partly through health insurance plans funded by the insured and government support. Skin cancer alone has occupied nearly 5 percent of Medicare's total cancer payments.[81]

The premature loss of life due to skin cancer also has economic implications. One study has asserted that "a person who died of melanoma between 2000 and 2006 died 20 years prematurely, compared to 17 years from other cancers".[82] A more recent report assesses average premature life loss at "20.4 years of potential life, compared with an average of 16.6 years for all malignant cancers".[83] On an individual level, financial losses in case of skin cancer disabilities and death are also significant. It is estimated that on average (between 2000 and 2006) people who died prematurely of skin cancer forwent US\$413,370 in lifetime earnings.[84] On the national level, the economic impact of lost years is estimated at US\$4.5 billion.[85] Meanwhile, "(a)nnual costs associated with lost workdays and restricted-activity days are estimated at US\$76.8 million for (non-melanoma skin cancers) and US\$29.4 million for melanoma".[86] Even sunburn, which can lead to skin cancer, accounts for a significant amount of lost work hours, resulting in an estimated economic impact for lost work and treatment in excess of US\$10 million.[87]

in United States Blacks. *Cancer Epidemiology, Biomarkers & Prevention,* 9, 291. Cancer Research UK (2014). *Skin Cancer Incidence Statistics.* Retrieved May 5, 2014, from Cancer Research UK: www.cancerresearchuk.org/cancer-info/cancerstats/types/skin/incidence/uk-skin-cancer-incidence-statistics.

79 Surgeon General's Report (2014), *op. cit. supra* at n.27 chapter 1, at 21, 25–28, 32–37.
80 *Id.* at 9.
81 *Ibid.*
82 Centers for Disease Control and Prevention (2011, November 11). *Melanoma Surveillance in the United States.* Retrieved November 30, 2013, from Cancer Prevention and Control: www.cdc.gov/cancer/dcpc/research/articles/melanoma_supplement.htm.
83 Surgeon General's Report (2014), *op. cit. supra* at n.27 chapter 1, at 9.
84 Ekwueme, D., Guy, G., Li, C., Rim, S., Parelkar and Chen, S. (2011). The Health Burden and Economic Costs of Cutaneous Melanoma Mortality by Race/Ethnicity – United States, 2000 to 2006. *J Am Acad Dermatol,* 133–143.
85 Surgeon General's Report (2014), *op. cit. supra* at n.27 chapter 1, at 9.
86 *Ibid.*
87 Amber, K. T., Bloom, R., Staropoli, Dhimam, S. and Hu, S. (2014). Assessing the Current Market of Sunscreen: A Cross-sectional Study of Sunscreen Availability in Three Metropolitan Counties in the United States. *Journal of Skin Cancer,* 7.

In addition to these costs, national and state public institutions are incurring expenses to prevent, research, educate, monitor, and otherwise take measures to reduce skin cancer injuries and deaths. The US Department of Health and Human Services (HHS) along with several federal agencies sets ten year policy goals and targets to reduce skin cancer incidence and mortality across America. The National Cancer Institute and the Centers for Disease Control and Prevention monitor trends in disease prevalence.[88]

Government agencies also run a number of public educational and awareness raising programmes about solar UV radiation and methods to avoid overexposure. The EPA and the National Weather Service jointly publish a UV Index. The EPA also implements an educational programme called SunWise.[89] The Agency for Healthcare Research and Quality facilitates healthcare for skin cancer patients and provides preventative and curative advice[90] and has recommended counselling for young adults aged between 10 and 24.[91] The Comprehensive Cancer Control Programs and Coalitions runs state and local programmes to educate about skin cancers and to develop solutions to reduce human sun exposure in outdoor recreational areas[92] and the National Park Service provides informational services for visitors.[93] On another level, the FDA sets standards and issues requirements for sun screen product labelling as well as indoor tanning devices.[94] In parallel, the Federal Trade Commission is responsible for investigating false, misleading, and deceptive advertising claims about such products and services.[95] However, despite all of these programmes and initiatives, the Surgeon General has issued his *Call to Action* to increase public resources and policy support for improved prevention and treatment to insure against "skin cancer as major public health problem".[96]

The individual's burden of skin cancer damage can be acute in both economic and non-economic terms. Costs of medical treatment for skin cancer have increased in recent years. A study published by the *American Journal of Preventative Medicine* estimated individual costs for melanoma at US\$4,780 per year and all skin cancers at US\$1,643 annually.[97] New cures for skin cancer are expensive.[98] Private and/or public health insurance

---

88   Surgeon General's Report (2014), *op. cit. supra* at n.27 chapter 1, at 73–75.
89   *Id.* at 77.
90   *Id.* at 76.
91   *Id.* at 35.
92   *Id.* at 75.
93   *Id.* at 78.
94   *Id.* at 75–76.
95   *Id.* at 76.
96   *Id.* at 1.
97   Guy, G., Machlin, S., Ekwueme, D. and Yabroff, K. (2014, November 9). *Prevalence and Costs of Skin Cancer Treatment in the US, 2002–2006 and 2007–2011.* Retrieved from www.ajpmonline.org/article/S0749-3797(14)00510-8/fulltext#tbl2fna.
98   Surgeon General's Report (2014), *op. cit. supra* at n.27 chapter 1, at 25.

premiums must be also calculated.[99] Still, according to the US Census Bureau about 50 million people were uninsured for health in 2010.[100] This situation points to the potential health costs burdened by the uninsured population and the probability of their avoidance of healthcare. The latter being also significant as early diagnosis increases chances of survival and reduces financial stress.[101]

In terms of prevention, as discussed above, citizens individually bear the costs of sun hats, protective clothing and sun screen cosmetics. The EPA's SunWise program advances that individuals who invest US$1 in such preventative measures create a personal saving of US$4 in the long run.[102] Still, it is not known exactly how much sun protection costs people individually and cumulatively on an annual basis. In 1987, the NRDC calculated that the individual prevention scheme would amount to an annual expenditure of US$8 billion annually.[103] Today, sun screen sales alone in the United States were estimated at US$1.4 billion in 2013 and are expected to climb to US$1.8 billion by 2018.[104] Additional costs for protective hats, clothing and sunglasses would escalate the total expenditure. For low income households in particular, these additional costs "may pose financial problems".[105] While these estimates require further data and refinement, they do elucidate the high volume of costs owing to increased skin cancer risks and incidence rates in the United States.

Still, it is difficult to attach a price tag to other losses. Assigning a value to premature loss of life, although possible,[106] may be morally problematic.[107] Such a matter is one which even individuals may not be able to assess

99 More study is needed to analyse cost sharing and distribution in the United States beyond the scope of this study.

100 American Cancer Society, Inc. (2014). *Economic Impacts of Cancer*. Retrieved from American Cancer Society: www.cancer.org/cancer/cancerbasics/economic-impact-of-cancer.

101 US Preventative Measures Task Force. (May 2012). *Recommendations Summary*. Retrieved from Skin Cancer: Counseling: www.uspreventiveservicestaskforce.org/Page/Topic/recommendation-summary/skin-cancer-counseling.

102 Surgeon General's Report (2014), *op. cit. supra* at n.27 chapter 1, at 32.

103 Andersen and Sarma (2002), *op. cit. supra* at n.37 chapter 1, at 80–81; Collins, C. (2010), *op. cit. supra* at n.36 chapter 1, at 198; Parson (2003), *op. cit. supra* at n.14 chapter 1, at 135. Benedick (1998), *op. cit. supra* at n.22 chapter 1, at 60–61.

104 Euromonitor International (2014). *Sun Care in the US*. Euromonitor International.

105 Surgeon General's Report (2014), *op. cit. supra* at n.27 chapter 1, at 9.

106 Non-economic costs assessable in wrongful death cases may include loss of "love, companionship, comfort, care, assistance, protection, affection, society, moral support, loss of the enjoyment of sexual relations and loss of training and guidance". CACI (California Civil Jury Instructions) 3921 *Wrongful Death (Death of an Adult)*. See also CACI 3922, *Wrongful Death (Parents Recovery for Death of a Minor Child)*.

107 See e.g. Ackerman, F. (2008, January). *Critique of Cost–Benefit Analysis, and Alternative Approaches to Decision-making*. Retrieved from Global Development and Environment Institute, Tufts University: www.ase.tufts.edu/gdae/Pubs/rp/Ack_UK_CBAcritique.pdf, at 4–7.

for themselves let alone for the lives of others.[108] Further, even if the disease is not fatal, it can affect a patient's quality of life.[109] That impact is equally hard to measure in financial terms.

In addition, avoiding the sun can also result in the loss of personal freedoms to enjoy outdoor recreational and employment activities. Public authorities and medical experts advise that people use sunscreen lotions, hats and protective clothing and stay indoors during peak day time hours (usually between 10am and 3pm depending on geographical location and seasons).[110] While sun protection methods may have preventative values, their efficacy relies on consistent and regular use as well as product safety.[111] Still, even then, they are not necessarily full proof against all skin cancers.[112] Most research agrees that sun avoidance especially during midday is the only sure way to avert skin cancer.[113] That imperative is reflected in the WHO's statement:

> To negate the adverse effects of increased UVR exposure due to ozone depletion, an alternative response to that of careful titration of sun exposure dose is, in theory, to recommend total sun avoidance and large-scale vitamin D supplementation.[114]

Such a prescription – complete sun avoidance[115] – is demanding and ultimately impacts on the freedoms and interests of people. To eliminate risk they may have to sacrifice employment or recreational activities or

108 *Id.*
109 Surgeon General's Report (2014), *op. cit. supra* at n.27 chapter 1, at 1.
110 See e.g. US EPA (2014, April 29). *SunWise.* www2.epa.gov/sunwise; University of California, San Francisco, School of Medicine, Department of Dermatology. (2007, May 4). *Sun Avoidance.* www.dermatology.ucsf.edu/skincancer/General/prevention/Sun_Avoidance.aspx.
111 Meanwhile, the chemical additives and other active ingredients such as nanoparticles may also be toxic and/or potentially increase other cancer risks. See National Cancer Institute (2014, February 27). *Skin Cancer Prevention.* Retrieved from National Cancer Institute: www.cancer.gov/cancertopics/pdq/prevention/skin/HealthProfessional/page4#Section_129; Environmental Working Group (2014). *The Trouble With Sunscreen Chemicals.* Retrieved from EWG's 2014 Guide to Sunscreens: www.ewg.org/2014sunscreen/the-trouble-with-sunscreen-chemicals/; Prevenslik, T. (2009). *DNA Damage and Cancer by Nanoparticles.* Retrieved from nanoqed 2014: www.nanoqed.org/resources/DNA.pdf.
112 McDaid, C. F. (2010). *Sun Protection Resources and Environmental Changes to Prevent Skin Cancer: A Systematic Review.* University of York; Bastuji-Garin, S. and Diepgen, T. (2002, April 30). Cutaneous Malignant Melanoma, Sun Exposure, and Sunscreen Use: Epidemiological Evidence. *British Journal of Dermatology,* 146(s61), 24–30.
113 US Preventive Services Task Force (2003). *Counseling to Prevent Skin Cancer: Recommendations and Rationale of the US Preventive Services Task Force.* Atlanta: Centers for Disease Control and Prevention.
114 World Health Organisation (2003), *op. cit. supra* at n.31 chapter 1.
115 *Ibid.*

otherwise modify their daily behaviour to avoid sun exposure. Practically speaking, people would be required to stay indoors for 4–7 hours during the mid-day particularly in summertime.[116] For children, who comprise the group most vulnerable to the sun's radiation, ensuring their daily protection is critical yet practically challenging[117] given their natural inclinations and need for outdoor mobility:[118] their normal childhood behaviour and freedom of action and play are impaired.[119]

Aside from these non-economic harms, it is possible to provide a preliminary estimate of damage costs based on the above calculable individual and government burdens of coping with and preventing skin cancer. Table 3.3 below attempts to do this. It makes a conservative assumption that the federal government will spend approximately US$1 million in 2015 on national skin cancer prevention and treatment programmes. It also suggests that each American will spend on average US$50 in 2015 on sun protection gear such as hats and clothing. Based on these estimated and assumed costs, the total private and public expenditure would be close to US$30 billion. If the melanoma increase rate at 67 percent based on the 1975 baseline is applied, then the total amount of increased costs to Americans would near US$20 billion. Applying a more conservative 1985 baseline increase rate of 47 percent indicates an expenditure in excess of US$14 billion.

3.3 Apportioning liability on a market share approach

The amount of liability which could be imposed on the defendant producers can be assessed further based on their market share production and sales of ozone depleting chemicals between 1976 and 1992 as presented in Chapter 2. Figure 3.2 recaptures this breakdown according to the known successor companies with the historic producers marked in parentheses.[120] However, this should be understood as an initial estimate as it does not capture accurately the pre-1986 domestic production levels as well as overseas markets.

In addition, the US total market share production in relation to total global production must also be taken into account. As introduced in Chapter 2, based on data compiled in the Appendix of this study, an estimation can be made. Table 3.4 illustrates this. It shows the cumulative sum of global and US industries' production of ozone depleting chemicals other than carbon tetrachloride between 1931 and 2012. It further breaks down production volume into three distinct time periods: (1) 1931–1975 – the period before the risk of stratospheric ozone loss was knowable; (2) 1976–1992 – the period when the risk was knowable but when US chemical producers are alleged to have not taken sufficient precautionary action to prevent chemical emissions, and (3) 1993–2012 – the period when regulations were imposed and enforced to phase out the production of most ODCs in the US and elsewhere. Accordingly, the table reveals that for the

Table 3.3 Estimated annual cost (2015) of skin cancer in the United States (US$, millions)

	Purpose of expenditure	Cost	Increased cost (1975 baseline)	Increased cost (1985 baseline)	Burden
Economic losses	Annual medical costs[1]	8,100	5,427	3,807	State/individual
	Loss of productivity (premature death)[2]	4,500	3,015	2,115	State/individual
	Employment absence[3]	116	78	55	State/individual
Non-economic	Premature death			–	Individual
	Disfigurement			–	Individual
	Personal (lifestyle restrictions)				Individual
Prevention	Personal (sunscreen)[4]	1,400	938	658	Individual
	Personal (protective gear)[5]	15,800	10,586	7,426	Individual
	Education	1	0.67	0.47	State
	Monitoring	1	0.67	0.47	State
	Screening	1	0.67	0.47	State
	Research (social, community planning)	1	0.67	0.47	State
	Research (medical)	1	0.67	0.47	State
Total		29,921	20,047	14,063	Total
Est. Total (State–public costs)		12,721	8,523	5,978	State
Est. Total (Individual, private costs)		17,200	11,524	8,084	Individual

Notes:
1   Surgeon General's Report (2014), *op. cit. supra* at n.27 chapter 1, at 9.
2   *Ibid.*
3   Amber, K. T., Bloom, R., Staropoli, Dhimam, S. and Hu, S. (2014). Assessing the Current Market of Sunscreen: A Cross-sectional Study of Sunscreen Availability in Three Metropolitan Counties in the United States. *Journal of Skin Cancer*, 7.
4   Euromonitor International (2014). *Sun Care in the US.* Euromonitor International.
5   Estimated as US$50 per person calculated by US 2013 population at 317,297,938.

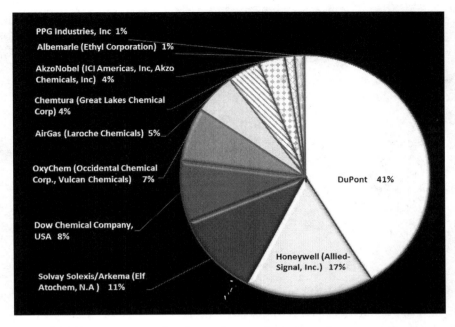

PPG Industries, Inc 1%

Albemarle (Ethyl Corporation) 1%

AkzoNobel (ICI Americas, Inc, Akzo Chemicals, Inc) 4%

Chemtura (Great Lakes Chemical Corp) 4%

AirGas (Laroche Chemicals) 5%

OxyChem (Occidental Chemical Corp., Vulcan Chemicals) 7%

Dow Chemical Company, USA 8%

Solvay Solexis/Arkema (Elf Atochem, N.A) 11%

DuPont 41%

Honeywell (Allied-Signal, Inc.) 17%

Figure 3.2 US corporate market share of ozone depleting substance production based on 1990 production allowances and estimated 1986 production levels

entire period, the share of US production is 38 percent. However, for the liability period suggested in this study, 1976–1992, the total share of US production relative to total global production between 1931 and 2012 is calculated at 22 percent.

Table 3.4 Total global and US ozone depleting chemical productions, 1931–2012, ODP tonnes

	Global production ODP tonnes	US production ODP tonnes	US total production share of total global production	US production share 1976–1992, against total global production	US production share 1976–1992, against total global production 1976–2012
1931–1975	8,804,440	4,486,496	51%		
1976–1992	18,084,085	6,680,672	37%		
1993–2012	4,117,303	640,465	16%		
Totals	31,005,828	11,807,632	38%	22%	30%

By applying these production and market share estimates to the data presented above regarding the scope and costs of skin cancer damages, it is possible to give an approximation of the amount of liability each company would bear. The amount of damages is based on Table 3.3 above which assessed the individual and public costs associated with preventing and coping with skin cancer incidences and deaths in the US. There, the annual private and public economic costs were approximated at US$30 billion in 2015. This includes individual household costs for skin cancer protection including sun screens, hats and clothing, which were approximated at US$17.2 billion. Based on these figures, the damage liability should be further calculated commensurate to the increased costs directly linked to increased skin cancer incidence and death rates between 1975 and 2015. The damages may be adjusted according to the following discount rates:

- Rate 1: The total market share of ozone depleting substances production by US companies between 1975 and 1992. This was calculated at 22 percent as the portion of all global production for the period 1931 to 2012.[121]
- Rate 2: The estimated increased rates of skin cancer incidence based on melanoma incidence rate estimates between 1975 and 2013 calculated at 67 percent (i.e. 67 percent of current skin cancer cases are presumed to be additional). This does not apply assumed higher non-melanoma incidence rates due to lack of publicly available data.
- Rate 3: A causal factor of 90 percent based on data presented in Section 3.2.3 above suggesting that between 80 percent and 90 percent of all skin cancers are caused by solar UV radiation.
- Rate 4: The individual market share of former and successor US chemical companies of ODC production as presented above.

116 US EPA (2014, April 29). *SunWise:* www2.epa.gov/sunwise.
117 Surgeon General's Report (2014), *op. cit. supra* at n.27 chapter 1, at 66–67; US EPA (2006). *Human Health Benefits of Stratospheric Ozone Protection.* Washington, D.C., at 32: "For the whole life exposure assumption, the risks of ozone depletion are borne primarily by the present population of adults who will experience these health effects as they age. It is children and future generations that will experience increased early life UV exposures and the associated incremental health effects later in their lives".
118 Cercato, M. *et al.* (2013), *op. cit. supra* at n.31 chapter 1; US Preventive Services Task Force. (2003, October), *op. cit. supra* at n.31 chapter 1.
119 Tran, A. D., Aalborg, J., Asdigian, N. L., Morelli, J. G., Mokrohisky, S. T., Dellavalle, R. P. *et al.* (2012). Parents' Perceptions of Skin Cancer Threat and Children's Physical Activity. *Prev Chronic Dis.*
120 This is based on production allowances stipulated in US federal regulation on Protection of Stratospheric Ozone 40 C.F.R. 82.5. This is an estimate of market share based on ODP equivalents not production weight.
121 This excludes production of carbon tetrachloride due to lack of sufficient publicly available data.

Table 3.5 applies these rates to assumed damage costs. In doing so, it distinguishes costs to public agencies and costs to both private persons and the government. It assesses the latter at amounting to around US$3.9 billion in 2015. Based on this figure and not accounting for inflation, the total liability over the next 15 years (2015–2030) would be close to US$60 billion. The bottom half of the Table 3.5 shows how those liabilities could be apportioned across the 11 former or successor ODC producer companies.

Again, this method of calculating liability costs requires further refinement and review. Additionally, market share assumptions must be validated as well as damage cost estimations. However, for the purposes of the *ozone layer case*, it provides a reasonable basis to consider how liabilities could be assessed and distributed amongst the chemical producers should a tort claim against these companies be made in the future.

Table 3.5 Market share liability calculations for ozone depleting chemical manufacturers (estimated annual base costs and 15 year projection, in US$ millions)

Liability discounts	Liability discount	Y 2015 Damage costs (private and public costs)	Years 2015–2030 Damage costs (private and public, excludes inflation, population growth)	Y 2015 Damage costs (public only)	Years 2015–2030 (public costs, excludes inflation, population growth)
Total damage costs		29,921	448,815	12,721	190,815
Rate 1: Industry's share of total layer global contribution to ozone depletion	22%	6,583	98,739	2,799	41,979
Rate 2: Increased incidence rate of melanoma between 1976 and 2013	67%	4,410	66,155	1,875	28,126
Rate 3: Percentage of skin cancer caused by solar UV radiation exposure	90%	3,969	59,540	1,688	25,314

Producer, successor corporation   Market share (percentage, estimated financial contribution, US$ millions)

Rates 4	Market share	Y 2015 Liability (private/public costs)	Years 2015–2030 Liability (private/public costs)	Y 2015 Liability (public costs only)	Years 2015–2030 Liability (public costs only)
DuPont	41%	1,627	24,411	692	10,378
Honeywell	17%	675	10,122	287	4,303
Solvay Solexis/Arkema[1]	11%	437	6,549	186	2,784
Dow Chemical	8%	318	4,763	135	2,025
OxyChem	6%	238	3,572	101	1,519
AirGas	6%	238	3,572	101	1,519
Chemtura	4%	159	2,382	68	1,013
Azko Nobel	4%	159	2,382	68	1,013
Albemarle	2%	79	1,191	34	506
PPG Industries	1%	40	595	17	253

Note:
1 There is insufficient data to assess the exact market share of each of these successor companies.

Part II
Liability tests

4 Negligence and strict product liability

This chapter discusses whether the conduct of companies in producing and marketing ODCs between 1976 and 1992 would be liable under the US common law theory of negligence and strict product liability. Given the similarities of these theories, they are discussed together but with special attention to questions of negligence given the predominance of this liability theory in the United States.

The US Restatement of Torts defines negligence as "conduct which falls below the standard established by law for the protection of others against unreasonable risk of harm".[1] To establish liability in negligence, a plaintiff needs to prove: (1) that the defendant had a legal duty or obligation to perform a reasonable standard of care toward her so as to protect her against an unreasonable risk; (2) that the defendant failed to meet that required standard of care; (3) that causation and proximate cause exist in relation to her injury and the defendant's conduct; (4) that the defendant could foresee the unreasonable risk as well as his duty toward the plaintiff to avoid that risk; (5) that she has suffered losses and damages as a result of (2).[2]

In contrast, the strict product liability theory as explained by the Restatement applies to: "One who sells any product in a defective condition unreasonably dangerous to the user or consumer or to his property is subject to liability for physical harm thereby caused to the ultimate consumer or to his property if (1) the seller is engaged in the business of selling such a product, and (2) it is expected to and does reach the user or consumer without substantial change in the condition in which it is sold."[3]

What differentiates the theories is the manifestation of fault. In negligence, it is essential to prove a defendant's deviated from an expected duty

---

1   Restatement (Second) of Torts (1965), § 282.
2   Restatement (Third) of Torts: Liability for Physical Harm (2005).
3   Restatement (Second) of Torts (1965) § 402A (1)(2). Further, this rule applies "although the seller has exercised all possible care in preparation and sale of his product, and (b) the user or consumer has not bought the product from or entered into any contractual relation with the seller."

of care e.g. as in producing and marketing a defective product, and causing the plaintiff's injury as a result.[4] In such cases, he may have intentionally caused harm or acted without reasonable care, foresight and precaution.[5] In contrast, strict product liability is focused "on the dangerous condition of the product as put into commerce"[6] as opposed to a tortfeasor's conduct.[7] The theory's rationale is to relieve that plaintiffs' burden of proving fault so as to achieve greater consumer protection and public safety.[8]

However, with regard to product liability, the theories possess identical features: causation, injury, and a product's foreseeable, unreasonable risk of harm must be established. Evidence must also be provided that a product is defective and that the product's defective condition "existed at the time the product left the control of the manufacturer or supplier".[9] This includes showing that the product is "unreasonably dangerous", or "more dangerous than an ordinary consumer would expect when used in an intended or reasonably foreseeable manner".[10] Under both theories, the defectiveness of complex products is often determined by weighing their risks against their utilities.[11] This involves probing whether substitute products are available, whether safer products are feasible and cost effective, and whether the product carries warning labels or not. It must be shown that the product's risks of harm must not be open and obvious[12] but generally foreseeable,[13] and reasonably known by the manufacturer based on

4   Prosser, W. L. (1971). *Handbook of the Law of Torts.* St Paul, Minnesota: West Publishing Company, at 142.

5   Holmes, O. W. (1881). *The Common Law.* Boston: Little, Brown and Company, at 94–6: Only by finding fault can liability be imposed and compensation awarded for injuries in a reasonable and just way.

6   *O'Keefe v. Boeing Company*, 335 F. Supp. 1104, 1118–1119, 1132 (SDNY 1971); *Barker v. Lull Engineering Co.*, 573 2d 443, 431 (Cal. 1978); *Campbell v. General Motors Corp.*, 649 2d 224, 32 Cal. 3d 112, 119 (Cal. 1982); *Cronin v. JBE Olson Corp.*, 501 2d 1153, 104 Cal. Rptr. 433, 8 Cal.3d 121, 133 (1972).

7   Hollingsworth (n.d.). *Framework for Toxic Tort Litigation.* Washington, D.C.: Washington Legal Foundation, at 293,301.

8   *Escola v. Coca Cola Bottling Company of Fresno*, 24 Cal. 2d 453, 462 (Cal. 1944); Priest, G. L. (1985, December). The Invention of Enterprise Liability: A Critical History of the Intellectual Foundations of Modern Tort Law. *The Journal of Legal Studies, 14*(3), at 462; Steiner, J. M. (1983). Putting Fault Back into Products Liability. In M. D. Bayles and B. Chapman (eds), *Justice, Rights and Tort Law* (179–209). Dordrecht/Boston: D. Reidel Publishing Company, at 204–205.

9   Hollingsworth, *op. cit. supra* at n.7, at 2, citing *McClaran v. Union Carbide Corporation*, 26 F. Appendix 869 (10th Cir. 2002) and *Flock v. Scripto-Tokai Corporation*, 319 F. 3d 231 (5th Cir. 2003).

10   *Id.* at 2, citing *Rivera v. Philip Morris, Inc.*, 395 F. 3d 1142 (9th Cir. 2005) and *Sigler v. American Honda Motor Company*, 532 F. 3d 469 (6th Cir. 2008).

11   *Id.* at 3, citing *Brown v. Raymond Corporation*, 432 F. 3d 640, 647 (6th Cir. 2005) and *Toms v. J. C. Penny Company*, 304 F. Appendix 121, 124 (3d Cir. 2008).

12   See also, End, J. (2000). The Open and Obvious Danger Doctrine: Where does it belong in our comparative negligence regime? *Marquette Law Review*, 84(445).

13   Restatement (Third) of the Law of Torts (1997), § 2(c)

available scientific and technical knowledge.[14] Finally, the plaintiffs will need to prove that their injuries were a result of the defective product. However, if this can be established, under the strict product liability theory, then the burden of proof should shift to the defendant.[15]

These criteria and concepts are unpacked in the following sections in relation to the *ozone layer case* to determine whether a finding of liability would be plausible under negligence and strict product liability theories and under what conditions. The following discussion seeks to probe the negligence and strict product liability of the producers of ODCs for their alleged failure to warn about the potential chemical risks, their failure to prevent direct emissions of the chemicals during manufacturing and pre-sale stages through the use of emission control technologies, the failure to take precautionary measures in reducing and not increasing the global market and demand for ozone depleting substances including the industry's failure to develop and market safe alternatives until the 1990s. In doing so, it also investigates whether the chemicals were defective products and posed an unreasonable risk of harm under both negligence and strict liability theories. Here, the common risk-utility test is applied. Further, issues of causation, proximate cause and the existence of injuries and damages are analysed. In exploring these concerns, special considerations are given to potential plaintiffs who would be individuals and those which would be US States. The argumentation relies on US tort case law and theory.

4.1 Existence and failure of legal duty of care

As presented in Chapter 2, the depletion of the ozone layer and subsequent human health damages, most notably estimations of increased skin cancer incidences and death were understood to constitute risks of unreasonable harm. This was established in the United States by Congressional and federal agency policy makers in their endangerment findings which have remained intact since the mid-1970s despite numerous uncertainties. Assuming this risk, the question here is whether or not the producers of ODCs had a duty to exercise reasonable care to protect vulnerable classes of people from such potential harms.

Under the negligence theory, an act or omission is subject to liability when it fails to conform to external standards imposed by society and creates unreasonable danger to others. The act may not be careless or even morally wrong *per se* but it would violate an expected standard of care or duty one person has toward another *as recognised by the law*.[16] That duty is essentially one's obligation to not violate the legally protected interests or

14   *Taylor v. Merck & Company* (WD Tennessee 2009).
15   *Barker v. Lull Engineering Co.*, 573 2d 443, 431–32 (Cal. 1978).
16   Prosser (1971), *op. cit. supra* at n.4, at 149–151.

rights of other people. It is a violation of these rights which gives rise to negligence.[17] Such duties of care can be informed by public statutes as well as common law. A duty of care is not necessarily satisfied by regulatory compliance, however, especially when the rules are deficient or non-existing.[18] Standards of care also can be gleaned from case law precedent, evidence of customary practice, industry standards and "knowledge of experts".[19] Industry practices or standards often serve as evidence in determining what a standard of care should be in negligence cases. In the *ozone layer case*, the standards of care incumbent on chemical producers can be deduced from these sources.

4.1.1 Duty to warn

In 1976, the Consumer Product Safety Commission and the Food and Drug Administration proposed regulations requiring that CFC containing products bear warning labels. Effective from 1977–1978, manufacturers had to label their aerosol products, warning of potential chemical dangers to the environment and human health.[20] The intention was to alert consumers to such risks thereby spurring reduced consumption and emissions. However, labelling requirements did not extend to upstream chemical products such as containers of CFCs sold to industrial and commercial users. They also did not affect non-aerosol and other essential products such as refrigerators, air conditioners, seat cushions, fire extinguishers and cleaning solvents.[21] Such duties to warn were imposed on producers from 1993.[22] From that year onward, any container in which ozone depleting substances were stored or transported[23] and introduced into interstate commerce was required to bear a warning label.[24] However, this mandate did *not* affect products or containers specifically bound for export.[25]

Accordingly, in the 1970s and 1980s, there was an apparent logical disconnect between requiring that fungible chemicals in one form

---

17   *Palsgraf v. Long Island Railroad Company*, 248 NY 339, 344–345 (NY 1928).

18   *Kendall v. Hoffman-LaRoche, Inc.*, 36 A. 3d 541, 554 (NJ 2012).

19   Prosser (1971), *op. cit. supra* at n.4, at 166–168.

20   16 C.F.R. 1401: Self Pressurized Consumer Products Containing Chlorofluorocarbons: Requirements to Provide the Commission with Performance and Technical Data; Requirements to Notify Consumers at Point of Purchase of Performance and Technical Data (CPSC); 21 C.F.R. 2.125: Use of ozone-depleting substances in foods, drugs, devices, or cosmetics (FDA).

21   *Id.*; US Consumer Product Safety Commission (1977, April 26). *FDA and CPSC Announce Fluorocarbon Labelling Plan*: www.cpsc.gov/en/Newsroom/News-Releases/1977/FDA-And-CPSC-Announce-Fluorocarbon-Labeling-Plan/.

22   40 C.F.R. §§ 82.100 – 82.124.

23   40 C.F.R. § 82.104(a)(1), 40 C.F.R. § 82.124(a).

24   40 C.F.R. § 82.106(a): "WARNING: Contains [insert name of substance], a substance which harms public health and environment by destroying ozone in the upper atmosphere".

25   40 C.F.R. § 82.106(b).

(aerosols) bear warning labels but not in another (non-aerosols). The risks both entailed were the same given that either product would have emitted the chemicals given that no disposal requirements were in place until the 1990s. The same disjoint is observed regarding products sold on the US market and those bound for export. Given that US stratospheric ozone protection policy was to curb *global* emissions, and that chemical releases were expected from *every product* containing them – regardless where products were sold, that goal would be defeated if users or consumers in the US and in other countries were not alerted to ozone depleting product dangers (assuming that such a warning would affect consumption). Therefore, even though regulations were silent on the need for ODCs as products to bear warning labels, from a policy perspective it is arguable that such products should have had an attached warning and that attaching warnings proactively, on a voluntary basis, would not have been penalised.

It terms of common law precedent, courts generally have recognised that product manufacturers have a duty to warn consumers and users about risks their products could cause to the environment and human health.[26] The policy implication is that "would be" users or consumers are ensured a reasonable basis to decide whether they desire to use or purchase the product in question.[27] In the *ozone layer case*, the impact of this objective may have been to decrease user demand and to bolster efforts of the user community to develop safe containment and capture technologies and/or alternative materials and products altogether. Although this presumption is not fully assured, in effect, this was what happened in the 1970s regarding aerosol products[28] and it was what started happening in the 1980s when evidence of ozone layer depletion became starker and the adoption of comprehensive regulations appeared imminent.[29]

Common law also supports that even if the probability of the ozone layer harm were low – such as a "one in a million" chance of harm occurring scenario, given the unreasonable nature of the harm and its potential lethal impact on the environment and human health, manufacturers may have still born a duty to disclose that risk of harm.[30] And, even if it is argued that the utility of chemicals outweighs their risks, the duty to warn still

---

26 *Davis v. Wyeth Labs, Inc.*, 399 F.2d 121 (9th Circuit 1968); *State Department of Environmental Protection v. Ventron Corporation*, 440 A.2d 455 (1981), aff'd in part 468 A.2d 150 (1983).

27 *Anderson v. Owens-Corning Fiberglas Corp.*, 53 Cal. 3d 987, 1003 (Cal. 1991); *Davis v. Wyeth Laboratories, Inc.* 399 F. 2d 121, 129–130 (9th Cir. 1968).

28 Andersen, S. O., Sarma, K. M. and Taddonio, K. N. (2007), *op. cit. supra* at n.5 chapter 2 table 2.3, at 156.

29 Rothenberg, S. and Maxwell, J. (1997). Industrial Response to the Banning of CFCs: Mapping the Paths of Technical Change. *Technology Studies*, 213–236, at 222–223: For example, Northern Telecom, AT&T, IBM and the Digital Equipment Corporation transitioned from CFC solvents to aqueous and other chemical substitutes and no-clean technologies.

30 *Davis v. Wyeth Laboratories, Inc.* 399 F. 2d 121 (9th Cir. 1968).

would have existed.[31] This is particularly true for products such as ozone depleting substances which may be deemed as *unavoidably unsafe*. Such products include those which, "in the present state of human knowledge, are quite incapable of being made safe for their intended and ordinary use."[32] Such products contain some risks which cannot be eliminated through any exercise of reasonable care. However, because they are extremely useful for society (e.g. vaccines) they can be placed on the market.[33] They are not considered defective or unreasonably dangerous if they are "properly prepared and marketed, and proper warning is given." Thus, primarily, a failure of the duty to warn renders an unavoidably unsafe product defective.[34] Courts have found drugs, asbestos and other like products to be both *unavoidably unsafe*[35] and defective when not accompanied by warning labels and instructions.[36] By analogy, ODCs may fall under this category of products as well. Presumably, consumers should have been presented with production information alerting them of possible harmful consequences. In support of this notion, in 1977, the New York Court of Appeals did endorse the public right to know about the potential dangers of chlorofluorocarbons in aerosol sprays.[37]

The duty to warn also extends to toxic or radiation contamination. This is relevant in the *ozone layer case* because the issue is not only the chemicals as unsafe products but also their release into the environment. Essentially, until 1993 when emissions controls were widely introduced, it was highly certain that once the chemicals were produced and unleashed into the market, they were emitted into the environment. Arguably, production and sale of the chemicals was tantamount to their contamination of the atmosphere and resulting, latent harms to human health. The attenuate duty to warn of such consequences has some case law basis.

Recent litigation concerning corporate liability for groundwater and public well contamination caused by MTBE seepage from underground storage tanks provides a useful basis to connect a product warning requirement with its environmental harms. In *In Re MTBE Prods. Liability Litig.*, the Second Circuit Court of Appeals found that the defendant Exxon had a duty to warn gas station operators as well as "city water providers and the public of dangers arising from the addition of MTBE into gasoline". Such a warning would have made a difference for example by encouraging the

31   *Borel v. Fibreboard Paper Products Corp.*, 493 F. 2d 1076 (5th Cir. 1973).
32   Restatement (Second) of Torts (1965), § 402 comment k.
33   *Ibid.*
34   *Ibid.*
35   *Borel v. Fibreboard Paper Products Corp.*, 493 F. 2d 1076, 1088 (5th Cir. 1973); *Anderson v. Owens-Corning Fiberglas Corp.*, 53 Cal. 3d 987, 1000 (Cal. 1991).
36   *Collins v. Eli Lily & Co*, 116 Wis. 2d 166, 196–197 (Wis. 1984).
37   *ATI, Inc. v. Ruder & Finn*, 42 NY 2d 454 (Court of Appeals of the State of New York October 6, 1977).

replacement of leaking storage tanks.[38] The court concluded that the company was negligent for its failure to warn.[39]

Another case which deals with failure to warn claims regarding environmental and human harms resulting from radiation fallout and contamination from nuclear testing is *Allen v. United States* (1984). In that case, local citizens claimed damages for radiation exposure and injuries. The court assessed that the government was obliged to inform the community of "the nature and extent of any hazards" which they were expected to accept and endure.[40] The court stated:

> (The people) were never fully and accurately informed of what it was they *were* exposed to, what it might entail in terms of long-term consequences, or how to keep the additional risk as low as was possible at that time. Consequently, many people were exposed to more radiation, *and greater risk,* than ever needed to be"[41] and were deprived of and wrongfully denied "an *opportunity* ... to protect themselves, at least as far as was practical; the opportunity to evaluate the question of risk for themselves and their children; the opportunity to choose to leave the area of increased risk, or to choose voluntarily to stay.[42]

The court further implored that the standard of care required is proportional to the potential danger of increased injury to innocent people stating that, "extraordinary risk demands extraordinary care".[43] The court emphasised the increased need for reasonable care when injuries to children are foreseen as they are more vulnerable and sensitive to ionizing radiation and because they are "less able to understand even commonplace risks than are adults".[44] While the court recognised that the human inability to control the impacts of nuclear radiation "(o)nce loosed in the air" "may not be negligence", it nevertheless concluded that negligence would be found if "the best, most stringent protective measures to warn of, lessen, and mitigate its risk" were not taken.[45]

In applying the courts' determinations in *Allen* and *MTBE* to the *ozone layer case*, it can be surmised that the ODC producers had not only a normal, but a heightened level of duty to warn about the dangers of ozone

---

38   *In Re MTBE Prods. Liability Litig.*, 725 F. 3d 65, 92, 101–104 (2d. Cir. 2013).

39   *Id.*; See also *Sterling v. Velsicol Chemical Corp.*, (WD Tenn. 1986) 647 F. Supp. 303, 316–317.

40   *Allen v. United States*, 588 F. Su 247, 356 (1984) (D Utah, 1984) reversed in *Allen v. United States*, 816 F. 2d 1417 (10th Cir. 1987), at 385, 390.

41   *Id.* at 403.

42   *Id.* at 403–404.

43   *Id.* at 353–354.

44   *Id.* at 353–356. Reaffirming this principle, see *Hall v. E. I. DuPont De Nemours*, 345 F. Supp. 353, 361, 366 (EDNY 1972); American Law Institute (1965). *Restatement (Second) of Torts* § 298, Comment (b).

45   *Id.* at 354.

depleting substance emissions. This is underscored by the potential dangers to children who are more vulnerable to the effects of increased solar UV radiation exposure and the increased likelihood of developing and dying from skin cancer later in life.[46]

Taken together, the duty to warn downstream chemical users and the public at large, conceivably would have had an influence both on driving technical innovations to ensure emissions controls as well as the development of safe alternatives and on consumer choices as well as the public's willingness to accept the consequences of continued, increased production, sale and emissions of the chemicals. As the ODC manufacturers apparently failed to provide such warnings and information, and rather promoted awareness that the chemicals were safe and posed no significant risk, it can be concluded that they were negligent in failing excessively to exercise these duties of reasonable care. That failure may also be construed as outrageous and morally deplorable suggesting that it amounts to gross negligence.[47]

However, such conclusions rely heavily on the knowledge of risk and attenuate reasonability of the producers throughout 1976–1992 in deflecting such duties.[48] Should the risk of harm have been genuinely unknowable, then the negligence cause is diminished. The policy rationale for this principle is to provide an incentive for manufacturers to improve their products by relieving them of liability for injuries caused by unknowable dangers their products may have had.[49] Ergo, how knowable were the risks of harm? As was presented in Chapter 2, some evidence suggests that the chemical manufacturers knew that an unreasonable risk of harm existed. Although the defendants in the *ozone layer case* could well argue, as they did back in the day, that the causes of impacts of ozone thinning, the causes of skin cancer and the causal connection between the two phenomena were scientifically uncertain.[50] Still, publicly available information suggests that they were unable to prove such uncertainties and that they did not completely exclude the risk. At minimum, the producers recognised a risk even if they assumed a low probability. Moreover, they were aware at least that the government had determined that risks of unreasonable harm existed in 1976 and that

---

46　Surgeon General's Report (2014), *op. cit. supra* at n.27 chapter 1, at 30; Oliveria, S., Saraiya, M., Geller, A. C., Heneghan, M. K. and Jorgensen, C. (2006, February). Sun Exposure and Risk of Melanoma. *Archives of Disease in Childhood*, 91(2), 131–138; English, D., Armstrong, B. K., Kricker, A. and Fleming, C. (1997). Sunlight and Cancer. *Cancer Causes Control*, 8, 271–283.

47　See Chapter 12.

48　*Brown v. Superior Court*, 44 Cal. 3d 1049, 1069 (Cal. 1988); *Borel v. Fibreboard Paper Products Corp.*, 493 F. 2d 1076 (5th Cir. 1973); *Bly v. Otis Elevator Co.*, 713F. 2d 1040 (4th Cir. 1983).

49　*Anderson v. Owens-Corning Fiberglas Corp.*, 53 Cal. 3d 987, 999 (Cal. 1991). As stated by the California Supreme Court: "...if a manufacturer could not count on limiting its liability to risks that were known or knowable at the time of manufacture or distribution, it would be discouraged from developing new and improved products for fear that later significant advances in scientific knowledge would increase its liability".

50　See Chapter 3.

the government never retracted that finding. It is therefore highly questionable how strong the "we didn't know" argument would prevail in limiting producer liability given the sheer magnitude of the risk involved.

This same issue was assessed also by the 1984 *Allen* court. There, the court recognised that a defendant's duty of care varies "according to the state of available scientific information at a given time" and that "(t)he exactness of hindsight is not the appropriate measure of foreseeability or degree of care". Further, "(n)o one, including the officers and employees of government, can be expected to guard against risks of harm which are not to be rationally anticipated, or which are so unlikely to cause injury that they may be reasonably disregarded". However, the court also affirmed that low probability of a risk is not a sufficient reason to relax or alleviate a duty of care.[51] In quoting William Prosser, the court explained:

[I]f the risk is an appreciable one, and the possible consequences are serious, the question is not one of mathematical probability alone. The odds may be 1000:1 that no train will arrive at the very moment that an automobile is crossing a railway track, but the risk of death is nevertheless sufficiently serious to require the driver to look for the train. It may be highly improbable that lightning will strike at any given place or time; but the possibility is there, and it requires precautions for the protection of flammables. As the gravity of the possible harm increases, the apparent likelihood of its occurrence need be correspondingly less.[52]

This rationale has been applied also in product liability cases where even if the risk of injury were one in a million, manufacturers would still need to disclose that risk.[53]

Moreover, in *Allen*, the court expounded that

a reasonable person, exercising great care in light of the best of available scientific knowledge, would err on the side of caution by assuming no "safe" threshold exposure to atomic radiation, i.e., that any degree of exposure equates with some corollary degree of biological risk, and by determining that every practicable step be taken to minimize unnecessary radiation exposure. The reasonable man would not, therefore, conclude if radiation dosage is kept at or near the "maximum permissible" limits …, there is no increased risk of injury.[54]

In addition, by nature of being engaged in the chemical business, specifically in the development and production of ODCs, the producers had

---

51 *Allen v. United States* (1984), *op. cit. supra* at n.40.69, at 356.
52 *Ibid.*
53 *Davis v. Wyeth Laboratories, Inc.* 399 F. 2d 121 (9th Cir. 1968).
54 *Allen v. United States* (1984), *op. cit. supra* at n.40.69, at 359–360.

superior knowledge of chemical risks and at minimum should have known the risks involved.[55] For example, in *Arnold v. Dow Chemical Company* (2001), the California Court of Appeal held that a pesticide company, by nature of being engaged in the pesticide development and marketing business[56] should have known about their product risks. The court stated: "As chemical and pesticide manufacturers, the defendants are presumed by law to be fully familiar with the known, published toxic effects of the active ingredients contained in their pesticide products, as well as of the 'inert ingredients' contained therein, and of the toxic organic solvent contained therein."[57] This sentiment rings true for ODC enterprises that would equally be imputed with the same duty to know.

Further given the magnitude risk and harm attached to stratospheric ozone loss, the producers not only should have but *must* have appreciated its potential given their conscious decision to market ODCs. In *Allen* the court determined that the government had capacity to know about the risks of nuclear testing as well as "an effective monopoly of the special skills, training and experience relevant to open-air atomic testing".[58] It reasoned that engaging in nuclear testing requires that one fully appreciates the risks involved and takes measures to prevent potential harms. Essentially, the knowledge of risk required to conduct an activity must be proportional to the degree of risk of harm involved: the greater the risk, the stricter the standard of care should be.[59] So too in the *ozone layer case*, it would seem that such standard of care should prevail given the catastrophic consequences of depleting the earth's protective shield against UV radiation.

4.1.2 Duty to prevent direct emissions in production and pre-sale stages

Core to the US stratospheric ozone protection policy was the approach to stem ODC emissions by eliminating the production, and sale of the chemicals. In the 1970s, these duties were imposed regarding the production and consumption of CFC containing aerosol products. Regulatory duties to prevent direct emissions of ODCs during production and pre-sale stages only began taking shape in the mid-1980s. In 1985, federal regulations regarding National Emission Standards for Hazardous Air Pollutants imposed requirements for chemical capture, leakage prevention and other like technology to be applied during the production and use of CFC-113,

---

55   *Sollami v. Eaton* (2002) 772 NE 2d 215: The Supreme Court of Illinois affirmed that, "(a) manufacturer has a duty to warn where the product possesses dangerous propensities and there is unequal knowledge with respect to the risk of harm, and the manufacturer, possessed of such knowledge, knows or should know that harm may occur absent a warning".

56   *Arnold v. Dow Chemical Company*, 91 Cal. A 4th 698, 737–738 (Cal. A 2001).

57   *Ibid.*

58   *Allen v. United States* (1984), *op. cit. supra* at n.40, at 338.

59   *Id.* at 354–355.

methyl chloroform and carbon tetrachloride.[60] In 1993, this duty was extended to include CFC-11, CFC-12 and methyl bromide.[61] Also, from that year onward, additional requirements were put in place to control downstream emissions from products. Those were imposed primarily on downstream chemicals handlers, technicians and end-users.[62]

Notwithstanding these rules, it is unclear whether ODC producers were ever obliged to prevent, or be responsible for accidental or intentional release during production or at any point prior to sale. Beginning in 1995, they were mandated to maintain records of spills or releases in quantities at or above 100 pounds.[63] However, regulations following Title VI of the Clean Air Act (protecting the ozone layer), address intentional and accidental release on the part of end-users not producers.[64] Elsewhere, the Act does require that "owners and operators of stationary sources[65] producing, processing, handling or storing (extremely hazardous) substances have a general duty…to identify hazards which may result from such releases using appropriate hazard assessment techniques, to design and maintain a safe facility taking such steps as are necessary to prevent releases, and to minimize the consequences of accidental releases which do occur."[66] This duty applies in relation to 189 hazardous substances which the EPA has identified. Among these, carbon tetrachloride, methyl chloroform and methyl bromide are included but all other CFCs and halon gases are omitted.[67] In fact, somewhat inexplicably, the above requirement is not intended to apply to ozone depleting substances i.e. ODCs are exempted from this provision of the law.[68]

On the side of common law, court rulings would support that a duty of care should exist to guard against the release of hazardous substances into

---

60   40 C.F.R. § 61.
61   40 C.F.R. § 63.
62   40 C.F.R. §§ 82.152, 82.154, 82.156, 82.2704.
63   40 C.F.R. § 82.13(f)(2)(xii).
64   In 1990, Congress established the National recycling and emission reduction program, under section 608 of the Clean Air Act: 42 U.S.C. § 7671. Subsequent regulations set rules for preventing end-use releases of refrigerants and halon gases including small/accidental releases and intentional venting: 40 C.F.R. §§ 82.154; 82.250(a); 82.270(b); 40 C.F.R. §§ 82.154 (1) (i)-(vi).
65   A stationary source is defined in the Clean Air Act as "any building, structure, facility, or installation which emits or may emit any air pollutant" (42 U.S.C. § 7411 (a)(3)) as well as "…equipment, … or substance emitting stationary activities (i) which belong to the same industrial group, (ii) which are located on one or more contiguous properties, (iii) which are under the control of the same person (or persons under common control), and (iv) from which an accidental release may occur" (42 U.S.C. § 7412 (2)(c)).
66   42 U.S.C. § 7412(r)(1),(2)A): "The term accidental release' means an unanticipated emission of a regulated substance or other extremely hazardous substance into the ambient air from a stationary source".
67   42 U.S.C. § 7412(r)(5).
68   42 U.S.C. § 7412 (b)(2): " No substance, practice, process or activity regulated under title VI of this Act shall be subject to regulation under this section solely due to its adverse effects on the environment". Note: It also excludes air pollutants "for which a national primary ambient air quality standard has been established".

the environment. In *Indiana Harbor Belt R. Co. v. American Cyanamid Co.* (1990), the court assessed that persons who exercise control over dangerous chemicals have a duty to ensure that those chemicals are contained and not released into the environment.[69] In this case, however, that duty was found for the train company which shipped the chemicals and was deemed responsible for ensuring their secure containment prior to delivery. The company's negligence was found for not meeting that duty when the chemicals escaped the train car in which they were contained. The court reasoned that the railroad industry business in shipping commodities was common and had an important social and economic purpose. That function included transporting chemicals and other products which could be harmful to the environment if not properly contained. Therefore, the railroad company had a duty to take precautions which were feasible to ensure safe containment by inspecting its holding facilities and employing technologies to prevent chemical releases.[70]

By analogy, this would equally mean the defendant ODC producers would have had a duty to prevent the chemical emissions under their control such as in manufacturing processes. However, this duty would be subject to the availability and feasibility of emissions capture and storage technology in the 1970s and 1980s.[71] Presuming that the chemicals were released and such technology was usable, then a clear case of negligence could be made. However, if ODC capture know-how was technically retarded,[72] then a stronger case of **strict liability for abnormally dangerous**

---

69   *Indiana Harbor Belt R. Co. v. American Cyanamid Co.*, 916 F. 2d 1174 (7th Cir. 1990).

70   *Id.* See also, *Edwards v. Post Transportation Co.*, 228 Cal. App. 3d 980 (App. 4th D. Cal. 1991): Sulphuric acid release during delivery operations can be prevented with reasonable care; *Sprankle v. Bower Ammonia & Chemical Co.*, 824 F. 2d 409, 415–41 (5th Cir., 1987): Escape of dry ammonia from storage tank can be prevented.

71   Mooz, W., Dole, S., Jaquette, D., Krase, W., Morrison, Salem, S. *et al.* (1982, March). *Technical Options for Reducing Chlorofluorocarbon Emissions.* Retrieved from Rand Corporation: www.rand.org/content/dam/rand/pubs/reports/2008/R2879.pdf: The 1982 study suggests, *inter alia*, that service techniques for mobile air conditoners be improved and that solvent use "improve equipment and operating practices, use carbon absorption recovery for pure CFC-113 and use external waste reclamation."; Knopeck, G., Zwolinski, L. and Selznick, R. (1989). An Evaluation of Carbon Absorption for Emissions Control and CFC-11 Recovery in Polyurethane Foam Proc Selznick, R. (1989). An Evaluation of Carbon Absorption for Emissions Control and CFC-11 Recovery in Polyurethane Foam Processes. *Journal of Cellular Plastics*, 164–172. Farmer, R. and Nelson, T. (March 1988). *Control Technology Overview Report: CFC-11 Emissions from Flexible Polyurethane Foam Manufacturing.* Research Triangle Park, NC: US EPA; Bishop, F. S. (1979). *Report on the Progress of Regulations to Protect Stratospheric Ozone: Report to Congress.* US Environmental Protection Agency, Office of Toxic Substances. Also See Wijmans, J. and Hans, G. (1993). *Treatment of CFC and HCFC Emissions.* Retrieved from United States Environmental Protection Agency: http://cfpub.epa.gov/ncer_abstracts/index.cfm/fuseaction/display.abstractDetail/abstract/1675/report/0.

72   Only DuPont appears to have reported the successful adoption and use of such know-how at some point after 1992. DuPont (2011), *op. cit. supra* at n.134 chapter 2.

activities might be made.[73] For example, in *State Department of Environmental Protection v. Ventron Corporation* (1981), the New Jersey Supreme Court found that although mercury was deemed useful to society, the inability to secure its safe disposal made processing activities abnormally dangerous.[74] Likewise in *Crawford v. National Lead Co.* (1989), the US District Court of Ohio determined that a uranium processing plant operator was strictly liable for emissions of harmful substances during processing which was an uncommon practice within society, abnormally dangerous, but nonetheless a valuable activity.[75] In numerous other cases, strict liability was found for the inability of companies to exercise reasonable care in preventing direct and indirect (through water) human exposure to toxic substances including beryllium,[76] chromium ore by-products,[77] perfluorooctanoic acid[78] and other "noxious chemicals".[79]

In sum, despite regulatory silence and inconsistencies, a fair amount of case law would support that a duty of care to prevent direct emissions was incumbent of the defendant producers. If the use of emissions control technologies would have been feasible but not employed, the case for negligence or strict liability may be supported. However, as with other technical questions associated with the *ozone layer case*, the public availability of such

---

73   Restatement (Second) of Torts (1965):§§ 519, 520. The theory holds: "One who carries on an abnormally dangerous activity is subject to liability of harm to the person, land or chattels of another resulting from the activity even though he has exercised the utmost care to prevent the harm"; (2) this strict liability is limited to "the kind of harm, the possibility of which makes the activity abnormally dangerous." In determining whether an activity is abnormally dangerous, the following factors are to be considered:

(a) the existence of a high degree of risk of some harm to the person, land or chattels of others;
(b) the likelihood that the harm that results from it will be great;
(c) the inability to eliminate the risk by the exercise of reasonable care;
(d) the extent to which the activity is not a matter of common usage;
(e) the inappropriateness of the activity to the place where it is carried on; and
(f) the extent to which its value to the community is outweighed by its dangerous attributes.

74   *State Department of Environmental Protection v. Ventron Corporation* 94 N.J. 473, 492–493 (1981); See also *T & E Industries, Inc. v. Safety Light Corporation* 123 N.J. 371, 394–395 (1991): Strict liability found for radium waste dumping; *Sterling v. Velsicol Chemical Corp.*, 647 F. Supp. 303, 307 (WD Tenn. 1986): Strict liability found of chemical wastes leaching into ground water and causing injuires.
75   *Crawford v. National Lead Co.*, 784 F. Supp. 439, 443 – 444 (Ohio, WD 1989).
76   *Schwartz v. Accuratus Corporation,* Dist. Court, ED Pennsylvania 2014, Civil Action No. 12-6189 (2014).
77   *Smith v. Honeywell International Inc.,* Dist. Court, D. New Jersey 2011, Civil Action No. 2:10-cv-03345 (SDW)(2011); *Interfaith Community Org. v. Honeywell International Inc.,* 263 F. Supp. 2d 796, 850–851 (D. NJ 2003).
78   *Rowe v. DuPont,* Dist. Court, D. New Jersey 2009, Civil Nos. 06-1810 (RMB), 06-3080 (RMB), No. 06-1810, 289, 06-3080, 256 (2009).
79   *Banks v. Ashland Oil Co.,* Dist. Court, ED Pennsylvania 2001, 127 F. Supp. 2d 679 (2001).

information is wanting. Further investigation or disclosure by the former producers would be needed to substantiate liability.

4.1.3 Duty to not produce and market defective products

In 1977, the EPA promulgated regulations which, *inter alia*, prohibited the manufacture of fully halogenated chlorofluoroalkanes (CFCs) for use as propellants in aerosol spray products deemed non-essential like hair spray.[80] The regulation was adopted as a precautionary measure to avoid unreasonable risks of harm to the population by reducing the volume of chemicals produced and sold in the US market.[81] The rule's intent was to control emissions by eliminating products which directly released CFCs into the environment upon use. The rule did not apply to CFC production for essential uses or other "contained" uses such as refrigeration and air-conditioning. The rule also did not affect the export of the raw chemicals nor did it have any impact on the production of CFCs overseas by US companies.[82] Aside from the latter (as a jurisdictional matter), the EPA had intended to propose a set of follow-up, more comprehensive rules by 1980 to address these limitations.[83] However, due to the well-known regulatory delays, stratospheric ozone protection laws and regulations were adopted a decade later.

In 1993, new regulations came into effect[84] under the EPA's authority following the 1990 Clean Air Act amendment to include Title VI.[85] These set out a clear policy for reducing and eventually eliminating ODC production and sale again with the stated intent to avoid environmental catastrophe let alone serious increases in skin cancer incidences and deaths. Initially, the rules necessitated that the production of the most potent ozone depleters be frozen and then phased out by 2000.[86] That schedule was then accelerated to achieve a complete production ban on most of the substances in the US by the end of 1995 with the exception of some essential uses, particularly methyl bromide.[87] According to the phase out plan, the federal government allocated and then incrementally reduced production and consumption allowances to producers and importers of ozone depleting substances. Production allowances were

---

80 21 C.F.R. 2.125; 40 C.F.R. 762: Regulations on Use of Fully Halogenated Chlorofluoroalkanes (EPA).
81 43 *Fed. Reg.* 11301 (17 March 1978)
82 *Ibid.*
83 *Ibid.*
84 40 C.F.R. §82: Protection of Stratospheric Ozone.
85 Clean Air Act: 42 U.S.C. § 7671.
86 Clean Air Act: 42 U.S.C. § 7671c; federal regulation on the Protection of Stratospheric Ozone: 40 C.F.R. §.82.7; 40 C.F.R. § 82.8. Regarding methyl bromide, production allowances, although small, were still being allocated in 2012, see 40 C.F.R. § 82.8 (c).
87 Clean Air Act: 42 U.S.C. § 7671e; federal regulation on the Protection of Stratospheric Ozone: 40 C.F.R. § 82.7.

granted to US chemical producers[88] while consumption (permission to market/export) allowances were allotted to both producers and importers.[89] Any company which produced, imported or sold larger quantities than allowed, would have been in violation of the regulation. Each excess kilogram accounted for a separate violation,[90] and each violation was subject to a fine of US$25,000 per day.[91]

However, similar to the EPA's 1978 regulation, such restrictions did not apply to overseas production or marketing activities of the chemical producing companies or their subsidiaries.[92] Such activities were under the jurisdiction of the country where production occurred. Under the terms of the Montreal Protocol, developing countries,[93] also known as Article 5 countries, were permitted to delay their phase out plans for a period of 10–15 years for the purpose of fulfilling their developmental needs. That is, whereas almost all ODC production in developed countries came to a halt by December 1995, production in developing countries was not required to reach a complete close until 2010.[94] This essentially meant that overseas production was permissible so long as it complied, *inter alia*, with the production and consumption quotas of Article 5 countries.[95]

Export controls on raw chemicals were first introduced from January 1993. In line with the Montreal Protocol, chemicals produced in the US could only be exported to countries which were party to the treaty.[96] Until 2005, federal regulations did not restrict the type or quantity of chemicals that could be exported. In fact, chemical companies were permitted to exceed their production allowance baselines by 10 percent to 15 percent for certain chemicals during specified time frames to meet the export market demands.[97] Chemical companies were only obliged to not exceed

88   40 C.F.R. § 82.5.
89   40 C.F.R. § 82.5, 82.6. The amount of allowances allocated varied according to the chemicals in accordance with the historical amount of production and imports reported in a specified baseline year as follows: CFC and halon gas – 1986; carbon tetrachloride, methyl chloroform, and other CFCs – 1989; methyl bromide and HBFC 22B1-1, 1991.
90   40 C.F.R. § 82.4 (b).
91   40 C.F.R. § 82.4(n)(2).
92   42 U.S.C. § 7671: The 1990 Clean Air Act amendments do not address overseas production.
93   Montreal Protocol (1987) § 5(1), *op. cit. supra* at n.18 chapter 1: developing countries (also known as "Article 5 countries") were defined as any country which consumed less than 0.3 kilograms of CFCs and halon gases per capita on the date at which the protocol became legally binding under the national laws of that country.
94   UNEP (2002). *Information Paper: The Montreal Protocol Control Schedule and its Evolution.* Retrieved from www.unep.fr/ozonaction/information/mmcfiles/3326-e.pdf.
95   Montreal Protocol (1987) § 5, *op. cit. supra* at n.18 chapter 1.
96   40 C.F.R. §82.4(l); 57 *Fed. Reg.* 33754. In the EPA's 1978 regulation, only the processing of CFCs into "aerosol propellant articles" was prohibited.
97   57 *Fed. Reg.* 33754, 60 *Fed. Reg.* 24969: CFCs: 10% (1992–1995), 15% (1996–2005) carbon tetrachloride and methyl chloroform: 10% (1992–1995), 15% (1996–2010); Halon gases 10% (1992–1993), 15% (1994–2002).

these additional production allowances.[98] After 2005, export caps were set along with a phase out schedule. CFC exports were required to cease by 2009 and methyl bromide by the end of 2014.[99]

In a nut shell, until 1993, the production, marketing and export of the chemicals for non-aerosol uses went unregulated. Also, at no time were any duties imposed with respect to the producers' overseas enterprises. Presumably, such duties would have been enforced by the host countries. Thus, in the *ozone layer case*, the question is whether any common law duties of care would have prevailed in lieu of such regulations.

The control of export and overseas activities of US companies is a subject for Congressional decision.[100] Production and emissions restrictions on certain products or sources is also a matter for the legislature to determine not the judiciary.[101] However, regarding duties of care in relation to marketing of defective, unsafe and unavoidable unsafe products, significant jurisprudence abounds.

Common law dictates a clear duty of product manufacturers to not introduce defective products into US commerce.[102] Products can be defective in their manufacture (a flaw which occurs during production), their design (pre-production error in design) or in not being accompanied by warning regarding reasonable dangers the product may pose. In all of these cases, it is expected that the manufacturer can correct or eliminate the defect and that he has a duty to do so. Defective product liability can be pursued under both strict product liability and negligence theories. Both rely on the risk-utility test[103] to assess product defectiveness which takes into account:

- the *gravity or magnitude of the risk* created by the defendant's conduct
- the *likelihood of the risk* eventuating in harm
- the *utility of the defendant's activity* and
- the *feasibility of the defendant taking precautions* to prevent against risks of or actual harm.[104]

98 40 C.F.R. §82.4(b)(1).

99 40 C.F.R. §§ 82.8, 82.11.

100 Fergusson, I. F. (2014). *The US Export Control System and the President's Reform Initiative.* Congressional Research Service; Winer, K. (1999). Doing it Right – Overseas: Compliance Programs Take on New Importance in a Global Economy. *ABA Section of Business Law, Business Law Today.*

101 Greenstone, M., List, J. A. and Syverson, C. (2012). The Effects of Environmental Regulation on the Competitiveness of US Manufacturing. NBER Working Paper No. 18392; *Massachusetts v. EPA*, 127 S.Ct. 1438.

102 Restatement (Second) of Torts (1965), §402 comment (a); *Alvarez v. Felker Manufacturing* (1964) 230 Cal. App. 2d 987; *O'Neil v. Crane Co.* (Cal. 2012) 266 P. 3d 987.

103 *Id. at* § 291; Mueller, D. B. and Metcalf, B. A. (2013). Adoption of the Risk-Utility Rule in Negligent Design Cases: Jablonski v. Ford Motor Co. *IDC Quarterly*, 23(4).

104 Restatement (Second) of Torts (1965), §§ 282, 402.

In weighing these factors, courts have also assessed whether the product "has failed to perform as safely as an ordinary consumer would expect when used as intended or in a reasonable way" whether the benefits of its design "outweigh the risk of danger inherent in such design",[105] and whether a safe alternative design is technically and economically feasible.[106] In negligence, the same inquiries are followed but with a focus on the defendant's conduct[107] i.e. his ability to adopt a safer alternative product or product design and his failure to do so.[108] Whereas, in a strict liability suit, the plaintiff may only need to show evidence that a safer alternative product existed.[109] Most but not all product liability cases are brought under strict liability theories. In practice, these tests have been applied in product liability suits involving harmful substances in products such as drugs (e.g. DES),[110] vaccines (e.g. defective DPT),[111] chemicals (e.g. pesticides),[112] and industrial materials (e.g. asbestos).[113]

In applying this logic to the *ozone layer case*, the question is whether ODCs would also qualify as defective products under negligence or strict liability theories. To this, as during the alleged liability period, the defendant producers would likely argue appositively. They would likely contend that the chemicals qualified as unavoidably unsafe products or as non-defective products on the basis that the utility of the chemicals was high and that it was financially and technically unfeasible to develop and market safe replacement substances. The following discussion revisits those arguments calling into question their authenticity. That is, given the utility of ODCs, how feasible was it between 1976 and 1992 for the chemical producers to avoid large scale emissions by introducing safe, alternative products or simply to halt product sales much earlier than they did? And if not, would it have at least been viable that they did not increase their production and marketing activities when the risk of ozone layer depletion became known? After all, since Union Carbide was able to cease its production of chlorofluorocarbons in 1977 despite the fact that it controlled more than 20

---

105 *Barker v. Lull Engineering Co.* (Cal. 1978) 573 P. 2d 443.
106 *Id.* at 431.
107 *O'Keefe v. Boeing Company*, 335 F. Supp. 1104, 1118–1119, 1132 (SDNY 1971); *Barker v. Lull Engineering Co.*, 573 2d 443, 431 (Cal. 1978); *Campbell v. General Motors Corp.*, 649 2d 224, 32 Cal. 3d 112, 119 (Cal. 1982); *Cronin v. JBE Olson Corp.*, 501 2d 1153, 104 Cal. Rptr. 433, 8 Cal. 3d 121, 133 (1972).
108 Restatement (Third) of Torts (1998): Products Liability § 2(b).
109 *Blue v. Environmental Engineering, Inc*, 828 NE 2d 1128 (Ill 2005).
110 *Collins v. Eli Lily & Co*, 116 Wis.2d 166 (Wis. 1984); *Sindell v. Abbott Laboratories*, 26 Cal.3d 588 (Cal. 1980).
111 *Morris v. Parke, Davis & Co.*, 667 F. Supp.1332 (CD Cal. 1987).
112 *Arnold v. Dow Chemical Company*, 91 Cal. A4th 698 (Cal. A 2001); *In Re Agent Orange Product Liability Litigation*, 373 F. Su2d 7, 19 (EDNY 2005).
113 *Borel v. Fibreboard Paper Products Corp.*, 493 F. 2d 1076 (5th Cir. 1973); *O'Neil v. Crane Co.*, 266 3d 987 (Cal. 2012); *Urie v. Thompson*, 337 US 163 (1949).

percent of the entire market,[114] would it not have been possible for other manufacturers to have followed suit? These questions rely on assessing how commonly used and useful the chemicals were to society some decades ago as well as the feasibility of introducing safe replacement chemicals and technologies. They also beg clarification regarding what the ODC producers understood regarding cost of risks involved in not developing safe alternatives.

Risk-utility assessment

Ozone depleting chemicals provided numerous benefits to society and were commonly used. As discussed above, CFCs were first developed in 1928[115] and later marketed in the post-World War II era as "safe" alternatives to other chemicals as they were non-toxic and inflammable.[116] They came to be used in a variety of commercial and industrial products such as refrigeration, air conditioning, fire extinguishers, gas propellants, foam blowing agents (e.g. for insulation and packaging), aerosol (hair, deodorant) sprays and cleaning solvents. As such, they were of significant value to industry and to society at large.[117] "By the early 1970s, 200,000 tonnes of CFCs were used in aerosols annually in the US and the typical US household contained 40 to 50 aerosol cans, half of them propelled by CFCs."[118]

In the 1970s and 1980s, of the numerous arguments put forward by the chemical industry to oppose regulatory controls on CFC production and use, the essential value of the chemicals to the economy was at the fore.[119] Leading the voice of industry in 1981, DuPont underscored the following benefits.

- **Refrigeration, in particular for the health sector and for processing, shipping, and keeping food fresh or frozen:**[120] Because "virtually all …

---

114 Palmer, A., Mooz, W., Quinn, T. and Wolf, K. (October 1980). *Regulating Chlorofluorocarbon Emissions: Effects on Chemical Production Support Document for Economic Implications of Regulating Chlorofluorocarbons Emissions from Non-aerosol Applications.* US EPA, Office of Pesticides and Toxic Substances. Washington, D.C., at 27, Table V-1; AFEAS (1993), *op. cit. supra* at n.108 chapter 2.

115 Morrisette, P. (1989), *op. cit. supra* at n.6 chapter 1.

116 See Barrett, S. (2007). *Why Cooperate? The Incentive to Supply Global Public Goods.* Oxford University Press at 75. Barret underscores the irony involved in the safety assumption.

117 Morrisette, P. (1989), *op. cit. supra* at n.6 chapter 1.

118 Parson (2003), *op. cit. supra* at n.14 chapter 1.

119 The DuPont Report, *op. cit. supra* at n.15 chapter 2, Volume I; Browne, M. W. (1990, July 17). Grappling with the Cost of Saving Earth's Ozone. *The New York Times;* Parson (2003), *op. cit. supra* at n.14 chapter 1, at 57: Beginning in 1979, DuPont distributed information to its CFC customers urging them to oppose regulator controls on the chemicals; Alliance for a Responsible CFC Policy (n.d.). *Q&A Chlorofluorocarbons and Ozone.* Retrieved May 21, 2014, from Legacy Tobacco Documents Library: http://legacy.library.ucsf.edu/tid/ema84c00/ pdf; Alliance for a Responsible CFC Policy (1986, October). Policy Statement. *CFC Alliance Newsletter.*

120 The DuPont Report, *op. cit. supra* at n.15 chapter 2, Volume 1 at II-5.

refrigeration equipment (was) designed for, and exclusively (used), CFC refrigerants", because "other refrigerants could not be substituted in this equipment", and because other refrigerants if available would be hazardous and therefore place public safety at risk, CFCs were essential and of great social value.[121]

- **Mobile air-conditioning:** 13 percent of all CFC-12 production was for "virtually all" motor vehicle air-conditioning. This was valuable to reduce summer "heat stress" which adversely impacts on "driver alertness" which generally is a key factor in causing "many of the 47,000 fatalities and 1,800,000 disabling injuries experienced annually in traffic accidents".[122] Therefore, CFC-12 was an "important asset in current programs to increase passenger safety in transportation".[123]

- **Employment and public and private revenue:** In 1975, the CFC business injected more than US$8 billion into the economy, enabling some 200,000 jobs.[124] In 1979, CFC sales were estimated at US$375 million "with more than 650,000 jobs related to CFC use and 240,000 domestic business locations using CFCs".[125] In 1981, employment dependency increased to some 780,000 jobs.[126] In 1985 and 1988, 10,000 American businesses provided goods and services using CFCs estimated at US$28 billion.[127] Domestic market chemical sales alone were valued at US$750 million. Meanwhile, chlorofluorocarbon dependant equipment was valued at US$135 billion.[128] Thus, eliminating CFCs would mean significant unemployment, loss of household income, increases of public unemployment subsidies and increased deaths on account of heart failure and suicide and medical costs due to hospitalisation and other required treatments to deal with the physical and emotional trauma of lost work.[129]

- **Energy savings:** CFCs were valuable in being more performance and energy efficient than possible but heavier substitute refrigerants such as ammonia and HCFC-22. Adopting either substitute would entail an

---

121 *Ibid.*

122 *Id.* at II-7: In defence of its heat stress argument, DuPont also cites a study by the National Highway Traffic Safety Administration which apparently concluded that "suitable air-conditioning equipment or other effective countermeasures should be available to drivers who will be exposed for extended periods of time to (heat stress) conditions". There is no discussion on "other suitable countermeasures" but presumably they would also exist.

123 *Id.*. at II-7 – II-8.

124 Maxwell, J. and Briscoe, F. (1997), *op. cit. supra* at n.23 chapter 2.

125 Andersen and Sarma. (2002), at 229–30, *op. cit. supra* at n.37 chapter 1.

126 The DuPont Report, *op. cit. supra* at n.15 chapter 2, Volume 1.

127 Parson (2003), *op. cit. supra* at n.14 chapter 1, at 175.

128 *Id.*: World-wide the figure was placed at US$385 billion; Browne, M. W. (1990, July 17). *Grappling with the Cost of Saving Earth's Ozone.* The New York Times; and Sarma (2002), *op. cit. supra* at n.37 chapter 1, at 230.

129 The DuPont Report, *op. cit. supra* at n.15 chapter 2, Volume 1 at V 50–51.

energy penalty of between an additional 27.9 or 49.8 billion gallons of oil.[130]

- **Industry switch costs:** Introducing chemical substitutes would require an investment of over US$10 billion to build new plants and retool manufacturing processes.[131]

Government agencies also recognised that banning CFCs would have economic consequences. A 1978 report by the US Department of Commerce concluded that such an embargo would have entailed high switch costs and the expense of having to eliminate "important goods and processes." It would have also affected "the jobs of millions of workers".[132]

Such utility arguments were and likely remain valid. However, the extent of their legitimacy may be called into question. Chapter 2 presented some evidence that safe replacement technology was available but expensive and that cheaper options were feasible but less safe and less efficient. Still, it is unsure what the economic impact of switching to safe alternatives would have been. The industry's dismal projections would need to be verified. Subsequent scholarship has suggested that the economic and social benefits of the replacement chemical business were not sufficiently counted and the switch costs were overstated. Both after the 1978 aerosol ban[133] and the 1990s regulations, actual transition costs were half if not lower than half what industry purported.[134] The energy savings question also must be re-examined[135] as greater efficiency of new cooling products and value for money to consumers were not sufficiently accounted.[136] And, in the absence of "studies showing how the damage attributable to these (ozone depleting) chemicals compared to the costs of limiting their use", the expenses of eliminating ozone depleters

130 *Ibid.*
131 Pool, R. (1989). The Elusive Replacements for CFCs. *Science*, 242, 666–68.
132 Rowlands, I. H. (1995), *op. cit. supra* at n.42 chapter 1, at 101 at 102.
133 Andersen, S. O. and Sarma, K. M. (2002), *op. cit. supra* at n.37 chapter 1, at 297–98.
134 Sprinz, D. and Vaahtoranta, T. (1994, Winter). The Interest-based Explanation of International Environmental Policy. *International Organization*, 48(1) 77–105, at 80, 93; Vanner, R. (2006, June). *Ex-post Estimates of Costs to Business of EU Environmental Policies: A Case Study Looking at Ozone Depleting Substances.* Policy Studies Institute; Pew Environment Group (2010). *Industry Opposition to Government Regulation.* The PEW Environmental Group; Percival, R. V. (1997), *op. cit. supra* at n.22 chapter 1, at 523; DuPont (2007). *DuPont Advocates Accelerated Phaseout of Ozone-Depleting Substances,* http://investors.dupont.com/phoenix.zhtml?c=73320&p=irol-newsArticle&ID=1050654&highlight=; Browne, M. W. (1990, July 17). *Grappling with the Cost of Saving Earth's Ozone.* The New York Times.
135 A good starting point for all these questions is the US EPA's 1981 assessment of the costs to the US economy associated with introducing a cap on CFC production in Palmer, A. and Quinn, T. (1981). *Economic Impact Assessment of a Chlorofluorocarbon Production Cap.* US EPA.
136 Andersen, S. O., Sarma, K. M. and Taddonio, K. N. (2007), *op. cit. supra* at n.5 chapter 2 table 2.3, at 229.

predominated the benefits of doing so.[137]

An informative case in this regard is *In Re: MTBE Prods. Liability Litig.* (2013). In that case, New York City plaintiffs alleged Exxon's liability for MTBE leakage into the city's ground water and wells. The plaintiffs' claims were based on multiple theories.[138] At trial, the jury had upheld most of the plaintiff's contentions except the design defect theory. Plaintiffs had argued that ethanol could have been a safer, feasible alternative but could not provide sufficient evidence to convince the jury that ethanol would have been the better choice. On appeal, Exxon contended that the jury's finding was tantamount to saying that MTBE was rather the safest, most feasible product available and as such had the company not used MTBE it would have not been in compliance with federal oxygenate requirements. The Court of Appeals disagreed. It determined that the jury's verdict was not an endorsement of MTBE as the safest available chemical but rather a conclusion that the plaintiffs had not provided adequate evidence to defend why ethanol was not a feasible, safer choice. The Court further resolved that Exxon's reasons for not using ethanol as an MTBE replacement i.e. that the supply of ethanol was insufficient and the costs of using ethanol were too high, were not sufficient enough to excuse its use as a safer alternative.[139] The Court's ruling provides some support for a similar risk utility assessment in the *ozone layer case*. It opens possibilities for plaintiffs to present safer product arguments and it suggests that higher economic costs of using alternative technologies would not necessarily render a finding that such an alternative would not be feasible. The latter is significant since the historical justifications of the chemical industry for delaying the introduction of safer replacements were largely focused on financial as opposed to technical feasibility issues.

Another factor which could have influenced the feasibility questions is the defendant producers' conduct in suspending research and development of safe alternatives for an estimated five to seven years in the 1980s.[140] DuPont along with Allied Signal and ICI Americas halted this work on the assumption that the risk of ozone layer depletion was negligible and on the

---

137 *Id.* at 102–103, 109 citing Markandya, A. (1991). Economics and the Ozone Layer. In D. Pearce, *Blureprint 2: Greening the World Economy*. London: Earthscan, at 64; Parson (2003), *op. cit. supra* at n.14, at 5: Parson underscores that one key issue in the debates at both national and international levels was whether "scientific evidence of risk was strong enough to proceed with potentially costly regulatory controls".

138 *In Re MTBE Prods. Liability Litig.*, 725 F. 3d 65, 79–83 (2d. Cir. 2013).

139 *Id.* at 97–101.

140 Maxwell, J. and Briscoe, F. (1997), *op. cit. supra* at n.23 chapter 2; But also see Parsons (2003) at 54–55, 175–177 recounting that DuPont spent US$10 million by 1979 and US$15 million by the mid-1980s; Andersen and Sarma (2002), *op. cit. supra* at n.37 chapter 1, at 199; The DuPont Report, *op. cit. supra* at n.15 chapter 2, Volume 1 at II-6. It is unclear when exactly what research was resumed or initiated by whom. DuPont is said to have restarted its alternative chemical research in 1988.

assessments that new chemicals would be too expensive and non-competitive.[141] According to DuPont's Freon Products Division Head: "There wasn't scientific or economic justification to proceed. How much do you trade a possible (environmental) risk for a (business risk) that is real?" Essentially, the company saw no market interest to switch to alternatives which they claimed would cost three times more than CFCs.[142] Later, at some point between 1986–88, the companies asserted that they resumed their research. Some joined forces to advance chemical substitutes and conduct safety tests.[143] Results began emerging during those years when Pennwalt first marketed a chemical replacement[144] and DuPont began patenting HCFC and HFC replacements in 1988.[145] These efforts enabled a healthy transition in the 1990s. Yet, the question remains whether this move could not have happened earlier.

Ultimately, in the *ozone layer case*, deciphering between what was actually known by industry in terms of the impacts of switching to alternative technologies will require a significant degree of disclosure on behalf of the chemical producers. That can be achieved at trial when the defendant companies would need to prove that safe alternatives were neither feasible nor available.

This discussion now turns to the question regarding how risks were and should be assessed in terms of material, economic and noneconomic damages and injuries. Court judgments generally do appreciate such risks particularly when injuries to human health and well-being are at stake. In *Arnold v. Dow Chemical Company* (2001), the California Court of Appeal assessed that the risk of danger inherent in pesticide chemicals[146] "outweighed the benefits of that design (ease of use, low cost of manufacture, rating as a general use pesticide)."[147] Here, the court's weighting of health risks over costs associated with pesticide production and marketability could provide for useful argumentation. Of course, in the *ozone layer case*, the sheer scale of harm anticipated was by far much greater than in *Arnold*, and probably any product liability case ever litigated. In fact, the *ozone layer case* is unique in involving a risk of harm which affects a global public good[148] and cannot be mitigated by human intervention. These factors along with evidence demonstrating increased incidences of and deaths from skin cancers and their associated economic and non-economic costs, may very well overshadow contentions that safe alternative chemicals were

141 *Ibid.*
142 Cagin, S. and Dray, (1993), *op. cit. supra* at n.41 chapter 1, at 225.
143 Benedick, R. E. (1998), *op. cit. supra* at n.22 chapter 1; Parson (2003), *op. cit. supra* at n.14 chapter 1, at 176, 193. Rowlands, I. H. (1995), *op. cit. supra* at n.42 chapter 1, at 117.
144 Parson (2003), *op. cit. supra* at n.14 chapter 1, at 127.
145 *Id.* at 177.
146 *Arnold v. Dow Chemical Company*, 91 Cal. A4th 698, 737 (Cal. A 2001).
147 *Id.*
148 See n.34 *supra.*

not feasible because they were expensive.[149]

To support this assertion, the Learned Hand formula may be applied. Introduced by Judge Hand in 1947,[150] this economic model to evaluate tort liability[151] aims to weigh costs of harm against costs of avoiding harm to assess liability. Risk values are determined by multiplying the *probability* (P) of a risk of injury occurring by the gravity of resulting *loss* (L) i.e. (PL). The cost of precaution to avoid that risk are represented by (B) or "the *burden* of taking adequate precautions".[152] Therefore, if the likelihood and gravity of a harm occurring are low and the precautionary costs are high, the defendant's liability may be mitigated: PL < B. However, if the magnitude of harm is great and some probability exists, and if precaution is cheap, then the defendant should bear liability. In either case, the reasonability of the defendant's actions can be inferred.

Applying this formula to the *ozone layer case* should bear a clear finding of liability since the enormous magnitude of potential harm posed by stratospheric ozone loss must always outweigh costs of precaution. This is particularly true as the alleged costs of harm include non-economic, invaluable losses such as infringements on individual and public rights to health, employment and enjoyment of the environment.[153] On that understanding, it would be difficult to say that ODCs were not defective, and the producers failed in their common law duty by increasing the market supply.

In hindsight, the risks of ODCs clearly outweighed their usefulness. During the 1970s and 1980s, that understanding was likely appreciated on a theoretical level. However, the fact that that did not translate into comprehensive laws and regulations soon after the aerosol bans were imposes, suggests that somehow the tally of costs and benefits was askew. One problem contributing to that imbalance was the limitation of policy makers to quantify and argue the risk. Although it could have been possible to calculate that risk in financial terms at that time,[154] efforts to do so were wanting until the mid-1980s. Until then, the costs benefit analysis largely favoured the bargain utility of ODCs.[155]

---

149 One argument against cost issues is made in *Doundoulakis v. Town of Hempstead*, 42 NY 2d 440, 368 NE 2d 24, 398 NYS 2d 401 (1977). The policy consideration was that "those who engage in activity of sufficiently high risk of harm to others, especially where there are reasonable even if more costly alternatives, should bear the cost of harm caused the innocent".

150 *United States v. Carroll Towing Co., Inc.,* 159 F. 2d 169 (2d Cir. 1947).

151 Twerski, A. and Hendereson, J. A. (2009). Manufacturer's Liability for Defective Product Designs: The Triumph of Risk-Utility. *Cornell Law Faculty Publications. Paper 794*, 1061 at 1065.

152 *Id.* at 174. Cf. Restatement (Second) of Torts (1965) §§ 291–293, 298.

153 See discussion in Chapter 3 estimating injury costs.

154 Megie, G. (2006). From Stratospheric Ozone to Climate Change: Historical Perspective on Precaution and Scientifc Responsbility. *Science and Engineering Ethics*, 12(4), 596–606, at 604.

155 Rowlands, I. H. (1995), *op. cit. supra* at n.42 chapter 1, at 101.

In 1984, the Natural Resource Defence Council (NRDC), a US non-governmental environmental organisation, petitioned the EPA to enact comprehensive regulatory controls of ozone depleting substances and the basis of the Agency's endangerment finding. The outcome was a settlement involving an agreed "Stratospheric Ozone Protection Plan" which required the EPA to conduct, *inter alia*, a comprehensive health and environmental damage assessment of the ozone layer depletion problem.[156] That report,[157] issued in 1987, projected future skin cancer damages to individuals, households, business, and the economy.[158] The report estimated that "the total cost of phasing out CFCs to the US economy would be US$28 billion and the economic benefits of damage avoided would be US$6.54 trillion – a benefit cost ratio of 240 to 1."[159]

Numerous scholars have reflected that the analysis was an important if not decisive factor in pushing the Reagan Administration to support regulatory controls on CFCs domestically and to endorse the Montreal Protocol.[160] The global agreement was necessary because the benefits of avoiding serious harm could not be achieved by US unilateral action alone. For example, while US domestic controls were projected to avoid two million deaths by 2165, international regulation would rescue five million

---

156 Liftin (1995), *op. cit. supra* at n.40 chapter 1; Benedick (1991), *op. cit. supra* at n.22 chapter 1, at 66. Doniger, D. and Quibell, M. (2007), *op. cit. supra* at n.36 chapter 1, at 4–5; Collins, C. (2010), *op. cit. supra* at n.36 chapter 1, at 166.

157 US EPA (1987). *Regulatory Impact Analysis: Protection of Stratospheric Ozone.* Washington, D.C.: US EPA.

158 Sunstein, C. R. (2007), *op. cit. supra* at n.22 chapter 1, at 80; Haas, P. M. (1992). Banning Chlorofluorocarbons: Epistemic Community Efforts to Protect Stratospheric Ozone. *International Organization,* 46(1), 187–224, at 219; Benedick (1991), *op. cit. supra* at n.22 chapter 1, at 63.

159 Andersen and Sarma (2002), *op. cit. supra* at n.37 chapter 1, at 230.

160 Haas (1992), *op. cit. supra* at n.587; Benedick (1991), *op. cit. supra* at n.22 chapter 1, at 63; DeCanio, S. (2003). Economic Analysis, Environmental Policy and Intergenerational Justice in the Reagan Administration. In *International Environmental Agreements: Politics, Law and Economics* (299–321). Netherlands: Kluwer Academic Publishers; Liftin (1995), Chapter 5, *op. cit. supra* at n.40 chapter 1; Doniger, D. and Quibell, M. (2007), *op. cit. supra* at n.36 chapter 1, at 4–5; Collins, C. (2010), *op. cit. supra* at n.36 chapter 1, at 160; Cagin, S. and Dray, (1993), *op. cit. supra* at n.41 chapter 1. The authors explain that one of the biggest setbacks in enacting comprehensive controls on ozone depleting substances was the political change from the Carter to the Reagan Administration. While under the former, significant strides were made to enact environmental regulation in the United States, under President Reagan's anti-regulatory policy most environmental laws came to a standstill; Gifford, D. G. (2013), *op. cit. supra* at n.2 chapter 3,, at 112, quoting Merrill, T. W. (1997). Agency Capture Theory and the Courts: 1967–1983. *Chicago-Kent Law Review,* 72, 1039 at 1053: The era was "characterised by widespread pessimism about the capacity of any government institution to achieve results that will promote public interest". Schultz, G. (2012). Economic Strength and American Leadership. In L. E. Ohanian, J. B. Taylor and I. J. Wright (eds), *Government Policies and the Delayed Economic Recovery.* Stanford, California, Hoover Institution Press, Stanford University, at 16. Reagan became a strong supporter of the Montreal Protocol which he saw as an "insurance policy" against environmental harms.

citizens and save approximately US$900 billion.[161] These benefits coupled with the decreasing switch costs to industry (as the feasibility of alternatives increased in the mid-1980s) are said to have tipped the scales in favour of eliminating ODCs.[162]

Why that resolve could have not emerged earlier may partially be due to limitations of cost benefit analyses frameworks used in developing US environmental policy, and the problem of economic discounting using traditional rates and devaluing long term costs of harm.[163] In the 1980s, both issues presented a fundamental challenge to enacting precautionary measures to address intergenerational equity concerns.[164] This problem of discounting was not overcome until 1987 when both liberal and conservative discount rates were applied, demonstrating that precautionary costs were significantly less than long term benefits. This finding supported regulatory action.[165]

However, limitations to regulatory frameworks for assessing and gauging long term costs of harm were and are a matter of concerning in developing environmental policy.[166] In promulgating rules to control ODCs pursuant to the aerosol bans, the EPA was required under the Clean Air Act to conduct an impact assessment according to a set list of criteria.[167] Those criteria included a review of the "direct or indirect effects upon the public health and welfare of changes in ... ozone in the stratosphere, and the

---

161 Sunstein, C. R. (2007), *op. cit. supra* at n.22 chapter 1, at 82–85.

162 *Ibid*; Rowlands, I. H. (1995), *op. cit. supra* at n.42 chapter 1, at 112–113, 118; Sprinz, D. and Vaahtoranta, T. (1994, Winter). The Interest-based Explanation of International Environmental Policy. *International Organization*, 48(1) 77–105, at 80, 95.

163 Rowlands, I. H. (1995), *op. cit. supra* at n.42 chapter 1, at 108.

164 *Id.* at 108, 206.

165 Sunstein, C. R. (2007), *op. cit. supra* at n.22 chapter 1, at 80; Haas (1992), *op. cit. supra* at n.587; Benedick (1991), *op. cit. supra* at n.22 chapter 1, at 63. See also DeCanio, S. (2003), *op. cit. supra* at n.160, at 309–312: The President's Council of Economic Advisors reviewed data provided in the above-mentioned. Applying a 2% market interest rate, the Council estimated that 993,000 deaths in the United States between 1986 and 2075 would be valued at US$1.3 trillion which could be avoided by a 20% cut in chemicals uses costing less than US$4 billion. This was the conservative, approved policy level conclusion. However, within the Council, projections were also considered using a simplified, intergenerational neutral, low discount rate. That cost benefit analysis demonstrated a savings of US$10 trillion. The astonishingly high numbers implied by either model effectively forged consensus with the Council that regulatory actions were imperative. From that point forward, those Council members and other strong politicians who had been opposed to regulation for years were no longer persuasive as they had "simply lost the substantive argument".

166 Parson (2003), *op. cit. supra* at n.14 chapter 1, at 44; Portney, R. (ed.) (1990). *Public Policies for Environmental Protection*. Washington, D.C.: Resources for the Future, at 219.

167 42 U.S.C. §7453; In the 1980s, the Regan administration staunchly supported deregulation. See Gifford (2013), *op. cit. supra* at n.2 chapter 3, at 112 quoting Merrill, T. W. (1997). Agency Capture Theory and the Courts: 1967–1983. Chicago-Kent Law Review, 72, 1039 at 1053: The era was "characterised by widespread pessimism about the capacity of any government institution to achieve results that will promote public interest.

probable causes of changes in the... ozone in the stratosphere".[168] However, the need to include the cost of those effects was not specified. In contrast, other criteria entailed a full economic impact analysis of more immediate and inflationary costs affecting industry, small business, competition, (un)employment, consumers and energy consumption.[169]

Guided by the assessment framework, the EPA did not produce a full damage appraisal until 1986 when it was compelled to do so as an outcome of the legal settlement it reached with the NRDC, as discussed above. Even in 1982, following a NAS report in which the Biological Effects Committee argued for skin cancer incidence rates and deaths to be factored into risk calculations in determining policy actions, the EPA avoided using such information to bolster its rationale for regulatory controls.[170] Some analysis suggest that the EPA's delay in doing so was also due to the Agency's internal lack of clarity regarding its mandate and its inexperience in fashioning a policy to deal with a problem like ozone layer depletion which entailed uncertain, long term harm to human health and environment unlike "air and water pollutants, hazardous wastes or industrial chemicals" having direct and immediate consequences.[171] Still, had the EPA's assessment framework demanded a thorough risk accounting, and had the Agency made substantive case regarding future environmental and human damages, the EPA may have been more successful much earlier on. For example, the Agency's 1979 economic feasibility study to back enhanced CFC regulatory controls did not address long term costs of harm.[172] Rather, the study's rule-making validation was defended on other grounds which met with an unsympathetic rebuttal from industry.[173] DuPont specifically discounted many of the EPA's calculations and justifications, thus

---

168 42 U.S.C. §7453 (a).

169 42 U.S.C. §7453 (e); § 7617

170 Parson (2003), *op. cit. supra* at n.14 chapter 1, at 93, citing National Academy of Sciences. (1982). *Causes and Effects of Stratospheric Ozone Reduction: An Update.* Washington, D.C.: National Academy Press.

171 Parson (2003), *op. cit. supra* at n.14 chapter 1, at 44, 93–94;.Portney, R. (ed.) (1990), *op. cit. supra* at n.166, at 219, 287.

172 Palmer, A., Mooz, W., Quinn, T. and Wolf, K. (1980). *Economic Implications of Regulating Chlorofluorocarbon Emissions from Nonaerosol Applications Prepared from the US EPA* Santa Monica: The RAND Corporation: The report specifically states: "Evaluation of the health and environmental effects of ozone depletion is beyond the scope of this study, and we have not attempted to weigh the costs of regulation against health and environmental benefits. Instead, we identify mandatory control policies that could be expected to reduce CFC emissions between now and 1990 without seriously curtailing the availability of the services provided by the final products made from CFCs". See also Parson (2003) *op. cit. supra* at n.14 chapter 1, at 87 who likewise reflects that public expenditure on ozone layer related research was concentrated on resolving questions of atmospheric science. That budget exceeded US$200 million. Funding for studies on the effects of ozone loss only amounted to US$1 million in the early 80s.

173 See e.g. Cagin, S. and Dray, (1993), *op. cit. supra* at n.41 chapter 1.

weakening the Agency's position in calling for increased regulatory controls.[174]

Arguably, these cost benefit analysis constraints remain an obstacle to precautionary environmental policy making in the US which calls into question the need for a reform of the assessment framework.[175] As will be discussed in Chapter 13, the *ozone layer case* could aid in rethinking that construct to meet equally pressing global environmental challenges.

Taking these issues into consideration in the *ozone layer case*, it is equally critical to assert that the chemical producers also had a duty of care to assess and understand the risks of the chemicals which they marketed. The EPA's delay in predicting future losses to American citizens and society cannot be used an excuse for the ODC producers not knowing what the economic and non-economic risks were prior to 1987 when the companies actually increased both the production and the very risks which their due diligence should have confirmed in the 1970s. As discussed, chemical procures did provide detailed assessments of the costs associated with removing CFCs from the market. However, their business as usual impact assessments categorically concluded that resulting damage, if any, would be negligible. Given that they were producing and selling the risk creating products, were their assessments sufficiently diligent? Was it reasonable that not they but a government agency conduct a comprehensive risk assessment more than a decade after the risk became known? More critically, was their analysis of risk fabricated to protect their commercial interests?

The literature reviewed in this study has not directly dealt with these questions. However, most scholars agree US chemical producers' and manufacturers' resistance to regulations and introducing alternative technologies in the 1970s and 1980s was fuelled by economic and business

---

174 The DuPont Report, *op. cit. supra* at n.15 chapter 2, (Volume 2).

175 Percival, R. V. (1997), *op. cit. supra* at n.22 chapter 1, at 518: Percival has discussed how court decisions may respect that federal agencies such as the EPA are authorised to "issue regulations designed to prevent harm before it occurs" by not requiring proof of actual harm *Ethyl Corp. v. EPA*, 541 F. 2d 1 (DC Circuit 1976) (*en banc*). However, in some instances courts have rather limited the authority of US federal agencies to impose precautionary regulations in the absence of quantitative risk assessments demonstrating existence of significant risk, and reduced risk as a result of the proposed regulatory action. In the *Industrial Union Department v. American Petroleum Institute* (The Benzene Case), 448 US 607 (1980), the US Supreme Court pronounced that "it was not enough simply to find that a substance caused harm before regulating it to the limit of feasibility. Instead, agencies first have to determine that the risks posed by a regulatory target are 'significant' and that the contemplated regulatory action would appreciably reduce them". Likewise, in *Corrosion Proof Fittings v. EPA* 947 F. 2d 1201 (5th Circuit 1991), the Fifth Circuit struck down the environmental agency's proposed regulation to phase out asbestos use on the basis "that the agency had not analysed all the costs and benefits not only of an asbestos ban, but for all intermediate alternatives".

interests.[176] They explain that the companies opposed unilateral regulations which would result in unfair competition in global markets[177] and supported a global agreement which they could influence given their technical power[178] and ensure the competitive advantage of their newly patented products in the international replacement chemical market.[179] However, whether such business interests influenced the defendant companies' risk assessment is not apparent. As discussed above, they vindicated their behaviour on the basis of their risk assessment. Still, it is fair to ask whether those assessments were genuine and appropriate, and constructed as means to justify their profitability.[180]

In sum, based on the foregoing discussion, a reasonable basis exists to conclude that the risk utility analysis could demonstrate that the risks of ODCs outweighed their utility even throughout the 1970s and 1980s. Accordingly, it is possible to surmise that ozone depleting chemicals were defective products. Ultimately, the case begs a judicial opinion to confirm or refute these assumptions.

---

176 Andersen and Sarma (2002), *op. cit. supra* at n.37 chapter 1, at 197–200, 229, 230; Benedick (1998), *op. cit. supra* at n.22 chapter 1, at 33–34; Dotto, L. and Schiff, H. (1978). *The Ozone War.* Garden City, New York: Doubleday; Maxwell, J. and Briscoe, F. (1997), *op. cit. supra* at n.23 chapter 2; Parson (2003), *op. cit. supra* at n.14 chapter 1, at 54–55, 175–177.

177 The DuPont Report, *op. cit. supra* at n.15 chapter 2, at 45.

178 Falkner, R. (2005), *op. cit. supra* at n.147 chapter 2, at 113, 129–130.

179 DeSombre, E. R. (2000). The Experience of the Montreal Protocol: Particularly Remarkable, and Remarkably Particular. *UCLA Journal of Environmental Law and Policy,* 19(1), 49–81, at 59, 70–71; Schreurs, M. (2004). *Environmental Politics in Japan, Germany, and the United States.* Cambridge University Press, at 18; Andersen and Sarma (2002), *op. cit. supra* at n.37 chapter 1, at 74, 199, 442; Parson (2003), *op. cit. supra* at n.14 chapter 1, at 54, 117–118, 158. However, in the early 1980s industry groups tried to block US participation in international negotiations, where also the Fluorocarbon Panel attacked the scientific evidence which the EPA argued to justify international chemical controls; Benedick (1998), *op. cit. supra* at n.22 chapter 1, at 317. While the aerosol bans initially sapped the international competitiveness of US companies, they induced technological development and innovation which gave the companies a future market advantage. Collins, C. (2010), at 196, *op. cit. supra* at n.36 chapter 1. Maxwell, J. and Briscoe, F. (1997), *op. cit. supra* at n.23 chapter 2; Miller, A. (1990, October). The Development of Substitutes for Chlorofluorocarbons: Public–Private Cooperation and Environmental Policy, *Ambio* 19(6/7), CFCs and Stratospheric Ozone, 338–340.

180 Collins, C. (2010), at 191, *op. cit. supra* at n.36 chapter 1: reflecting more broadly on this concern, Collins has argued that the weighting of costs and benefits was hostage to the "subjective set of values, assumptions and beliefs" of stakeholders which are shaped by their "political allegiances and ideological-philosophical proclivities". He elaborates that, "Activist policy makers with strong environmental ethics place a much higher value on the long-range health and ecological costs of atmospheric disruption than free market conservatives; while the situation is reversed when valuing the costs of regulation. Those with a large stake in manufacturing CFCs or producing fossil fuels ... will tend to downplay health and environmental consequences while concerning themselves mainly with the immediate economic costs of any particular policy response."

4.2 Causation

Proving causation in the *ozone layer case* presents numerous challenges. Ultimately, it demands establishing a nexus between the defendants' alleged conduct and the plaintiff harms. While scientifically that connection can be deduced, it nevertheless involves a series of natural and non-natural occurrences over long periods of time. Figure 4.1 attempts to illustrate this complexity.

To simplify this challenge, causation may be assessed by a three tier approach drawing on the above figure. In the first instance, it would require showing *factual causation* or an objective assessment that the cause of harm and the harm itself are related.[181] This can be shown by applying the "but for" test, as in "but for" the defendant's action, "the plaintiff's damages would not have occurred". Second, plaintiffs would need to prove that their particular injuries are directly linked to the environmental damages created by the defendants' conduct. Finally, the causation test would require showing that the defendants' conduct was a substantial factor in causing the plaintiffs' harm. Each of these approaches is discussed below.

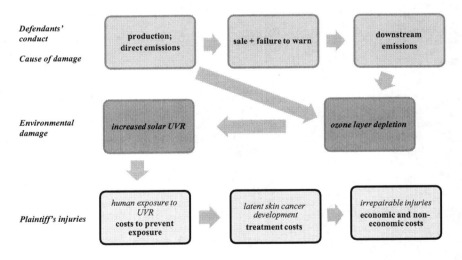

Figure 4.1 Causal link between ODC production and skin cancer damages

181 Prosser (1971), at 237–238, *op. cit. supra* at n.4: "It is a matter of what has in fact occurred... in a very real and practical sense, the term embraces all things which have so far contributed to the result that without them it would not have occurred.... On the other hand, an act or omission is not regarded as a cause of an event if the particular event would have occurred without it".

4.2.1 Factual causation

In the *ozone layer case*, factual causation can best be approached by applying the "but for" test. The proposition would be:

> But for the defendants' increased production and sale of defective ozone depleting products,
> *and/or*
> But for the defendants' failure to mitigate chemical emissions during production and pre-sale stages,
>
> └──►the plaintiffs' injuries i.e. increased risk of developing of dying from skin cancer, increased incidences and death and associated losses, would not have occurred.

In terms of both scientific fact and policy determinations, this test must show the causal link between the two occurrences even if the link is remote and even if other factors may have contributed to the plaintiffs' harms. Evidence presented in Chapter 2 showed that the causal connection between ODC emissions and skin cancer growth was appreciated in the 1970s. More recent studies by UNEP,[182] the WHO and the EPA state counterfactually the catastrophic harms which would have resulted if measures to control the production and emissions had not be taken globally. In the US alone, it is estimated that 6.3 million skin cancers have been avoided

---

182 UNEP (n.d.). *Key Achievements of the Montreal Protocol to date 1987–2012.* http://ozone.unep.org; US EPA (2006). *Human Health Benefits of Stratospheric Ozone Protection.* Washington, D.C. WMO (2010). *Scientific Assessment of Ozone Depletion: 2010, Global Ozone Research and Monitoring Project-Report.* See chapter 6 at 37; US EPA (2010). *Ozone Layer Protection – Science.* www.epa.gov/spdpublc/science/ods/index.html; US EPA (2011, May). *Benefits of the CFC Phaseout:* www.epa.gov/ozone/geninfo/benefits.html; Australian Government, Department of the Environment (n.d.). *The Ozone Layer.* www.environment.gov.au/protection/ozone/ozone-science/ozone-layer; Fahey, D. W. and Heggin, M. I. (2010). Twenty Questions and Answers about the Ozone Layer: 2010 Update. In WMO, *Report of the 2010 Assessment of the Scientific Assessment Panel.* Geneva: World Meteorological Organisation; World Health Organisation. (2003), *op. cit. supra* at n.31 chapter 1; Farman, J. (2002), *op. cit. supra* at n.40 chapter 1; Ando, M. (1990). Risk evaluation of stratospheric ozone depletion resulting from chlorofluorocarbons (CFC) on human health. *Nihon Eiseigaku Zasshi,* 45(5), 947–53; Skin Cancer Foundation (2014). *Ozone and UV: Where Are We Now?:* www.skincancer.org/prevention/uva-and-uvb/ozone-and-uv-where-are-we-now; MacKie, R. M. (1996). *Skin Cancer: An Illustrated Guide to the Aetiology, Clinical Features, Pathology and Management of Benign and Malignant Cutaneous Tumours.* London: Martin Dunitz Ltd.; Slaper, H., den Elzen, M., de Woerd, H. and de Greef, J. (1992). *Ozone Depletion and Skin Cancer Incidence: An Integrated Modelling Approach.* Rijksinstituut voor Volksgezondheid en Milieu RIVM; Slaper, H., Velders, G. J., Daniel, J. S., de Gruijl, F. F. and van der Leun, J. C. (1996). Estimates of Ozone Depletion and Skin Cancer Incidence to Examine the Vienna Convention achievements. *Nature,* 256–8.

between 1990 and 2165.[183]

Such factual causation was established between ODC emissions and human injuries in *Covington v. Jefferson Country* (2004). In that case, two Idaho residents sued a public landfill owner and relevant local government authority for the wrongful disposal of white goods, leakage of CFCs and property contamination in violation of federal rules. Although the suit revolved around whether the plaintiffs had standing to advance their claims, the Ninth Circuit Court did affirm that they had sufficiently demonstrated their injuries and that the defendant's failure to follow federal procedures and prevent CFC emissions satisfied the proof of causation requirement.[184] Better explained by Judge Gould in his concurring opinion, the question of legal causation for standing purposes was substantiated by facts of scientific theory[185] and US stratospheric ozone protection policy. He affirmed on the basis of science that "the release of CFCs degrades the stratospheric ozone layer,... [which] gives humans necessary protection from otherwise life-threatening ultraviolet-B radiation".[186] Therefore, the landfill emissions would contribute to the plaintiffs' risk of exposure to increased harm.[187] And, politically, "(b)y proscribing the unregulated release of CFCs and by authorizing citizen suits to enforce this prohibition, Congress unmistakably expressed a belief that the release of CFCs causes injury to residents of the United States".[188]

Clearly, the Ninth Circuit Court's ruling and Judge Gould's opinion support the causation challenge in the *ozone layer case*. However, the court was judging the operations of a local landfill operator which were noncomplaint with *existing* federal regulations. The question is whether the court would have found causation based on common law duties of care in say 1983 before federal policy on the ozone layer protection had been agreed. Equally, what would be a court's conclusion today?

Climate change cases offer some insight to this question given their similar challenges in proving causation between anthropogenic greenhouse gas emissions and atmospheric disturbances and harms to people, their property and the environment. In some suits, causal links were established to affirm standing of plaintiffs. In *Massachusetts v. EPA* (2007), the US Supreme Court determined that Massachusetts' receding coast line among other physical impacts was traceable to global warming to which major US fossil fuel reliant corporations contributed.[189] The Court impressed: "The

183 UNEP (n.d.). *Key Achievements of the Montreal Protocol to date 1987–2012.* http://ozone.unep.org/new_site/en/Information/Information_Kit/Key_achievements_of_the_Montreal_Protocol_2012.pdf.
184 *Covington v. Jefferson County,* 358 F. 3d 626, 640–41 (9th Cir. 2004).
185 *Id.* at 649–650.
186 *Id.* at 649.
187 *Id.* at 652.
188 *Id.* at 655.
189 *Massachusetts v. Environmental Protection Agency,* 127 SCt. 1438 (2007).

risk of catastrophic harm, though remote, is nevertheless real".[190] In the same way, factual causation was found in *Connecticut v. American Electric Power Company. Inc.* (2009)[191] and *Comer v. Murphy Oil* (2009).[192]

More recently, however, in *Environmental Council v. Bellon*, the Ninth Circuit Court rejected plaintiffs' injunctive relief claims that Washington State agencies regulate for in-State oil refineries on the basis that they had not sufficiently established causation. The plaintiffs did argue that "greenhouse gas emissions from the State's five oil refineries" amounted to 5.9 percent of the State's total emissions and as such were a significant contributor to global warming impacting on the State.[193] They claimed that the State's failure to set and apply reasonably available control technology standards "contributed to greenhouse gas pollution and caused their members to suffer recreational,[194] aesthetic, economic[195] and health injuries".[196] However, the Ninth Circuit Court did not agree. The Court asserted:

> Plaintiffs' causal chain – from lack of (reasonably available control technology) controls to Plaintiffs' injuries – consists of a series of links strung together by conclusory, generalized statements of "contribution", without any plausible scientific or other evidentiary basis that the refineries' emissions are the source of their injuries. While Plaintiffs need not connect each molecule to their injuries, simply saying that the Agencies have failed to curb emission of greenhouse gases, which contribute (in some undefined way and to some undefined degree) to their injuries, relies on an "attenuated chain of conjecture" insufficient to support standing.

The Court went on to say that it is not possible to qualitatively or quantitatively assess the impact of local emissions on local populations given the vast number of greenhouse gas sources existing globally.[197] Further, the Court opined that the same standing requirements applied by the US Supreme Court in *Massachusetts v. EPA* did not apply because in that case the plaintiffs were US States which were exercising "a procedural right to challenge the rejection of its rulemaking petition" and which have a special

---

190 *Id.* at 1458.
191 *Connecticut v. American Electric Power Co.* (2009), *op. cit. supra* at n.8 chapter 3, at 346–47.
192 *Comer v. Murphy Oil USA* (2009), *op. cit. supra* at n.38 chapter 1.
193 *Environmental Council v. Bellon*, 732 F. 3d 1131, 1135, 1136 (9th Cir. 2013).
194 *Id.* at 1140–1141. Glacial and snow melting has reduced enjoyment of natural environment, snowshoeing, skiing, backpacking, hiking, mountaineering and glacier climbing.
195 *Id.* at 1141. "(F)looding and decreased water availability will further reduce the benefits from and enjoyment of … property."
196 *Ibid.* Increased respiratory problems including asthma are induced by "higher air temperatures and ozone pollution — exacerbated by global warming."
197 *Id.* at 1143–1144.

position and interests as sovereign entities.[198] Such relaxed rules are not available to citizens because they are not States.[199]

Essentially, the ruling does not provide for great optimism and could foreclose on citizens bringing climate change related cases in the future. It may also impact on the viability of the *ozone layer case* even if the sources of emissions are more easily identifiable, and verifiable data can show chemical production volumes attributable to a handful of US chemical producers, the total problem of ozone layer depletion was not caused by those companies alone. Another upshot of the *Bellon* ruling may be to direct that US States (on behalf of their citizens) rather than classes of skin cancer victims should pursue compensation pleas.

4.2.2 Causation of plaintiffs' injuries

The second more challenging test in terms of evidence is proving that the plaintiffs' injuries were a result of the environmental damage caused by the defendants' conduct. For citizen plaintiffs, this means defending that one's skin cancer or risk of skin cancer is attributable to exposure to increased levels of solar UV radiation. One case which can provide some guidance in this respect is *Allen v. United States* (1984). In that epic law suit, the Utah District Court was tasked with determining whether the plaintiffs' injuries of cancer and leukaemia were caused by radiation exposure due to nuclear fallout from the government's weapon testing programme, and not any other sources. To do this, the court applied and assessed the following criteria.

- probability, length and degree of the plaintiff's exposure to the harm
- existence of a signature injury or injury that be attenuate to the type harm (radiation) caused including expected latency[200]
- assessment of the number and degree to which other factors contribute to the injury
- plaintiff's geographical proximity to the harm site
- plaintiff's physical vulnerability to the harm
- retroactive assessments of the intensity of the harm (radiation)

---

198 *Id.* at 1145.
199 *Id.* at 1146.
200 *Allen v. United States* (1984), *op. cit. supra* at n.40, at 405–406, 415: The Court recognised that the longer the latency period, the higher probability that intervening causes will "obscure the factual connection between the plaintiff's injury and the defendant's purportedly wrongful conduct". However, the Court also opined that "where it is evident that the influence of the actor's negligence is still a substantial factor, mere lapse of time, no matter how long, is not sufficient to prevent it from being the legal cause of the other's harm".

- increased incidence rate of disease[201]
- absence of any other intervening causes.[202]

In the *ozone layer case*, applying these criteria is possible and may be sufficient to establish causation. Referring back to data presented in Chapter 3, because skin cancer is a signature disease of sun exposure, plaintiffs would need to prove that their disease was not triggered by other sources of UV radiation e.g. indoor tanning or by a special genetic condition. Assessing solar UV radiation necessarily must discount background radiation levels which may be surmised from skin cancer incidence rates at 1975 levels as well as other scientific data.[203] Additionally, because skin cancer is largely connected to sun exposure and sun burn during childhood, some medical history or life accounting may be needed. Medical proof of one's genetic disposition to skin cancer as well as evidence regarding where one has lived or worked could also be relevant. Such information may also be necessary if one claims loss of recreational and employment freedoms due to a future risk of developing skin cancer.

However, proving physical injury in connection with toxic or radiative substances is usually quite taxing for plaintiffs particularly when their disease is latent. Plaintiffs have been moderately successful in suits involving drugs (e.g. DES),[204] vaccines (e.g. defective DPT),[205] chemicals (e.g. pesticides),[206] and industrial materials (e.g. asbestos).[207] However, in many more cases, such as the *Agent Orange* litigation,[208] failure to establish proximate cause has quashed the ability of plaintiffs to pursue product liability claims.[209] Potential *ozone layer case* plaintiffs can take guidance from these experiences although the one most applicable would seem to be the *Allen* case.

201 *Id.* at 322, 405: The Court assessed the increased risk of cancer to the plaintiff group by comparing their risk relative to the same risk in other populations. The risk was assessed by comparative incidence rates.
202 *Id.* at 429–443.
203 See Chapter 3 §§ 3.2.3, 3.3 *supra*.
204 *Collins v. Eli Lily & Co,* 116 Wis. 2d 166 (Wis. 1984); *Sindell v. Abbott Laboratories,* 26 Cal. 3d 588 (Cal. 1980).
205 *Morris v. Parke, Davis & Co.,* 667 F. Supp.1332 (C.D. Cal. 1987).
206 *Arnold v. Dow Chemical Company,* 91 Cal. A4th 698 (Cal. A 2001); *In Re Agent Orange Product Liability Litigation,* 373 F. Su 2d 7, 19 (EDNY 2005).
207 *Borel v. Fibreboard Paper Products Corp.,* 493 F. 2d 1076 (5th Cir. 1973); *O'Neil v. Crane Co.,* 266 3d 987 (Cal. 2012); *Urie v. Thompson,* 337 US 163 (1949).
208 See Schuck, H. (1988). *Agent Orange on Trial: Mass Toxic Disasters in the Courts.* Cambridge: Harvard University Press: Although the product liability theory was advanced in litigation against chemical manufacturers, the plaintiffs (often the estate of deceased US war veterans) could not prove that the chemicals caused their diseases. Ultimately, some suits failed because defendant chemical companies successfully argued the government contractor defence. Still, the New York Court hearing the case approved a settlement of US$180,000 million.
209 *In Re Agent Orange Product Liability Litigation,* 597 F. Supp. 740, 782–783 (EDNY 1984); *In Re Agent Orange Product Liability,* 611 F. Supp. 1267 (EDNY 1985), aff'd, 818 F. 2d 187 (2d Cir.).

For US State plaintiffs, while the burden of proof is more relaxed, it would require them to establish a connection between their concrete injuries owing to ozone layer depletion. Here, the main challenge would be to demonstrate that they have suffered unreasonable interferences with public health and safety and/or bear increased public expenditures and losses owing to costs of increased skin cancer incidence and death rates.

4.2.3 Defendants' conduct in causing the plaintiffs harm

In the *ozone layer case*, the producers of ODCs have been named as defendants given their role in creating the source of chemical emissions that have contributed to depleting the ozone layer. It cannot be disputed that those handful of US companies did this. However, the defendants were not the only companies which produced the chemicals over the last century. According to data submitted in Chapter 3, US companies are estimated to have produced 38 percent of total (calculable) historical global production. As discussed there, this production share is discounted to 22 percent to reflect production during the period for which liability is alleged in this study. For causation, the questions which arise are: (1) whether that share of production substantially caused the plaintiffs' increased risks of developing and dying from skin cancers, and if so; (2) how much did that particular share contribute to what degree of stratospheric ozone loss and increased solar UV radiation to which the plaintiff was exposed and experienced an increased risk of developing skin cancer? Perhaps more simply, to what percentage of the plaintiff's harm did the defendant's share of production contribute? And is the answer to that question sufficient to establish causation?

In other cases, courts have dealt with similarly complex causation issues where multiple tortfeasors and often multiple causes of injury have existed. Many have applied the substantial factor test which takes into consideration:

- "the number of other factors which contribute in producing the harm and the extent to which they produce it"[210]
- "whether after the event and looking back from the harm to the actor's negligent conduct it appears highly extraordinary that it should have brought about the harm"[211]
- "whether the actor's conduct has created a force or series of forces which are in continuous and active operation up to the time of the harm, or has created a situation harmless unless acted upon by other forces for which the actor is not responsible".[212]

---

210 Restatement (First) of the Law Records (1942) § 433 (a).
211 Id. at § 433 (b).
212 *Id.* at § 433 (c).

Court opinions have developed this test further. In *Allen*, the court considered whether the government's conduct in carrying out nuclear weapons tests was a substantial factor in causing the plaintiff's harm. In doing so, it also applied market share and alternative liability theories[213] to advance and simplify that a defendant's negligent conduct can be a substantial factor in causing a victim's injury,[214] stating:

> Where by a preponderance of the evidence, the plaintiffs establish that the defendant's conduct negligently or wrongfully breached the duty of care, and that the conduct materially augmented or increased the risks of injury, and contributed to the harm suffered by the plaintiffs, the defendant shall be held liable.[215]

Further, the Court supported that the burden of proof should be shifted to the government to demonstrate that its nuclear fallout caused by its tests did not cause the plaintiffs' injuries.[216] According to the Court, this approach would address the "indeterminate plaintiff" problem which is common to cases involving victims of toxic chemicals and wastes where the

---

213 *Allen v. United States* (1984), *op. cit. supra* at n.40, at 410–413. The Court cites e.g. *Summers v. Tice*, 33 Cal. 2d 80 (Cal. 1948); *Oliver v. Miles*, 144 Miss. 852, 110 So. 666, 50 ALR 357 (1927); *Ybarra v. Spangard*, 1542d 687 (Cal. 1944); *Basko v. Sterling Drug, Inc.*, 416 F. 2d 417 (2d Cir. 1969); *Sindell v. Abbott Laboratories*, 26 Cal. 3d 588, 611–612 (Cal. 1980). *McAllister v. Workmen's Compensation Appeals Board*, 69 Cal. 2d 408, 4452d 313, 71 Cal. Rptr. 697 (1968): Smoke inhalation during 32 year employment as a fire fighter determined as a cause of deceased's lung cancer notwithstanding years of smoking. In the words of the Court:" given the present state of medical knowledge, we cannot say whether it was the employment or the cigarettes which 'actually' caused the disease; we can only recognize that both contributed substantially to the likelihood of his contracting lung cancer."; *Krumback v. Dow Chemical Co.*, 676 2d 1215 (Colo. 1983), *In Re Leroy A. Krumback*, W.C. No. 2-923-974, (Ind. Comm. Colo. 1984): proximate cause established based on evidence demonstrating that there was a "reasonable probability" that the deceased's colon cancer and death were caused by cut resulting from falling glass". Also in contrast, *Kramer Service, Inc. v. Wilkins*, 184 Miss. 483, 186 So. 625 (1939): "No probability that plaintiff's skin cancer was caused by cut resulting from falling glass".
214 *Allen v. United States* (1984), *op. cit. supra* at n.40, at 412, citing the Restatement (Second) of Torts: "If two forces are actively operating, one because of the actor's negligence, the other not because of any misconduct on his part, and each of itself sufficient to bring about harm to another, the actor's negligence may be found to be a substantial factor in bringing it about."
215 *Id.* at 357–358. The Court stated: "If it can be established that the Government negligently or wrongfully breached that duty, and that a rational factual connection exists between the Government's conduct and the plaintiffs' injuries, then law and public policy require that liability be imposed upon the party creating this particular risk. Even where there remains the possibility that the injury would have occurred in the absence of defendant's conduct – which is always a possibility in every case of cancer or leukaemia – doing justice between the parties requires that the party creating a materially increased risk of that harm bear at least the economic burden of its consequences."
216 *Id.* at 412–413.

relationship between cause and injury may not be established with absolute certainty.[217] From this, the *Allen* court sets out:

> Where a defendant who negligently creates a radiological hazard which puts an identifiable population group at increased risk, and a member of that group at risk develops a biological condition which is consistent with having been caused by the hazard to which he has been negligently subjected, such consistency having been demonstrated by substantial, appropriate, persuasive and connecting factors, a fact finder *may* reasonably conclude that the hazard caused the condition absent persuasive proof to the contrary offered by the defendant."[218] [Moreover,] "the plaintiff need not prove his case beyond a reasonable doubt. In fact, 'He is not required to eliminate entirely all possibility that the defendant's conduct is not a cause.'"[219] It is enough that he introduces evidence from which reasonable men may conclude that it is more probable that the event was caused by the defendant than that it was not. *The fact of causation is incapable of mathematical proof,* since no man can say with absolute certainty what would have occurred if the defendant had acted otherwise.[220]

The Court's opinion has obvious value for the *ozone layer case* as it speaks directly to radiation induced injuries and hails that negligent conduct suffices as a substantial factor to establish causation. Assuming that negligence could be proven, the ruling would also relax the causation requirement by permitting that the burden of proof rest with the defendants to show that their activities did not cause the plaintiffs' harm. However, the problem remains that unlike in *Allen*, the *ozone layer case* is targeted at multiple defendants that partially contributed to the destruction of a global public good which has had adverse effects on the environment and human health. Would it then be possible to establish that their conduct if proven negligent caused the plaintiffs' injuries?

To aid in answering this question, a number of liability theories have been developed by courts in response to common law tort claims where multiple tortfeasors have caused, likely caused or contributed to risks of harm and injuries suffered by innocent victims.[221] These include Joint and

---

217 *Id.* at 413.
218 *Id.* at 415.
219 *Id.* at 416.
220 *Ibid.*
221 *In re Methyl Tertiary Butyl Ether Products Liability Litigation, 379 F. Supp. 2d. 348, 371 (S.D.N.Y. 2005);* Restatement (Second) of Torts (1965) § 433B (2): Where the tortious conduct of two or more actors has combined to bring about harm to the plaintiff, and one or more of the actors seeks to limit his liability on the ground that the harm is capable of apportionment among them, the burden of proof as to the apportionment is upon each such actor.

Several Liability,[222] Industry-Wide Liability,[223] Market Share Liability,[224] Risk Contribution Liability[225] and "Commingled Product" Market Share Liability theories.[226] Of these the most relevant to the *ozone layer case* is the latter which has emerged in answer to the similarly complicated problem of harms caused by toxic soups of chemicals which are released into the environment where they commingle.[227] The theory was developed through toxic tort litigation regarding health damages caused by groundwater contaminated with Methyl tertiary butyl ether (MTBE).[228] It posits that when the precise harm-causing product and its supplier are known, liability can be established even if it cannot be verified *how much of the product in its commingled state has contributed to a specific injury*.[229] The theory advances that:

> When a plaintiff can prove that certain gaseous or liquid products (e.g., gasoline, liquid propane, alcohol) of many suppliers were present in a completely commingled or blended state at the time and place that the risk of harm occurred, and the commingled product caused a single indivisible injury, then each of the products should be deemed to have caused the harm ... (and) ... all of the suppliers can be held

---

222 Restatement (Second) of Torts (1965), § 433B(3): Where the conduct of two or more actors is tortious, and it is proved that harm has been caused to the plaintiff by only one of them, but there is uncertainty as to which one has caused it, the burden is upon each such actor to prove that he has not caused the harm. See *Ybarra v. Spangard*, 1542d 687 (Cal. 1944). *Summers v. Tice*, 33 Cal. 2d 80 (Cal. 1948). *Maddux v. Donaldson*, 362 Mich. 425, 431 (Michigan, 1961).

223 *Hall v. E. I. DuPont De Nemours*, 345 F. Supp. 353, 372, 373, 378, (EDNY 1972): Joint liability amongst industry members could be established if the defendants maintained "joint control of risk" demonstrated by: (1) The defendants' awareness of and "joint capacity to reduce or affect those risks", (2) "an explicit agreement and joint action among the defendants" but necessarily a joint venture or profit-sharing agreement, (3) "evidence of defendants' parallel behaviour sufficient to support an inference of tacit agreement or cooperation," and (4) "evidence that defendants, acting independently, adhered to an industry-wide standard or custom" (including codes and practices).

224 *Collins v. Eli Lily & Co*, 116 Wis. 2d 166, 194–196 (Wis. 1984): To establish causation, a plaintiff need not prove that a company's specific product caused her injury but provide evidence that any number of companies likely did produce and market that same fungible product, that such product caused her injury, and that the conduct of those companies was tortious under negligence and/or strict liability theories.

225 See Worley, L. L. (2006). The Iceberg Emerged: Wisconsin's Extension of Risk Contribution Theory Beyond DES. *Marquette Law Review*, 90.

226 *In Re Methyl Tertiary Butyl Ether Products Liability Litigation* (2005), *op. cit. supra* at n.221, at 377.

227 But see also the concept suggested in the Judge Andrew's dissenting opinion on proximate cause in *Palsgraf v. Long Island Railroad Company*, 248 NY 339, 352 (NY 1928).

228 *In re Methyl Tertiary Butyl Ether Products Liability Litigation* (2005), *op. cit. supra* at n.221, at 377.

229 *Id. at 379.*

(severally) liable for any harm arising from an incident of contamination.[230]

Accordingly, under this theory, a plaintiff must show that defendants' products were in fact present in the environment or in a particular place when and where an injury occurred, and that the commingled product caused the plaintiff's single, indivisible injury. Plaintiffs are expected to identify defendants "in good faith" by having "conducted some investigation".[231] Additionally, it must be shown that the defendants' conduct was tortious under negligence and/or strict liability theories. Should the plaintiff be able to provide evidence establishing these facts, the burden of proof then shifts to the defendants[232] who must "prove by a preponderance of evidence" that their "product was not present at the relevant time or in the relevant place, and therefore could not be part of the new commingled or blended product".[233] To increase the possibility of wider shared liability and a more equitable distribution of damages, the theory qualifies that defendants can implead other companies who (they assess) have also contributed to the injury.[234] This enables that a "pool of defendants"[235] is established which "can reasonably be assumed could have caused the plaintiff's injuries".[236]

As the *MTBE* case and the commingled theory speak to the *ozone layer case* on a number of similar grounds, both could be usefully employed to support that ODC producers have contributed to increased skin cancer injuries as a result of their commingling in the atmosphere and eating away at the ozone layer. As presented in Chapter 2, all US producers are known as a matter of public record during the liability period in question. While the American companies were not the only producers, theoretically the defendants could implead others to ensure that liability is apportioned fairly. It would also be possible that the plaintiffs sue all of the chemical producers world-wide. Even if this would unravel a number of other jurisdictional, legal and accountability issues beyond the present *ozone layer case*, it would be possible and it may be quite important. In any event, a finding of negligence would be critical. This includes establishing proximate cause as discussed next.

---

230 *Id.* at 377–78.
231 *Ibid.*
232 *Sindell v. Abbott Laboratories*, 26 Cal. 3d 588, 612 (Cal. 1980); *Collins v. Eli Lily & Co*, 116 Wis. 2d 166, 189, 197–98 (Wis. 1984).
233 *In Re Methyl Tertiary Butyl Ether Products Liability Litigation* (2005), *op. cit. supra* at n.221, at 379.
234 *Collins v. Eli Lily & Co*, 116 Wis.2d 166, 195 (Wis. 1984).
235 *Id.* at 198.
236 *Sindell v. Abbott Laboratories*, 26 Cal.3d 588, 611–612 (Cal. 1980).

4.3 Proximate cause

Once causation is established and once it is relatively clear that a standard of care exists, negligence theory demands that proximate cause be established. This involves assessing the extent to which a defendant could *foresee* that his conduct would result in an unreasonable risk of harm. A defendant's foreseeability is judged according to his constructive knowledge about a risk and his capability to know that risk "through the exercise of reasonable care".[237] This includes a defendant's ability to foresee intervening causes (natural or anthropogenic events) which follow from his conduct and influence a plaintiff's resulting harm. Intervening causes form part of the risk which the defendant creates. If the defendant can anticipate such causes, then he should take precautions to guard against them.[238] The defendant must also be able to foresee who will be harmed as a result of his actions.[239] He must know that he has a duty toward those potential victims to safeguard their legally protected interests or rights.[240] On this understanding, proximate cause is a policy question because it turns on what precautionary and reasonable care duties are or are not expected amongst actors within society.[241]

In applying this logic to the *ozone layer case*, the questions are two-fold but invariably interlinked: First, could the defendant chemical producers have foreseen that their alleged conduct could have resulted in future skin cancer related damages to the plaintiffs i.e. US residents and States? Second, did the companies have a duty of care toward this class of present and future victims?

Evidence presented in Chapter 2 suggests that the companies had sufficient information to be aware of the potential unreasonable risks their chemicals posed as well as intervening causes. Even if it would be argued disingenuously that skin cancer victims have only themselves to blame e.g. for sunbathing and swimming outdoors, that type of popular behaviour could have been foreseen as an intervening cause. Rather, the critical issue regarding their foreseeability is the *uncertainty* of what was known about the risks at stake.[242] In the 1970s and 1980s, that uncertainty meant that the risk

---

237 Prosser (1971), *op. cit. supra* at n.4, at 270–272. American Law Institute (1965). Restatement (Second) of Torts § 441, 447, 449; *Loftin v. McCranie,* 47 So. 2d 298, 302 (Fla. 1950); *Hall v. E. I. DuPont De Nemours,* 345 F. Supp. 353, 367 (EDNY 1972); *Boeing Airplane Company v. Brown,* 291 F. 2d 310, 317–318 (9th Cir. 1961); See Stevenson, M. K. (2011). Minnesota Negligence Law and the Restatement (Third) of Torts: Liability for Physical and Emotional Harms. *William Mitchell Law Review,* 37(3) at pp 1112–14 discussing *Harpster v. Hetherington,* 512 NW 2d 585, (Minn. 1994).

238 *Id.*

239 Prosser (1971), *op. cit. supra* at n.4, at 244.

240 *Palsgraf v. Long Island Railroad Company,* 248 NY 339, 343–34 (NY 1928); Chapman, B. (1983). Ethical Issues in the Law of Tort. In M. D. Bayles and B. Chapman (eds), *Justice, Rights and Tort Law* (13-43). Dordrecht/Boston: D. Reidel Publishing Company, at 25.

241 Chapman, B. (1983), *op. cit. supra* at n.240, at 25.

242 *Ibid.*

could have been very high as science later confirmed, or it could have been extremely low as the companies urged. The only certainty was that an unreasonable risk of harm potentially existed, and the type of harm involved teetered on being catastrophic. Given this, the question is how that type of uncertainty can be understood in assessing foreseeability and proximate cause. Moreover, it raises policy questions regarding the duty of care necessitated by such risks and begs the proposition that foreseeability was not only possible but inescapable in the *ozone layer case.*

In a number of cases similar questions have been grappled with by courts in determining proximate cause.[243] They have involved situations where the defendants' conduct was remotely connected to plaintiffs' harm, where intervening causes were involved and where the foreseeability of harm was not simple. In many of those cases, the judicial assessment of the defendant's foreseeability of harm has relied on the defendant's duty of care toward the plaintiff. The duty of care imposed on the defendant has been informed by the gravity of harm involved, the innocence of and the need to protect the plaintiff, the possibility of that harm affecting wider segments of the population, and the negligent behaviour of the defendant.[244] Ultimately, such cases have involved policy decisions or the application of policy rules. Thus, while a defendant's actual ability to foresee future harm is relevant, it has often been assessed as secondary to the duty of care imposed on the defendant which tells rather what the defendant was expected to have foreseen given those policy related considerations.

In *Johnson v. Kosmos Portland Cement Co.* (1933), the owner of an oil and rock barge was found negligent for failing to ensure crew safety.[245] The barge owner did not take the necessary precautions to prevent the build-up of gases in the vessel's hold when the barge was struck by lightning causing an explosion which killed everyone on board.[246] Proximate cause was determined on the basis that the company had allowed the presence of flammable gases which created a dangerous condition in which anything even a match or torch could have ignited and caused an explosion. It just so happened that the explosion was set off by a lightning bolt.[247]

Similarly, in *Bangor & AR Co. v. Ship Fernview* (1978), a chemical company's production and emissions of SO_3 and SO_2 were found to have proximately caused a ship crashing into and damaging a docking pier.[248]

---

243 Harris, O. F. (1986). Toxic Tort Litigation and the Causation Element. *Southwestern Law Journal*, 909, 911–12.
244 *United States v. Carroll Towing Co., Inc.,* 159 F.2d 169 (2d Cir. 1947); *Palsgraf v. Long Island Railroad Company,* 248 NY 339, 345 (NY 1928).
245 *Id.* at 195–7.
246 64 F. 2d 193, 194 (6th Cir. 1933).
247 *Id.* at 195–7.
248 *Bangor & AR Co. v. Ship Fernview,* 455 F. Supp. 1043, 1046 (D. Main 1978).

The chemical company's emissions mixed with natural water vapours causing abnormally heavy fog and acid mist. The wind blew the thick mist to the
harbour creating poor visibility conditions for the ship operator who was
unable to manoeuvre his vessel with clear vision thereby wrecking into the
docking pier.[249] The Court found that the defendant was negligent in causing the damage because the company failed to record, monitor and control
the escape of the sulphur gases beyond an accepted emissions limit.[250]
Finding negligence, the Court also ruled there was proximate cause on the
basis that no other factor could have influenced the formation of heavy fog
at the harbour[251] and on the common law rule "that a manufacturer who
negligently emits steam or other opaque gas which obstructs visibility on
public highways, airways, or waterways is liable for damages proximately
caused by such negligent emissions". [252] In both *Johnson* and *Bangor,* the
defendants could not foresee who the plaintiffs would be or their
injuries.[253] In fact, the probability of either disaster happening was low.
Rather, their public safety duty to prevent the development of dangerous
conditions was what triggered the policy expectation that they take precautions despite clear foreseeability.

In product liability cases, similar conclusions have been reached. In a
number of jurisdictions, courts have held that product manufacturers
have a duty to foresee harms their product may cause not only to the
direct consumers but also to bystanders.[254] The rationale suggests that
because product manufacturers have advanced technical know-how in
today's society, they have a duty toward consumers and users to ensure

---

249 *Id.* at 1046.

250 *Id.* at 1057–1058.

251 *Id.* at 1060.

252 *Id.* at 1057–1058, citing *Lavelle v. Grace,* 34 A. 2d 498, 500–01 (1943); Restatement
(Second) of Torts (1965) § 37.

253 *Atlas Chemical Industries, Inc. v. Anderson,* 514 SW 2d 309, 320 (1974) reversed in *Atlas
Chemical Industries, Inc. V. Anderson,* 524 SW 2d 681 (1975) In discussing gross negligence
perpetrated against unknown victims, the court provides the example that when one
throws a grenade into a crowd, he expects that people will be injured but does not know
who exactly. He nevertheless must be held accountable.

254 The Restatement (Third) of Torts, §§ 1, 2; *Caruth v. Mariani,* 11 Ariz. A 188, 463 2d 83,
85 (1970); *Berrier v. Simplicity Mfg., Inc.,* 563 F. 3d 38 2009 (Court of Appeals, 3rd Circuit
April 21, 2009) at 55–56; In *Darryl v. Ford Motor Company,* 440 SW 2d 630 (Supreme Court
of Texas. April 23, 1969), the court stated: "There is no adequate rationale or theoretical
explanation why non-users and non-consumers should be denied recovery against the
manufacturer of a defective product. The reason for extending the strict liability doctrine
to innocent bystanders is the desire to minimize risks of personal injury and/or property
damage. A manufacturer who places in commerce a product rendered dangerous to life
of limb by reason of some defect is strictly liable in tort to one who sustains injury because
of the defective condition." See also, *Greenman v. Yuba Power Products, Inc.,* 59 Cal. 2d 57
(Cal. 1963), *Codling v. Paglia,* 32 NY 2d 330 (1973); *Elmore v. American Motors Corp.,* 70 Cal.
2d 578 (Cal. 1969); *Toombs v. Fort Pierce Gas Company,* 208 SO 2d 615 (Fla. 1968); *West v.
Caterpillar Tractor Company, Inc.,* 336 SO 2d 80 (Fla. 1975).

their safety, this includes the ability to foresee, warn and prevent potential harms from their products.[255] In *In Re MTBE Prods. Liability Litig.* (2013), a similar logic was employed. There, the court affirmed the jury's finding that Exxon should be held liable for both negligence and strict liability for the contamination of New York City's groundwater and wells caused by the release of MTBE containing gasoline from underground storage tanks. The jury's verdict that the company had breached its duty of care to the city was reached, in part, based on Exxon's superior knowledge as the gasoline manufacturer and based on "(e)vidence of Exxon's timely knowledge of the particular dangers of MTBE, combined with evidence about remedial measures available as early as the 1980s...".[256] However, that evidence was not conclusive regarding what Exxon knew as to: (1) the health effects and migration capacity of MTBE, (2) the above ground spillage and underground tank leakage potentials of MTBE containing gasoline, (3) the degree to which ground water had already been contaminated in the 1980s and thereafter.[257] That is, despite some uncertainties, the defendant's duty to not pollute public water supplies was affirmed.

What can be gleaned from these cases is that the foreseeability requirement to establish proximate cause is inherently linked to the duty which the defendant owes to the plaintiffs and that duty is a matter of policy, as prefaced above.[258] In *Bangor*, the finding of proximate cause was simplified by an existing common law rule which prescribed that proximate cause is established by the negligent emissions of chemicals into the environment which obstructed visibility and endanger public safety.[259] In the *MTBE* case, such an explicit tenet was not stated with regard to ground water contamination but was ostensibly implied. In the *ozone layer case*, the question is whether a court would decipher or pronounce a similar directive regarding the negligent pollution of the atmosphere. A court would need to recognise that the defendant chemical manufacturers did have a duty of care toward future generations to ensure public health and safety by not contributing to the unreasonable risk of ozone layer depletion. Should that duty be cleared, given the magnitude of risk involved, questions regarding scientific uncertainty should be resolved. The companies' general awareness of the risk and their superior knowledge of their products as well as alternatives should be sufficient to establish proximate cause – if their conduct is deemed negligent.

---

255 *Codling v. Paglia*, 32 NY 2d 330, 340 (1973).
256 *In Re MTBE Prods. Liability Litig.*, 725 F. 3d 65, 92 (2d. Cir. 2013).
257 *Id.* at 91–94: The evidence reviewed is in relation to the punitive damage question. Most documentation appears to be speculative or consist of uncertainties.
258 *Johnson v. Kosmos Portland Cement Co.*, 64 F. 2d 193, 195–97 (6th Cir. 1933).
259 *Bangor & AR Co. v. Ship Fernview*, 455 F. Supp. 1043, 1057–1058 (D. Main 1978), citing *Lavelle v. Grace*, 34 A. 2d 498, 500–01 (1943); Restatement (Second) of Torts (1965) § 37.

Of course, it could still be argued that defendants exercised reasonable care by researching and monitoring the scientific validity of the ozone problem throughout the 1970s and 1980s and by investing in developing safe alternatives during 1974–1980. Further, because a number of companies turned to support ozone layer protection policy by restarting the search for replacement chemicals in the late 1980s, their behaviour was rather commendable. Moreover, it can also be asserted that in the 1970s and 1980s scientific uncertainty about the causes and harm of ozone layer depletion was so profuse that no duty of care could have or should be imposed on the defendants, and thus, they did not act negligently. As discussed elsewhere, all of these statements are perfectly defensible.

However, the question remains whether the duties of care exhibited by the companies amounted to the reasonable level of care an ordinary person would have expected given the potential magnitude of risk involved. In that context, the conduct alleged to be negligent deserves review. Moreover, the upshot of the uncertainty argument would be to probe whether their conduct was "inadvertent" and whether the eventuating harm has been accidental.[260] Although common sense[261] should enlighten that ozone loss over Antarctica the size of North America was not an accident, it could be one conclusion. Ultimately, this is a policy question which, if and when the *ozone layer case* would be tried, would test the limits of tort law.[262]

4.4 Existence of injuries and damages

In Chapter 2, the scope and type of damages which the *ozone layer case* plaintiffs would likely claim were presented. The type of proof of injury, however, varies as to whether the plaintiffs are individuals or US States. Individual plaintiffs would need to prove that they have or will suffer an injury or

---

260 *Palsgraf v. Long Island Railroad Company*, 248 NY 339, 345 (NY 1928). In this landmark case, Long Island Railroad Co., a train company, was not found negligent for failing to ensure the safety of a passenger who was injured in an accidental explosion on the company's premises. The accident occurred when a company employee pushed a passenger onto a train causing his concealed package of fireworks to fall and explode. Tremors from the blast caused a platform scale to fall over and injure the plaintiff. Because the plaintiff's damage was unforeseeable as caused by an inadvertent act, so too, no duty could be assumed on the part of the defendant.

261 *Id.* at 354:

262 *Id. at* 349–351. "Due care is a duty imposed on each one of us to protect society from unnecessary danger, not to protect A, B or C alone.... Everyone owes to the world at large the duty of refraining from those acts that may unreasonably threaten the safety of others. Such an act occurs. Not only is he wronged to whom harm might reasonably be expected to result, but he also who is in fact injured, even if he be outside what would generally be thought the danger zone....Unreasonable risk being taken, its consequences are not confined to those who might probably be hurt". Chapman (1983), *op. cit. supra* at n.240, at 25.

invasion to their person or property[263] showing that their personal, physical and emotional being and integrity and/or legally protected interests have been violated.[264] They will need to verify that they have incurred general, special or nominal damage or loss, economic or non-economic, which is representative of their injuries by assigning it a monetary value.[265]

Plaintiffs could also claim wrongful death injuries on behalf of family members or other close relations who have died prematurely. Proof of injury in these cases will vary by State.[266] In California, juries are instructed to assess both economic such as lost household income and non-economic damages including loss of "love, companionship, comfort, care, assistance, protection, affection, society, moral support, loss of the enjoyment of sexual relations and loss of training and guidance". However, the injury would not extend to pain and suffering.[267]

For US State plaintiffs, the showing of injury is different as they would be representing State citizens and public interests under the *parens patriae* doctrine[268] and/or statutory authorities.[269] They will need to show that skin cancer prevalence is an invasion to public safety or health which is specialised, in that it does not affect all persons but certain individuals or groups. The State plaintiffs can rely on a number of successful tort cases and settlements reached regarding lead paint, tobacco and hang guns where public interest injuries were evidenced. In such cases both abatement costs and economic losses[270] including public health care treatment and disease prevention costs were recoverable[271] for past, present and future damages caused by the defendants' acts.[272]

263 American Bar Association (2004). *Chapter Thirteen: Personal Injury.* Randon House. New York, at 3.

264 Buckley, W. R. and Okrent, C. J. (2004). *Torts and Personal Injury Law.* Clifton Park, NY: Thomson/Delmar Learning at 45–46; Sargent Shriver National Center on Poverty Law (2013). 9.1 Damages. In Sleasman, *Federa Practice Manual for Legal Aid Attorneys*; *Dillon v. Legg*, 68 Cal. 2d 728 (1968); *Consolidated Rail Corp. v. Gottshall*, 512 US 532 (1994); *Metro-North Commuter Railroad Co. v. Buckley*, 117 S Ct. 2113 (1997). *Borel v. Fibreboard Paper Products Corp.*, 493 F. 2d 1076 (5th Circuit 1973).

265 *Id.*

266 Buckley, W. R. and Okrent, C. J. (2004), *op. cit supra* n.693, at 344–345; Thomas Reuters (2014). *Wrongful Death Overview.* Retrieved from FindLaw: http://injury.findlaw.com/torts-and-personal-injuries/wrongful-death-overview.html.

267 CACI (California Civil Jury Instructions) 3921 *Wrongful Death (Death of an Adult). See also* CACI 3922, *Wrongful Death (Parents Recovery for Death of a Minor Child).*

268 *Georgia v. Tennessee Copper Co.*, 206 US 230 (1907). *Snapp v. Puerto Rico ex. Rel. Barez*, 458 US 592, 603, 607 (1982). See also Kanner, A. (2005), *op. cit. supra* at n.4 chapter 3, at 102–109; Gifford, D. G. (2013), *op. cit. supra* at n.2 chapter 3, at 123.

269 *People v. Atlantic Richfield Co.*, No. 1-00-CV-788657 (Cal. A 2014) at 1, 6.

270 *Minnesota v. Ri-Mel, Inc.*, 417 NW 2d 102, 112 (Minn. Ct. A 1987).

271 *Texas v. American Tobacco Co.* 14 F. Supp. 2d 956, 962; See also Gifford, D. G. (2013), *op. cit. supra* at n.2 chapter 3, at 131–132, 138–168, 176–186.

272 *Davis v. Blige*, 505 F. 3d 90, 103 (2d Cir. 2007).

For example, in the lead paint case, *People v. Atlantic Richfield* (2014), California county and city representatives alleged that lead causes grave harm, is injurious to health, and interferes with the comfortable enjoyment of life and property.[273] The plaintiffs provided evidence demonstrating that exposure to lead in household paint causes serious health problems, in particular with respect to children, that lead paint was still prominent in pre-1978 households and that exposure to lead under such circumstances continued to cause human injuries.[274] The plaintiffs did not attempt to recoup future health care costs but rather abatement costs largely to rid households of lead paint.[275]

Also, in *Texas v. American Tobacco* (1997), the plaintiff State sued tobacco companies and public relations firms "to recover costs incurred in providing medical care and other benefits to its citizens, including costs associated with the Medicaid program, as the result of the citizens' use of cigarettes and smokeless tobacco products".[276] A year later, the State entered into a settlement agreement with the defendants whereby compensation to the tune of US$2,255.9 million would be used partially to recoup indigent healthcare service expenses and more fully to cover longer term healthcare needs.[277] Meanwhile, that same year the more comprehensive Master Settlement Agreement covering the majority of US States was concluded enabling over US$200 billion to support State programmes and facilities to treat and prevent tobacco use and eventuating lung cancers.[278]

Further, a number of municipalities have sued firearm manufacturers, distributors and dealers for injuries resulting from marketing guns in ways that unreasonably facilitate their unlawful possession and use. Legal counsel for Chicago (Illinois),[279] Cincinnati (Ohio)[280] and Gary (Indiana)[281] brought tort claims asserting similarly "that defendants' conduct is the direct and proximate cause of deaths and injuries to ... residents and is a significant and unreasonable interference with public safety and health and the public's right to be free from disturbance and reasonable apprehension of danger to person and property".[282] In terms of damages, all plaintiffs demanded compensation for a combination of personal and

---

273 *People v. Atlantic Richfield Co.*, No. 1-00-CV-788657 (Cal. A 2014) at 7, 11.
274 *Id.* at 11, 14–19.
275 *Id.* at 100–108.
276 *State of Tex. v. American Tobacco Co.*, 14 F. Supp. 2d 956, 960 (Dist. Court, ED Texas 1997).
277 Tobacco Settlement Proceeds (1988). Retrieved from Texas Department of State Health Services: www.dshs.state.tx.us/tobaccosettlement/tobsett.shtm.
278 Office of the Attorney General (2014). *Master Settlement Agreement*. Retrieved from State of California Department of Justice: http://oag.ca.gov/tobacco/msa.
279 *City of Chicago v. Beretta USA Corp.*, 785 NE 2d 16, 1st Div. (Ill. Appellate Court, 1st Dist. 2002).
280 *City of Cincinnati v. Beretta USA Corp.*, 95 Ohio St. 3d 416 (Oh. 2002).
281 *City of Gary ex rel. King v. Smith & Wesson Corp.*, 801 NE 2d 1222 (Ind. 2003).
282 *City of Chicago v. Beretta* (2002), *op. cit. supra* at n.279, at 31.

public damage costs including medical care and treatment for victims, disability, pension and works compensation benefits, lost tax revues, property values and productivity, as well as crime prevention and correction expenses.[283] In these cases, the courts approved that the cities could proceed on their tort claims.[284]

283 *Id.* at 22; *City of Gary ex rel. King v. Smith & Wesson Corp.* (2003), *op. cit. supra* at n.281, at 1242; *City of Cincinnati v. Beretta USA Corp* (2002), *op. cit. supra* at n.282, at 342.
284 *Id.* at 31; *Id.* at 421; *Id.* at 1235.

5 Public nuisance

In the *ozone layer case*, plaintiffs may also bring claims under the public nuisance theory. The theory directs that a person who creates "an unreasonable interference with a right common to the general public", should be liable for that interference.[1] One crucial element of this theory is the unreasonable nature of the interference[2] i.e. it must be either intentional, or "unintentional and otherwise actionable under the principles controlling liability for negligent or reckless conduct or for abnormally dangerous activities".[3] The "intentional" nature of an activity relates to whether an actor knows or is substantially certain that a public right will be interfered as a result of his conduct.[4] Unreasonableness also depends on "the magnitude of the interference it creates" which can be evidenced by "a substantial and continuing interference with a public right".[5]

Another key aspect of public nuisance is that involves the infringement of a public right – which is common to all members of the general public[6] – such as "public health, the public safety, the public peace, the public comfort or the public convenience".[7] Such interference may be "proscribed by a statute, ordinance or administrative regulation".[8] It is often one that is continuing, i.e. that may have produced a "permanent or long lasting effect".[9] A public nuisance would be caused, for example, when polluting a lake makes the lake unusable for public recreation, and/or destroys the lake's ecosystem. The public rights of members of the lake

---

1   Restatement (Second) of Torts (1977) § 821B(1)
2   *Id.* at § 822 Comment (j): "Liability is imposed only in those cases where the harm or risk to one is greater than he ought to be required to bear under the circumstances, at least without compensation. "
3   *Id.* at § 821 B Comment (e).
4   *Id.* at § 825.
5   *State v. Lead Industries Association*, 951 A.2d 428, 447 (RI 2008).
6   *Id.* at § 821B Comment (g).
7   *Id.* at § 821B (2)
8   *Ibid.*
9   *Ibid.*

community to enjoy the lake's benefits are infringed.[10]

Finally, for individual plaintiffs, the theory requires that they must demonstrate that they have suffered "harm of a kind different from that suffered by other members of the public" in the exercise of that public right.[11] As a rule, personal injuries being "special and peculiar" are considered to qualify a kind of harm which is "different from that suffered by other members of the public".[12] Most public nuisance cases are brought by local or State government actors, however, and this requirement does not apply to them.[13] Still, it is the invasion of plaintiff's interests which is the "essential element of an actionable nuisance".[14]

In appearance, the *ozone layer case* would seem to match many of these criteria and thus would be arguable under the public nuisance theory. By comparing the *ozone layer case* with other environmental cases, the following sections explore the extent to which the theory could realistically be applied to attach liability to companies which produced, sold and emitted ODCs. This examines issues concerning public interference, particular injury and unreasonableness of activity.

5.1 Interference with public rights

In the *ozone layer case*, it is evident that ODCs[15] have damaged two correlative, essential public goods – the earth's ozone layer and "safe" sunlight i.e. an environmental condition where it is possible to be outdoors without an

10   *Id.* at § 821B Comment (g): Conversely, a public nuisance would not result if for the only reason that the same pollution "merely deprives 50 or a hundred lower riparian owners of the use of the water for purposes connected with their land". Cf. *Pennsylvania Coal Co. v. Sanderson*, 113 Pa. 126 (1886).

11   *Id.* "It is not, however, necessary that the entire community be affected by a public nuisance, so long as the nuisance will interfere with those who come in contact with it in the exercise of a public right or it otherwise affects the interests of the community at large".

12   *Id.* at § 821C Comment (d).

13   *Id.* § 821B Comments (b) and (d); Gostin, L. O. (2008). *Public Health Law: Power, Duty, Restraint.* Berkeley: University of California Press, at 471; Bearden, D. M. (2012). *Comprehensive Environmental Response, Compensation, and Liability Act: A Summary of Superfund Cleanup Authorities and Related Provisions of the Act.* Congressional Research Service, at 2.

14   *Wood v. Picillo*, 443 A. 2d 1244, 1247 (RI 1982); Prosser (1971), *op. cit. supra* at n.4 chapter 4, at 573–4.

15   Here the *ozone layer case* is again peculiar as while it could involve product liability, it departs from other such cases where defective products generally cause injuries to individual consumers but cannot be construed to affect the public at large even if injuries are wide spread by many products. See Gifford (2013), *op. cit. supra* at n.2 chapter 3, at 146 discussing how "the manufacture and distribution of products rarely, if ever, causes a violation of a public right as such a right has been understood in the law of public nuisance".

abnormal risk to human health.[16] Depletion of stratospheric ozone has resulted in increased amounts of solar ultraviolet radiation reaching earth to which human beings are unnaturally exposed.[17] That exposure has increased skin cancer incidences in the United States and globally.[18] Skin cancer patients bear economic and non-economic costs.[19] Meanwhile, persons at risk of contracting the disease particularly children are compelled to adapt their lifestyles so as to avoid sunlight exposure particularly during midday hours. Such behavioural changes may have negative impacts on their health and development.[20] This reality can impact also on adults regarding their employment decisions, recreational choices and enjoyment of the environment.[21] Hence, public rights to health, safety and convenience are interfered with and particularised harms are recognisable.

Court rulings have recognised that water and air are public goods which should be protected in the public health and safety interests. Interferences with these interests have constituted public nuisances.[22] Most public nuisance litigation involving toxic torts and public health right infringements have involved the contamination of public waterways and land.[23] Most probably due to causation challenges, there are far fewer cases which have dealt with air pollution as a public interference, which can be drawn on in support of the *ozone layer case*.[24]

One example is *In Re StarLink Corn Products* Liability Litigation (2002).

16 Barrett, S. (2007), *op. cit. supra* at n.34 chapter 1; Blackden, C. M. (2009), *op. cit. supra* at n.34 chapter 1; Choi, E. K. and Hartigan, J. C. (2008), *op. cit. supra* at n.34 chapter 1; *Edwards v. Post Transportation Co.*, 228 Cal. App. 3d 980 (App. 4th D. Cal. 1991); Ferroni, M. and Mody, A. (2002), *op. cit. supra* at n.34 chapter 1; *Fischer v. Johns-Manville Corp.*, 512 A. 2d 466 (NJ 1986); Campbell, H. E. *et al.* (2012), *op. cit. supra* at n.34 chapter 1; Barkin, J. S., *et al.* (1999), *op. cit. supra* at n.34 chapter 1; Jones, R. J. (2002), *op. cit. supra* at n.34 chapter 1.

17 World Meteorological Organization (2010), *op. cit. supra* at n.22 chapter 3, see Chapter 2.

18 World Health Organisation (1998). Global Solar UV Index: Fact Sheet No. 133. Retrieved August 23, 2012, from www.who.int/inf-fs/en/fact133.html.

19 See Chapter 3 at §3.2.3 *supra*.

20 Cercato *et al.* (2013), *op. cit. supra* at n.31 chapter 1; US Preventive Services Task Force (2003, October). *Counselling to Prevent Skin Cancer*. Retrieved from US Preventive Services Task Force: www.uspreventiveservicestaskforce.org/3rduspstf/skcacoun/skcarr.htm.

21 See Chapter 3 at §3.2.3 *supra;* US Preventive Services Task Force (2003). *Counseling to Prevent Skin Cancer: Recommendations and Rationale of the US Preventive Services Task Force.* Atlanta: Centers for Disease Control and Prevention.

22 *State v. Schenectady Chemicals, Inc.*, 103 AD 2d 33 (1983) citing *Matter of City of Johnstown v. Water Pollution Control Bd. of State of NY*, 12 AD 2d 218, 220 (1961). In *Schenectady*, a defendant company was found liable under public nuisance law for the seepage of chemical waste into the public water supply. The company was made to pay for clean-up costs even though an independent contractor had disposed of the affluence 15–30 years previously.

23 *State v. Schenectady Chemicals, Inc.*, 103 AD 2d 33, 37 (1983).

24 By comparison, private nuisance claims have been brought against fertiliser and smelter companies for their emissions of sulphur dioxide which caused farmers to lose profitability from crops and crops growing. *E. Rauh & Sons Fertilizer Co. v. Shreffler,* 139 F. 2d 38 (6th Cir. 1943); *United Verde Copper Co. v. Ralston,* 46 F. 2d 1 (9th Cir. 1931).

In that case, plaintiffs sued the manufacturers and distributors[25] of a genetically modified corn seed[26] on the public nuisance theory. The seed was designed to produce a protein toxic to certain insects[27] and to grow corn for animal feed and ethanol production. However, it was unfit for human consumption.[28] The nuisance was created when pollen from the corn plants was blown by the wind and infested other varieties of corn affecting the entire corn supply. The plaintiffs alleged that the resulting contamination interfered with the public's right to safe food.[29] The defendants filed a motion to dismiss the plaintiffs' claim on the basis that it did not plead a specialised harm but rather harm affecting the general public. The Court disagreed affirming that the nuisance did affect the public's right to safe food and that the harm to the plaintiffs as a group of commercial corn enterprises was particular, not general.

Following the Court's decision to deny the defendants' motion, however, no court judgement was reached in further proceedings as litigants reached a settlement agreement in 2003.[30] Nevertheless, *Starlink* supports the *ozone layer case* in advancing that product manufacturers can be liable for creating a public nuisance when their product is emitted into the air and results in invasions of public rights and causes harms to specific groups of people. Although in the *ozone layer case*, the causal link is more complex, the analogy is relevant.

Climate change suits, having close resemblance to the *ozone layer case*, also provide for useful argumentation that emissions of substances into the atmosphere can amount to public nuisance. In *Massachusetts v. EPA* (2007), a group of ten States,[31] local governments, and private organisations filed a petition questioning whether the EPA had authority to regulate greenhouse gas emissions from new motor vehicles.[32] The plaintiffs alleged that the emissions contributed to global warming – "the most pressing environmental challenge of our time".[33] Although the petitioners did not allege

25 *In Re StarLink Corn Products Liability Litigation*, 212 F. Supp. 2d 828, 838–834 (ND Ill. 2002).
26 Centers for Disease Control and Prevention (2001, June 11). *Investigation of Human Health Effects associated with Potential Exposure to Genetically Modified Corn:* US Department of Health & Human Services: www.cdc.gov/nceh/ehhe/Cry9CReport/pdfs cry9creport.pdf.
27 *Ibid.*
28 US EPA (2008, April). Starlink™ Corn Regulatory Information. Retrieved from United States Environmental Proetction Agency: www.epa.gov/opp00001/biopesticides/pips/starlink_corn.htm.
29 *In Re StarLink Corn Products Liability Litigation*, 212 F. Supp. 2d 828, 848 (ND Ill 2002).
30 Organic Consumers Association (n.d.). *US Farmers to Get $112 Million for GE Starlink Corn Contamination.* Retrieved from www.organicconsumers.org/Corn/starlink.cfm.
31 *Massachusetts v. EPA*, 127 S Ct 1438, 1446 (2007). States included California, Connecticut, Illinois, Maine, Massachusetts, New Jersey, New Mexico, New York, Oregon, Rhode Island, Vermont and Washington.
32 *Ibid.*
33 *Ibid.*

public nuisance, their claims were premised on the notion that greenhouse gas emissions lead to global warming impacts including sea level rise and temperature increases which ultimately would endanger public health and welfare.[34] The Supreme Court's standing review affirmed that traceable links exist between non-regulated emission sources and environmental impacts.[35] On that basis, the Court clarified that the EPA did have statutory authority to regulate the emissions.[36] The case is important because it has paved the way for similar suits where States and individuals have demanded injunctive relief and damages in applying public nuisance theory.

In subsequent climate change cases, plaintiffs have brought claims specifically on the public nuisance theory.[37] Notably, in *Connecticut v. American Electric Power* (2009), the Second Circuit Court upheld that State plaintiffs had standing to bring a public nuisance claim against US power companies for their contribution to global warming.[38] Specifically, the Court agreed with the plaintiff's assertion that the defendants' emissions "constitute a substantial and unreasonable interference with public rights in the plaintiffs' jurisdictions, including, *inter alia*, the right to public comfort and safety, the right to protection of vital natural resources and public property, and the right to use, enjoy, and preserve the aesthetic and ecological values of the natural world".[39] Although the Supreme Court reversed the Second Circuit's opinion in 2011 on grounds of federal common law pre-emption, the latter Court's opinion maintains value as the possibility for public nuisance suits at the State level still exists (at the time of this writing).[40] However, the challenge for plaintiffs bringing State common law claims now appears to be around establishing causation, which US States may be in a better position to pursue.[41] Still, for the purpose of this discussion, the above rulings have advanced that large emissions sources which contribute to global atmospheric changes can create public nuisances by interfering with public rights.

5.2 Particularised harms

To establish a public nuisance, plaintiffs to the *ozone layer case* will equally be tasked with showing that their injuries resulting from the public interference are specialised and peculiar. As introduced above, citizen

---

34   *Id.* at 1455–1458.

35   *Id.* at 1455.

36   *Id.* at 1462.

37   *Comer v. Murphy Oil USA* (2009), *op. cit. supra* at n.38 chapter 1; *Native Village of Kivalina v. Exxon Mobile*, 696 F. 3d 849 (9th Cir. 2012).

38   *Connecticut v. American Electric Power Co.* (2009), *op. cit. supra* at n.8 chapter 3, at 353.

39   *Id.* at 352.

40   *Am. Electric Power Co. v. Connecticut*, 131 S. Ct. 2527, 180 L. Ed. 2d 435, 72 ERC 1609 (2011).

41   *Environmental Council v. Bellon*, 732 F.3d 1131 (9th Cir. 2013).

plaintiffs should be able to prove their harm in a number of ways. Concrete financial losses due to skin cancer remediation and prevention can provide evidence of special damage that is different from and not shared by the general population. For those inflicted with the disease, the challenge is less daunting since each person's skin cancer is fundamentally unique. While establishing such harm invariably will encounter causation hurdles, as discussed in the previous chapter, the intention of the public nuisance theory may prevail in the plaintiff's favour. As stated by the Supreme Court of Rhode Island in *Wood v. Piccolo* (1982), "(t)he essential element of an actionable nuisance is that persons have suffered harm or are threatened with injuries that they ought not have to bear." In that case, the Court recognised a wide range of harms suffered by the plaintiffs including "physical symptoms of exposure to toxic chemicals", restricted reasonable use of property and threats to "aquatic wildlife and human beings with possible death, cancer, and liver disease".[42]

For US State plaintiffs, the challenge of establishing particularised harm should be relatively straight forward. As discussed above, they would be able to assess increased financial costs and losses owing to the skin cancer epidemic and the need to prevent its vulnerable citizens, in particular children, from unhealthy sun exposure. While numerous court precedents would support such claims, one of the most compelling is the US Supreme Court's ruling in *Georgia v. Tennessee Copper Co.* (1907). There, Justice Holmes asserted that US States have the right to defend their land and citizens from external sources of environmental and human harms,[43] specifically air pollution.[44]

5.3 Unreasonableness of interference

To further establish a public nuisance, plaintiffs will need to show that the defendants knew or were substantially certain that increasing the production and market of ODCs would lead to infringements of public safety and health. This issue which imputes what the defendants knew and should have known has been discussed at length in Chapters 2 and 4. There it was

---

42 *Wood v. Picillo*, 443 A. 2d 1244, 1247 (RI 1982).

43 206 US 230, 237: The Court stated: "...the state has an interest independent of and behind the titles of its citizens, in all the earth and air within its domain. It has the last word as to whether its mountains shall be stripped of their forests and its inhabitants shall breathe pure air. It might have to pay individuals before it could utter that word, but with it remains the final power".

44 206 US 230, 238: The Court further pronounced: "It is a fair and reasonable demand on the part of a sovereign that the air over its territory should not be polluted on a great scale by sulphurous acid gas, that the forests on its mountains, be they better or worse, and whatever domestic destruction they have suffered, should not be further destroyed or threatened by the act of persons beyond its control, that the crops and orchards on its hills should not be endangered from the same source".

proposed that sufficient knowledge was available in the 1970s to know that public rights could be threatened although much scientific uncertainty prevailed. However, given the magnitude of potential harm involved, it was further posited that the certainty requirement should be relaxed. Still, what the defendants knew and did not know for sure cannot be known based on publicly available sources. Additional disclosure and testimony by corporate management would be needed.

However, it may be that proving the unreasonableness of the interference requires less preoccupation with the defendants' conduct as opposed to the harm which was predicated. The public nuisance theory may be interpreted more along the lines of a strict liability as opposed to a negligence approach. This would inevitably be a policy decision. For example, in *Wood v. Piccolo,* local landowners brought a public nuisance action against a chemical waste dump facility for severe environmental contamination.[45] The pollution was described as "a chemical nightmare" causing harmful health impacts to the plaintiffs.[46] In reviewing the case and satisfied that causation was evinced, the Rhode Island Supreme Court found for the plaintiffs on the unreasonableness of the harm predicated by the defendants displacing the need to establish negligence.[47] The ruling effectively overturned the State common law precedent which had purported that pursuing a public nuisance grievance should require establishing a defendant's fault.[48] The *Wood* decision affirmed a new policy of environmental protectionism stating

> ...decades of unrestricted emptying of industrial effluent into the earth's atmosphere and waterways has rendered oceans, lakes, and rivers unfit for swimming and fishing, rain acidic, and air unhealthy. Concern for the preservation of an often precarious ecological balance, impelled by the spectre of "a silent spring", has today reached a zenith of intense significance.[49]

Should this policy prevail and the negligence showing be relaxed, plaintiffs in the *ozone layer case*, in particular US States could have a fairly strong case in showing an unreasonable interference. As discussed, it would be difficult to prove that destruction of the ozone layer was not unreasonable. Further, the atmospheric disturbance must amount to "a substantial and continuing

45   *Wood v. Picillo*, 443 A 2d 1244, 1245–46 (RI 1982).
46   *Id. at* 1246–47.
47   *Id.* at 1249. The Court affirmed that "negligence is not a necessary element of a nuisance case involving contamination of public or private waters by pollutants percolating through the soil and traveling underground routes".
48   *Id.* at 1248–49. As the Court reflected, the precedent set in *Rose v. Socony-Vacuum Corp.* (1934) had affirmed that "the defendant could with impunity contaminate the plaintiff's drinking water if the defendant polluted non-negligently".
49   *Ibid.*

interference with a public right".[50] In applying the rationale provided the Restatement (Second) of Torts §834 Comment (e),[51] it may be construed that the defendants' increased production, sale and emissions of ODCs between 1976 and 1992 has contributed to the loss of stratospheric ozone – a condition which continues,[52] will continue to impact on public health and safety, and cannot be abated by the defendants.

In sum, a reasonable possibility exists for *ozone layer case* plaintiffs to be successful in bringing their claims under the public nuisance theory. This could relieve some thorny issues in proving negligence – which will require more concrete evidence regarding what the companies knew and did in the 1970s and 1980s. Plaintiffs will still need to establish causation, however. As discussed, US State plaintiffs would have an advantage in doing so.

50   *State v. Lead Industries Association,* 951 A 2d 428, 447 (RI 2008).
51   Restatement (Second) of Torts (1965) §834 Comment (e): "...if the activity has resulted in the creation of a physical condition that is of itself harmful after the activity that created it has ceased, a person who carried on the activity that created the condition or who participated to a substantial extent in the activity is subject to the liability for a nuisance, for the continuing harm. His active conduct has been a substantial factor in creating the harmful condition and so long as the condition continues the harm is traceable to him. This is true even though he is no longer in a position to abate the condition and to stop the harm. If he creates the condition upon land in his possession and thereafter sells or leases it to another, he is subject to liability for invasions caused by the condition after the sale or lease as well as for those occurring before".
52   World Meteorological Organization (2007) and (2010), *op. cit. supra* at n.21 chapter 3.

Part III
Defences

6 Statutes of limitation and repose

As discussed in the preceding chapters, defendants in the *ozone layer case* would likely contend that scientific uncertainty largely influenced their conduct throughout the 1970s and 1980s. In addition to these arguments, the defendants may also raise a number of defences to limit their alleged liability. This chapter begins by discussing one of those defences, namely, that the *ozone layer case* would be barred due to State statutes of limitation. Other defences including federal and State law pre-emption, regulatory compliance, downstream responsibility, and open and obvious dangers are addressed in preceding chapters.

Statutes of limitation and repose could limit the possibility of *ozone layer case* tort claims at the State level given the long time period which has elapsed since ozone depleting substances were produced and sold by the defendant companies.

Generally, a statute of limitations dictates the time period within which a suit may be commenced based on the time when a plaintiff discovers an injury. Statutes of repose provide a time limit for initiating litigation but are bound to the time when an alleged misconduct took place not when the injury occurs. In terms of product liability, this means that the repose period begins to run when the defective product was first sold and may end even before an injury becomes manifest.[1] The policy rationale for these statutes is to provide greater surety to plaintiffs that they can bring tort claims and under what conditions.[2] Statutes of repose aim to ensure fairness in addressing long term injuries and liabilities and to ensure economic stability. Repose rules bring "certainty and closure to stale claims, thereby reducing the burden on the judicial system, as well as freeing commercial resources that would have been invested in the economy had they not remained set aside to cover outstanding continent liabilities". Repose limits aim to avoid unfair liability assessments where evidence and causality issues

---

1   La Fave, D. J. (2005). Remedying the Confusion between Statutes of LKimitations and Statutes of Repose in Wisconsin: A Conceptual Guide. *Marquette Law Review*, 88, 927–945, at 928.
2   Ferrer, A. A. (2006). Excuses, Excuses: The Application of Statutes of Repose to Environmentally-Related Injuries. *B.C. Envtl. Aff. L. Rev*, 33, 345–381, at 348–349.

are blurred due to the passage of time.[3] On the downside, such statutes may end up reducing deterrence of environmental harms by providing tortfeasors with immunity from liability. They may also lead to ineffective responses to environmental contamination by giving polluters an incentive to cover up problems and then forgo their contribution to financing clean-up operations.[4]

In the US, statutes of limitation and repose vary according to each State's statutory and common laws. Statutes of limitations for personal injury and product liability are legislated in all 50 US States.[5] The laws generally provide for a limit of one to six years within which a plaintiff can bring a claim after injury is discovered. Meanwhile, statutes of repose concerning product liability and affecting toxic tort litigation are also imposed in a limited number of States including North Carolina,[6] Oregon[7] and Alabama.[8] Because of this narrow reach, the practical challenges in dealing with time bars in the *ozone layer case* are more likely around statutes of limitations as opposed to repose laws.[9] As with other tort law theories, the degree to which statutes of limitation will impact on the *ozone layer case* will

---

3   *Ibid.*; Evans, J. E. (2013). See Repose Run: Setting the Boundaries of the Rule of Repose in Environmental Trespass and Nuisance Cases. *Wm. & Mary Envtl. L. & Pol'y Rev.* (38) 119, 119–167 at 134–137.

4   *Id.* at 371–372; *Ibid.*

5   Kroll, E. M. and Westerlind, J. M. (2011). *Arent Fox LLP Survey of Damage Laws of the 50 States including the District of Columbia and Puerto Rico.* Washington, D.C.: Arent Fox LLP.

6   NC Gen. Stat. § 1–52(16).

7   Rev. Stat. § 12.115(1).

8   *Abrams v. Ciba Specialty Chems. Corp.*, 659 F. Supp. 2d 1225) (SD Ala. 2009); Showalter, J. (2014). Supreme Court Decides CTS Corp. v. Waldburger Evaluating Whether CERCLA Precludes State-Law Statutes of Repose. *The National Law Review.*

9   However, in *CTS Corp. v. Waldburger*, 134 S. Ct. 2175 (2014), the US Supreme Court may widen that scope. The Court determined that the statute of limitations provision in the federal Comprehensive Environment Response and Liability Act (CERCLA) which permits a three year discovery rule for cases involving environmental contamination, does not apply to statutes of repose. (The CERCLA rule has benefited plaintiffs bringing claims in States where statutes of limitations impose stricter time bars and would otherwise pre-empt their cause of action.) This means that State statutes of repose will prevail over the federal grace period thus foreclosing on the possibility for citizens to pursue toxic tort claims. The ruling does not have a direct impact on the *ozone layer case* as the CERLA's aim is impose responsibility for environmental contamination clean-up costs rather than a compensation scheme for health injuries suffered as a consequence of environmental pollution (see note below). However, legal experts have warned that the ruling may prompt States to legislate new statutes of repose to insulate potential tortfeasors from liability. If this happens, as in States where statutes of repose are enacted, the *ozone layer case* would be quashed. That outcome can and should spark a debate on the short and long term economic and deterrence advantages which statutes of repose are poised to achieve. The critical questions are whether or not the repose policies will incentivise environmental pollution and create unfeasible financial burdens on future generations, and whether such policies will lead to an estrangement of the polluter pays principle. See also, Percival, R. (2014). *Opinion Analysis: Court's Narrow Reading of Superfund's Preemption Provision Leaves Victims of Toxic Exposure Without Legal Recourse.*

depend on whether the plaintiffs are US citizens or States.

As introduced above, plaintiffs will need to defend that they discovered their injuries within the statutes of limitations period. If they bring actions under the public nuisance theory, they would be able to argue that the nuisance is a continuing one. Accordingly, even if their injuries are discovered long after the harm causing incident took place, the continuing nuisance doctrine impresses that a new cause of action is created each day until the damage is abated.[10] This leniency is permitted because in many tort suits involving environmental contamination, the appearance of damage or injury may only be discovered years after the damage causing activity has ceased. In the *ozone layer case*, the theory would aid plaintiffs whose ability to bring a claim would have otherwise been extinguished decades ago. However, there are several caveats.

First, the plaintiffs must defend that their discovery of injury is ripe for adjudication. For citizen plaintiffs, the discovery date is likely when they are diagnosed with skin cancer or when they learn of that risk and are forced to change their behaviour accordingly. Following that date, they would have a certain number of years to initiate legal action. The problem with this is that the time bar would exclude persons who have had skin cancer already for several years as well as families of deceased skin cancer victims. For those persons, it may be possible to overcome this hurdle if they could argue successfully that they did not know their increased skin cancer was caused by ODC emissions. This issue evokes two additional considerations. First, it calls into question whether skin cancer patients should have known that their disease is attributable to such chemicals. Second, it begs whether they could have known that such emissions were negligent. Presumably, people will know that being in the sun causes sun burn. However, they may not know what their increased risks of developing skin cancer are and why, and how that relates to the ozone layer and the former ODC industry.

Such lack of awareness and knowledge may be difficult to prove, however. One case which demonstrates this challenge is *Edward Hines Lumber Co. v. Vulcan Materials Co.*, (1987). The Illinois District Court dismissed a strict product liability claim for environmental property

www.scotusblog.com/2014/06/opinion-analysis-courts-narrow-reading-of-superfunds-preemption-provision-leaves-victims-of-toxic-exposure-without-legal-recourse; Note: Percival, R. (2014). Argument Preview: Law School Clinic Seeks to Preserve Day in ourt for Victims of Polluted Well Water. Supreme Court of the United States Blog: When the CERCLA was being drafted, an expert working group recommended that the Act provide administrative compensation to victims of exposure to hazardous substances. Such a scheme would have supported such victims taking into account the various legal barriers they face including statutes of limitations, and proving causation. However, Congress rejected the proposal on account of difficulties involved in providing administrative compensation.

10   *Ibid.*; 17 Carmody-Wait 2d, NY Prac, § 107:43, at 315 "The right to maintain an action for a public nuisance continues as long as the nuisance exists; no one can obtain a prescriptive right to maintain a public nuisance".

damage and clean-up caused by the sale of toxic chemicals by the defendant chemical manufacturers to the plaintiff for his lumber and wood treating business. The plaintiff alleged that "the defendants were negligent in the manufacture and sale of ... chemicals (pentachlorophenol, creosote, chromated copper arsenate) due to their failure to conduct safety tests and inspections, to instruct purchasers regarding conditions and methods of the chemicals' safe use and to warn the users of the dangers associated with the chemicals.[11] The Court asserted that the Arkansas statute of limitations, which "begins to run when the negligent damage occurs not from the time the full extent of the injury is ascertained", barred the plaintiff's claim.[12] Because the plaintiff had noticed that the products he purchased were toxic and would cause environmental damage years in advance of his claim, the court determined that the point at which the alleged negligence had occurred was when the plaintiff became aware of the problem and thus his possibility to sue the chemical manufacturers had expired.[13]

For US States, proving an acceptable discovery date of injury will be equally challenging as they too will be imputed for having knowledge about skin cancer prevalence within their jurisdictions. The EPA publishes a concise overview of health impacts owing to ozone layer depletion.[14] The Agency produces information papers on skin cancer prevalence in each State.[15] Still, although this public data exists, it does not explicitly connect the chemical producers' alleged negligent conduct and the skin cancer problem facing individuals and State governments. A clear example of this is the Surgeon General's 2014 report on skin cancer which urges public measures to prevent skin cancer across America. The report states:

> UVB radiation has intermediate levels of energy and can cause sunburn and direct DNA damage. Ozone and other components of the atmosphere absorb more than 90 percent of UVB from the sun, but the amount absorbed varies widely depending on time, location, season, and weather. *Certain chemical and carbon emissions also have caused depletions in stratospheric ozone since the 1970s, and evidence suggests that this decrease has led to an increase in ground-level UVB levels. Further study is needed to determine whether ozone depletion is contributing to the increasing incidence of skin cancers worldwide.*[16]

11 *Edward Hines Lumber Co. v. Vulcan Materials Co.*, 669 F. Supp. 854, 856 (US District Court, ND Illinois, ED August 31, 1987).

12 *Id.* at 857, 861.

13 *Id.* at 858–860.

14 US EPA (2011). *Health and Environmental Effects of Ozone Layer Depletion.* Retrieved from Ozone Layer Protection: www.epa.gov/ozone/science/effects/index.html.

15 US EPA (2014). *Skin Cancer Facts for your State.* Retrieved from SunWise: www2.epa.gov/sunwise/skin-cancer-facts-your-state.

16 US Department of Health and Human Services (2014). *The Surgeon General's Call to Action to Prevent Skin Cancer.* Washington, D.C.: US Dept of Health and Human Services, Office of the Surgeon General, at 11 (emphasis added).

As the US Surgeon General is recommending further research to establish this link, it could be that such a peer-reviewed, official report could do this and serve as critical evidence of discovery for any and all *ozone layer case* plaintiffs. The report could herald the "ripeness" of the *ozone layer case* in showing the increased rates of skin cancer incidence and deaths as verifying the real damage caused by unharnessed production and sale of ODCs in the 1970s and 1980s.

In support of this suggestion is the Second Circuit Court's decision regarding New York City's claim against Exxon for MTBE contamination of city water wells. In the 2013 *MTBE* case, the statute of limitations debate was over whether the city's tort claim was unripe and/or overly ripe. On one hand, the defendant Exxon argued that the city's claim was unripe because contamination had not yet occurred. On the other hand, the company argued that the city had known about the contamination much earlier and, as such, the statute of limitations had expired, foreclosing on the city's claim. Ultimately, the Court found that the city's claim was just ripe. The city's suit was timely because the city brought its claim after damage was discovered and within the State's three year statute of limitations period. The cty based its discovery on the date when it learned that MTBE concentration in well water "rose to a level at which a reasonable water provider would have treated the water." While Exxon refuted the city's discovery argument, the company was unable to provide sufficient evidence proving otherwise. The city's discovery plea prevailed.[17]

A second problem faced by the ozone depletion case plaintiffs may be to demonstrate that their injuries derive from a nuisance which is continuing but not permanent. A permanent nuisance is understood as an invasion, usually of land, which cannot be abated.[18] However, if a nuisance involving contamination can be shown to naturally repair over time, then it may be considered abatable.[19] Still, if abatement measures are financially infeasible,[20] or if the invasion serves a socially beneficial purpose,[21] a nuisance may be considered permanent. The latter refers to a nuisance created which is deemed to be "integral to an enterprise vital to the development of the state".[22] However, recent court rulings suggest that this qualification for permanence may be outdated.[23]

---

17 *In Re MTBE Prods. Liability Litig.*, 725 F. 3d 65, 74–77 (2d. Cir. 2013).

18 *Id.*; *Hoery v. US*, 64 3d 214 (Col. 2003); *Mangini v. Aerojet-General Corp*, 12 Cal.4th 1087 (Cal. 1996).

19 *Arcade Water Dist. v. United States*, 940 F.2d 1265, 1268 (9th Cir. 1991).

20 *Mangini v. Aerojet-General Corp*, 12 Cal. 4th 1087, 1223 (Cal. 1996).

21 *Hoery v. US*, 64 3d 214, 220 (Col. 2003).

22 *Ibid.*

23 *Id.* at 219–220. This concept derives from early 20th century nuisance cases involving the construction of ditches and railroads which were considered important for society as a whole. They were also physical constructions which could not easily be removed. However, in *Cook v. Rockwell Int'l Corp.*, 358 F. Su 2d 1003, 1013 (D. Colo. 2004) followed

In the *ozone layer case*, the depletion of the ozone layer is likely not to be construed as permanent because science suggests that the ozone concentrations will recover eventually. Further, it is possible that skin cancer prevention measures are taken to avoid future prevalence of the disease. And, while ODCs may have provided social benefits in their use, they have no value in the stratosphere.

Nevertheless, it could be argued that the continuing current problem is permanent as it is humanly and financially impossible to "clean-up" the stratosphere and ensure sufficiently against increases in skin cancer incidence and death rates. If these harms are deemed permanent, that determination could influence the scope of damage compensation and could also impact on statutes of limitations.[24] This is because if a nuisance is permanent, the cause of action does not accrue. Therefore, plaintiffs who know or "reasonably should know of a permanent injury," must bring their claims within the period a statute of limitations allows.[25] Given the time bar, plaintiffs practically are foreclosed on bringing an additional future claim beyond what the statute permits. As a result, damage awards are affected. In some cases where similar issues have been raised, courts have supported lump sum payments to plaintiffs for past, present and future damages.[26] The policy behind this one-off approach is to achieve a compromise between compensating plaintiffs and avoiding that defendants are subject to ongoing liability.[27]

The final challenge encumbered by plaintiffs may be also to argue that their burden to comply with statutes of limitation should be relieved i.e. that as a matter of public policy, strict foreclosure on citizens' suits or actions brought by US States should be unwarranted. Precedent does exist in some States for legislature and courts to override such statutes particularly when physical injury is involved. Such practices were adopted in a number of asbestos cases. Policy makers and judges deemed it unfair that plaintiffs who discovered their lung cancer only later in life and long after asbestos manufacture ended in 1970, be barred from pursuing damage claims.[28]

---

by *Cook v. Rockwell Internat'l Corp.*, 580 F. Supp. 2d 1071 (D. Colo. 2006) rev'd and remanded on other grounds, 618 F. 3d 1127 (10th Cir. 2010), cert. denied (2012), hereinafter, *Cook v. Rockwell* (2004), the Colorado District Court did not consider the "the alleged presence of plutonium ... on Plaintiffs' and class members' properties" to be a permanent nuisance precisely because such alleged presence did not "serve a socially beneficial purpose".

24 *Cook v. Rockwell* (2004) *at* 1010; (D. Colo. 2004). References cited are *Cook IX*, 273 F. Supp. 2d at 1210–11; *Cox*, 236 SE 2d at 74; Harper, Law of Torts § 1.7, at 1:31–33; Dobbs, Law of Torts § 57, at 115 and n.1.

25 *Burley v. Burlington Northern & Santa Fe*, 2733d 825, 844 (Mont. 2012).

26 *Kornoff v. Kingsburg Cotton Oil Co.*, 45 Cal. 2d 265, 271 (Cal. 1955).

27 *Id.*

28 Gifford, D. G. (2013), *op. cit. supra* at n.2 chapter 3, at 52.

In *Borel v. Fibreboard Paper Products Corp.* (1973), the Fifth Circuit Court determined that the cause of a plaintiff's action to seek compensation for personal mesolethema injury caused by years of asbestos exposure accrued when the effects of that exposure became manifest i.e. when Borel, the plaintiff discovered or was diagnosed with the cancer. The Borel court based its decision on other court rulings "in cases involving similar injuries resulting from exposures to deleterious substances over a period of time", most notably the United States Supreme Court's verdict in *Urie v. Thompson* (1949).[29] Quoting that *Urie*, the Borel court impressed:

(Any other rule) would mean that at some past moment in time, unknown and inherently unknowable even in retrospect, (the plaintiff) Urie was charged with knowledge of the slow and tragic disintegration of his lungs; under this view Urie's failure to diagnose within the applicable statute of limitations a disease whose symptoms had not yet obtruded his consciousness would constitute waiver of his right to compensation at the ultimate day of discovery and disability.[30]

While asbestos case examples are extraordinary in US case law, their similarities (sources of harm being products which cause latent injuries) with the *ozone layer case* make them useful precedents based on which courts could rely to relax statutes of limitation.

Similarly, statutes of limitation may be eased for State governments. In some jurisdictions, State laws provide for governmental immunity from statutes of limitations and repose. Further, in a number of States, the common law doctrine of *nullum tempus occurrit regi* may still apply. Literally meaning "no time runs against the King," the doctrine exempts "certain governmental bodies from statutes of limitations, laches, and statutes of repose."[31] Although controversial, *nullum tempus* has been revived "by State attorneys general on behalf of governmental bodies seeking reimbursement for public expenditures for injuries caused by products such as tobacco, lead paint, and firearms".[32] This principle could enhance the ability for relevant US States to succeed as plaintiffs in the *ozone layer case*.

29 *Borel v. Fibreboard Paper Products Corp.*, 493 F. 2d 1076, 1101 (5th Cir. 1973) citing *Urie v. Thompson*, 337 US 163, 169 (1949). The case involved a dispute as to whether the statute of limitations would bar a locomotive fireman who had contracted silicosis from seeking compensation for his injuries.
30 *Id.* at 1102.
31 Mack, J. (2006, April). Nullum Tempus: Governmental Immunity to Statutes of limitations, Laches, and Statutes of Repose. *Defense Counsel Journal.*
32 *Ibid.*

7   Federal and state law pre-emption under the Clean Air Act

Another argument against the *ozone layer case* is that it is pre-empted by federal law under the Clean Air Act. The policy of federal pre-emption derives from the United States Constitution which empowers Congress to pass federal laws which supersede State laws and policies.[1] The policy exists primarily to ensure that national policy goals set by the legislative branch are achievable in ways that are fair, organised and harmonised across all 50 States.[2] Accordingly, federal law pre-emption means that once federal laws are enacted which prohibit or set standards for a private or public activity such as driving motor vehicles, labelling cigarettes, or polluting the environment, State courts are limited in passing judgment which would undermine those laws.

Not all federal laws pre-empt State laws, however. This includes laws for the protection of the ozone layer which are enshrined under Title VI of the Clean Air Act. While the Supreme Court has determined that the Clean Air Act (CAA) pre-empts federal common law actions,[3] current precedent

---

1 United States Constitution, Article 6(2) (the Supremacy Clause) E.g. *Comer v. Murphy Oil USA* (2009), *op. cit. supra* at n.38 chapter 1, at 869: "Under the separation of powers of the Constitution and the Supreme Court's cases, a question or subject matter that is committed by the Constitution, or by constitutional federal laws or regulations, exclusively to Congress or the president is not capable of being decided by a federal court".

2 Slaughter, J. B. and Auslander, J. M. (2008). Preemption Litigation Strategies Under Environmental Law. *Natural Resources & Environment*, 22(4), at 2: The rationale recognises that Congress and federal agencies are best placed to promulgate laws and regulations because they have the expertise and resources to assess risks and benefits of national policy choices to protect the public. See Schwartz, V. E. and Silverman, C. (2010). Preemption of State Common Law by Federal Agency Action: Striking the Appropriate Balance that Protects Public Safety. *Tulane Law Review*, 84, 1204.

3 *Am. Electric Power Co. v. Connecticut*, 131 S Ct. 2527 (2011): The Supreme Court determined that federal common law claims under the Clean Air Act are displaced. *Native Village of Kivalina v. Exxon Mobile*, 696 F. 3d 849, No. 09-17490 at 11646 (9th Cir. 2012). The Court affirmed: "...the Supreme Court has held that federal common law addressing domestic greenhouse gas emissions has been displaced by Congressional action. That determination displaces federal common law public nuisance actions seeking damages, as well as those actions seeking injunctive relief".

affirms that State statutory and common law claims may not be pre-empted.[4] This should include pleas for injunctive relief, abatement measures and non-accidental damage compensation.[5] Although State common law pre-emption may be pre-empted in the future, at present that conclusion is not supported.

Moreover, and specific to the *ozone layer case*, Title VI of the Clean Air Act expressly does not pre-empt State level tort actions. Under this Title, § 614(a) provides:

> Notwithstanding section 116, during the two year period beginning on the enactment of the Clean Air Act Amendments of 1990, no State or local government may enforce any requirement concerning the design of any new or recalled appliance for the purpose of protecting the stratospheric ozone layer.[6]

---

4   In *American Electric Power Co. v. Connecticut* 131 S Ct. 2527, 2531 (2011), Justice Ginsburg left open the issue whether State law would be pre-empted by the Clean Air Act. In *Native Village of Kivalina v. Exxon Mobile Corp.* 696 F. 3d 849, 863 (9th Cir. 2012), Judge Pro considered possibilities of State common law actions based on Supreme Court precedent. Pursuant to these rulings, in *Bell v. Cheswick Generating Station (Bell II)*, 734 F. 3d 188 (3d Cir. 2013) and *Merrick v. Diageo Americas Supply, Inc.*, No. 14-6198 (6th Cir. 2015), the Third and Sixth Circuit Courts have both affirmed the State common law right to bring nuisance claims under the Clean Air Act. Although a petition was submitted to the Supreme Court to review the Bell case non pre-emption verdict, the Court denied to grant certiorari. This is now understood as an endorsement that state law will not be pre-empted by federal law. See, Romey, M. G., Potash, A. and Fuoco, G. (2014). US Supreme Court Allows to Stand Ruling That Sources of Air Pollutants are Subject to State Common Law Tort Claims. Latham's Clean Energy Law Report.

5   CAA, 42 U.S.C. § 7604 (e) states, "Nothing in this section shall restrict any right which any person (or class of persons) may have under any statute or common law to seek enforcement of any emission standard or limitation or to seek any other relief" Although see restrictions regarding damage claims for accidental releases in 42 U.S.C. § 7411 (r), (r) 6. In *Native Village of Kivalina v. Exxon Mobile Corp.* 696 F. 3d 849 (9th Cir. 2012), a group of Alaskan natives brought public and private nuisance claims for damages suffered as a result of climate change against a selection of major greenhouse gas emitting enterprises. While the case was pre-empted as a federal law claim on other grounds, the Ninth Circuit Court did not determine that the plaintiffs' damage claims were moot. In *Merrick v. Diago Americas Supply, Inc.*, No. 14-6198 (6th Cir. 2015), although plaintiffs claimed injunctive relief, the court reviewed the legislative history of the CAA to conclude that damage claims would be admissible. Finally, cases brought under other federal laws have resulted in the award of compensation and/or punitive damages. See *International Paper Co. v. Ouellette*, 479 US 481 (1987); *Exxon Shipping Co. et al. v. Baker et al. (the Exxon Valdez case)*, 554 US 471 (2008); *Silkwood v. Kerr–McGee Corp.*, 464 US 238 (1984). However, pursuant to the Supreme Court's ruling, the Court of Appeals for the Tenth Circuit "reversed the plaintiff's award, holding that Oklahoma's workers' compensation act precluded Silkwood's recovery for personal injury". See Koenig, T. and Rustad, M. (2003). *In Defence of Tort Law*. New York: New York University Press, at 197.

6   CAA 42 U.S.C. § 7671m(a).

Further, Title VI § 618 qualifies that:

> For purposes of section 116, requirements concerning the areas addressed by this title for the protection of the stratosphere against ozone layer depletion shall be treated as requirements for the control and abatement of air pollution.[7]

Finally, § 116 stipulates:

> ...nothing in this Act shall preclude or deny the right of any State or political subdivision thereof to adopt or enforce (1) any standard or limitation respecting emissions of air pollutants or (2) any requirement respecting control or abatement of air pollution; except that if an emission standard or limitation is in effect under an applicable implementation plan or under section 111 or 112, such State or political subdivision may not adopt or enforce any emission standard or limitation which is less stringent than the standard or limitation under such plan or section.

Reading these provisions together, States or local governments should not be pre-empted in their legislative or judicial actions to enact and impose rules which are better than federal law requirements. However, between 1990 and 1992, States would not have been permitted to enforce product design directives for appliances. Appliances are defined under the pursuant federal regulations as "any device which contains and uses a refrigerant[8] and which is used for household or commercial purposes, including any air conditioner, refrigerator, chiller, or freezer".[9] This provision is both explicit and time-bound, making it an unusual provision in the Act.[10] However, this provision does not affect the claim against the chemical producers in the *ozone layer case* but only appliance manufacturers between 1990 and 1992. Hence, plaintiffs' tort claims at the State level would not be pre-empted.

That finding is bolstered by the fact that prior to 1990 during the liability period (1976–1992) proposed in the *ozone layer case*, the Clean Air Act also did not pre-empt State common law actions. The 1977 Clean Air Act Amendments under former Title I, Part B: Ozone Protection § 159 read:

---

7   CAA 42 U.S.C. § 7671q.
8   40 C.F.R. § 82.152 Refrigerant has also been defined as "any substance consisting in part or whole of a class I or class II ozone-depleting substance that is used for heat transfer purposes and provides a cooling effect".
9   40 C.F.R. § 82.3.
10   Speculatively, this requirement may have been written in as a placeholder for product design rules under contemplation. However, the provision now seems enigmatic since no prohibitions were ever adopted for the manufacture of such appliances but rather their sale and distribution – which was prohibited in 2002, see 40 C.F.R. § 82.

(a) Nothing in this part shall preclude or deny any State or political subdivision thereof from adopting or enforcing any requirement respecting the control of any substance, practice, process or activity for purposes of protecting the stratosphere or ozone in the stratosphere except as otherwise provided in subsection (b).

(b) If a regulation of any substance, practice, process, or activity is in effect under this part in order to prevent or abate any risk to the stratosphere, or ozone in the stratosphere, no State or political subdivision thereof may adopt or attempt to enforce any requirement respecting the control of any such substance, practice, process, or activity to prevent or abate such risk, unless the requirement of the State or political subdivision is identical to the requirement of such regulation. The preceding sentence shall not apply with respect to any law or regulation of any State or political subdivision controlling the use of halocarbons as propellants in aerosol spray containers.[11]

Essentially, this meant that pursuant to regulation being enacted, no State or local government was barred from imposing any laws or court judgements either with respect to aerosol sprays[12] or non-regulated substances. Because this law remained in effect until it was repealed in 1990, and because no regulations were enacted until that point, there is strong consistency and support that State common law claims as in the *ozone layer case*, were not and are not pre-empted.

---

11   CAA 42 U.S.C. § 7459 [repealed].
12   The regulations concerned are the 1978 ban on aerosol sprays put forth by the EPA and FDA and the 1977 warning label requirements mandated by the FDA and CPSC. See Chapter 4 § 4.1.3 *supra*.

8   Regulatory compliance defence

The *ozone layer case*'s defendants could also argue the regulatory compliance defence. They submit that because regulations regarding the manufacture and sale of ODCs for primarily non-aerosol uses were not enforceable until 1992, they were not under any regulatory duty to curtail their business operations. In the absence of regulations, their conduct was legally compliant.

While this defence is plausible, court precedent concurs that regulatory compliance may not be an excuse should it be established that common law duties of care would prevail despite the regulatory silence.

This precept derives from State common law tort cases, where courts have found certain actors negligent even when acting in compliance to federal rules. In *Silkwood v. Kerr-McGee* (1979),[1] the plaintiff claimed that a nuclear fuel processing plant was liable under negligence and strict liability theories for personal injuries caused by the plant's failure to prevent its employees from radiation exposure. One key issue in the case concerned whether the defendants' compliance with federal regulations would relinquish its liability. The defendants argued that they were not liable since they had "*no* common law duty to contain plutonium within the walls of their facility"[2] and that they had complied with "federal regulations controlling the facility".[3] The district court found these claims legally unsupportable. It held that federal regulation stipulates its relationship with State common law and often permits that States apply rules which are stricter than federal law mandates. In State jurisdictions, compliance to federal law can be evidence of a defendant's "exercise of reasonable care but is not conclusive" nor does it absolve tortfeasors of liability for injuries they have caused – such as in the field of aviation and drug manufacture.[4]

Likewise, in *McLane v. Northwest Natural Gas Co.,*[5] the Oregon Supreme Court imposed strict liability for the explosion of a natural gas storage tank,

1   *Silkwood v. Kerr-McGee Corp.*, 485 F. Supp. 566 (WD Okla. 1979).
2   *Id.* at 571.
3   *Id.* at 576.
4   *Id.* at 578–579.
5   *McLane v. Northwest Natural Gas Co.*, 255 Or. 324 (Or. 1970).

notwithstanding the fact that State law "expressly permitted such storage of natural gas". Also, in *Tinnerholm v. Parke Davis & Co.* a drug manufacturer was not exempted from liability for its failure to exercise due care in testing its products prior to putting them on the market on the basis that no such regulatory duties existed.[6] In asbestos cases, courts have determined that the common law duty to warn existed even if regulatory requirements were not in place at the time asbestos was produced and marketed.[7] Most recently, in *In Re MTBE Prods. Liability Litig.*, Exxon's negligence was found in not having prevented the contamination of groundwater caused by leakage of subterranean tanks containing MTBE gasoline which the companies had supplied to service stations for almost 25 years beginning in the 1980s.[8] The ruling was sustained even though the use of MTBE was not regulated until 2005.[9]

On the basis of these precedents, plaintiffs could argue that even if such regulatory duties were lacking, State common law duties to mitigate unreasonable risks of harm, namely resulting skin cancer injuries, nevertheless prevail. State courts would then need to determine whether the companies were obligated to reduce chemical production, warn about the chemical dangers and prevent emissions.

Even if strong arguments could be made that such common law duties were not incumbent on the chemical producers on the basis of scientific uncertainty and lack of resolve of policy makers to impose rules, plaintiffs could contend that the very corporate social responsibility policies of the defendants[10] as well as the 1976–77 regulations both set the scope of what should have been expected of the chemical producers. The regulatory duties prescribed in the 1970s and in the 1990s are strikingly consistent in terms of their purpose to reduce not increase the production and sale of ODCs and to require the use of warning labels. That common thread is bolstered by the fact that despite various scientific, political and economic

6   *Tinnerholm v. Parke Davis & Co.*, 285 F. Supp. 432 (SDNY 1968) at n.12.
7   *Borel v. Fibreboard Paper Products Corp.*, 493 F. 2d 1076, 1090 (5th Cir. 1973). The Court stated: But even more importantly, a manufacturer has a duty to test and inspect his product. The extent of research and experiment must be commensurate with the dangers involved. A product must not be made available to the public without disclosure of those dangers that the application of reasonable foresight would reveal. Nor may a manufacturer rely unquestioningly on others to sound the hue and cry concerning a danger in its product. Rather, each manufacturer must bear the burden of showing that its own conduct was proportionate to the scope of its duty.
8   *In Re MTBE Prods. Liability Litig.*, 725 F. 3d 65, 78. (2d. Cir. 2013).
9   *Id. at 82.*
10   For example, DuPont's corporate policy commits to a "business process responsible for the management of a product throughout its existing life cycle focusing on the health, safety and environmental issues at each phase". Part of this commitment involves developing safety and hazard information and labels regarding its products and services concerning their use, storage and handling E. I. DuPont Nemours and Company (2014). Product Stewardship: www.dupont.com/corporate-functions/our-approach/sustainability/commitments/product-stewardship-regulator/articles/product-stewardship.html.

uncertainties which delayed the adoption of comprehensive stratospheric ozone protection laws and regulations, policy makers never revoked the 1978 rules, the 1976 endangerment finding and the mandate of the EPA to propose further regulations. This suggests that even if enhanced regulatory duties were not put into effect until 1993, it was the policy intention laid down in the 1970s that should have been heeded.

9 Downstream liability question

One of the most palpable defences in the *ozone layer case* is that downstream actors should bear liability not the chemical producers. The defendants could argue that companies which purchased and used ODCs to manufacture and sell their own products are responsible for chemical emissions because they either released large quantities of the chemicals in producing their goods e.g. foam blowing, or they sold products which would eventually leak all of the chemicals in the absence of any recovery technology or policy. Based on the **sophisticated intermediary defence theory**,[1] they could also say that such downstream companies were "knowledgeable user(s)".[2] Hence, the producers relied on those companies to warn about product risks.[3] Downstream manufacturers, not the chemical producers had the primary duty to protect citizens from the potential, unreasonable risks of harm which the chemicals posed.[4]

This argument would be persuasive since it attaches responsibility to the point of emissions rather than production. It changes the dynamics around product liability in the *ozone layer case* by shifting the defective product from the chemicals to the goods manufactured with the chemicals. It also reopens the question as to where the emission source is to be located. Essentially, the argument highlights the key complexity of establishing liability in the *ozone layer case* as it is simultaneously a product liability suit and a negligent "direct spiller" action.

The easiest solution to this problem would be to offer that Congress and federal agencies answered the question by identifying the production and sale of ODCs as the source of harm. The 1990 amendments to the Clean Air Act and corollary federal regulations clearly ordered that the chemicals

---

1   *Macias v. State of California* (1995) 10 Cal.4th 844.
2   *Goodbar v. Whitehead Bros.*, (WD Va. 1984) 591 F. Supp. 552; *Akin v. Ashland Chemical* (10th Cir. 1998) 156 F. 3d 1030, 1036–1037; *Higgins v. E. I. DuPont de Nemours, Inc.*, 671 F. Supp. 1055, 1058 (D Md. 1987): The "knowledgeable industrial purchaser is the only one in a position to communicate an effective warning to the ultimate user".
3   Rest. 2d Torts § 388, comment n.; *Adkins v. GAF Corp.* (6th Cir. 1991) 923 F. 2d 1225, 1230.
4   *Goodbar v. Whitehead Bros.*, (WD Va. 1984) 591 F. Supp. 552; *Higgins v. E. I. DuPont de Nemours, Inc.*, 671 F. Supp. 1055 (D Md. 1987).

be phased out and eliminated. However, the rules also required that warning labels be placed on both the containers in which the chemicals were sold as well as the products which were manufactured with the chemicals. Regulatory duties were thus imposed on both the chemical producers and downstream manufacturers. As the duty to warn on the part of the chemical producers is a key liability allegation in the *ozone layer case*, it would be a fair argument that the chain of responsibility includes the downstream actors since they marketed the majority of products which consumers would have purchased directly.

The questions then can be posed as to what actors a court of law of law would attach liability and ultimately whether the defendant producers could successively shift their responsibility to escape liability in the *ozone layer case*. In their defence, courts have held that a product manufacturer's liability ends when it sells its product to intermediaries for distribution.[5] In *Vandermark v. Ford Motor Co.* (1964), the Supreme Court of California determined that automobile manufacturers were obliged to ensure that their "cars delivered to the ultimate purchaser free from dangerous defects". The court perceived the manufacturers of finished products as the "strategic link in the complex chain of production and distribution and held that they could not delegate their duty backward to the manufacturers of component parts, or forward to dealers and distributors".[6] The precedent speaks strongly in favour of downstream goods manufacturers as opposed to the chemical producers.

However, in other tort cases where similar issues have been raised, courts have applied tests to ascertain which actors in a supply chain bear a duty of care to protect the public from unreasonable risk of harm which their products could cause. Applied to the chemical producer defendants, the tests would probe: Did their product or conduct create a risk of great magnitude? Were they in a superior position and relied on by others to mitigate that risk?[7] Did they anticipate that downstream actors would not exercise proper care in mitigating that risk and that serious harm would follow? Conversely, could they anticipate that downstream actors were competent and could be relied on to assume a duty of care to protect the public from the harms caused by ODC releases?[8] Did they provide warnings and information about product dangers to intermediaries?[9] Did they delegate their duty of care to other actors?[10] Finally, did they exercise control

---

5   *Cavan v. General Motors Corp.*, 571 2d 1249 (Or. 1977).
6   *Vandermark v. Ford Motor Co.*, 61 Cal. 2d 256 (Cal. In Bank. 1964).
7   Prosser (1971), *op. cit. supra* at n.4 chapter 4, at 177.
8   *Ibid.*
9   Restatement (Second) of Torts § 388; *Selma Pressure Treating Co. v. Osmose Wood Preserving Co.* (1990) 221 Cal.App.3d 1601, 1623; Borel v. Fribreboard Paper Products Corp., (5th Cir.1973) 493 F.2d 1076, 1093.
10   Prosser (1971), *op. cit. supra* at n.4 chapter 4, at 176.

over or participate substantially in the activity, product or instrumentality that causes injury?[11] On all these counts, an affirmative conclusion that the chemical producers bear primary responsibility can also be reached.

In support of this conclusion, many courts have found that liability should rest with the actors who are the source of dangerous chemical emissions or are the primary suppliers of hazardous chemical products.[12] Although not many, such cases bear important precedent for the *ozone layer case*. For example, in *In Re MTBE Prods. Liability Litig.* (2013), the Court of Appeals determined that Exxon was liable for New York City's ground and well water contamination for supplying MTBE containing gasoline to service stations. The finding was reached on the basis that the company knew that station storage tanks would leak and that consequently its gasoline would leach into groundwater and surrounding property. The court determined that Exxon's actions as supplier also constituted a public nuisance.[13] In this case, it was expected that Exxon being in a superior position was relied on to exercise precaution in ensuring that its product did not adulterate subterranean water sources. Part of that duty meant ensuring secure underground gasoline storage. The other part meant to refrain from using MTBE as a gasoline additive. This logic employed in the MTBE case can be applied to the *ozone layer case*. Ostensibly, like Exxon, it may be determined that the defendant chemical producers were depended on and expected to ensure that their products did not leach into the environment. Similarly, because they must have known that their chemical products would eventually be released by downstream users or applications, the chemical producers also had a duty to take precautionary measures to prevent emissions.

A relatively recent decision by the California Supreme Court on an asbestos case has advanced this thinking. In *O'Neil v. Crane Co.* (2012), plaintiffs sued two companies which made valves and pumps for United States Navy warships. The plaintiffs claimed compensation for physical

11   *Hawkins v. Evans Cooperage Co., Inc.*, 1985, 766 F. 2d 904 (5th Cir. 1985): The activity must have been in the control of the defendant at the time of plaintiff's injury. *Heinrich v. Goodyear Tire and Rubber Co.*, 532 F.Supp. 1348 (D. Maryland. 1982): The defndant must have "the right or duty to control, if not actual control over, the activity causing the harm;" American Law Institute (1979). *Restatement (Second) of Torts* § 834 Comment (g) cited in Gifford (2013), *op. cit. supra* at n.2 chapter 3.

12   *State v. Schenectady Chemicals, Inc.*, 103 A.D.2d 33, 38 (1983): A chemical company's liability was not excused even though the company's independent contractor and not the company itself had disposed the waste; *United States v. Hooker Chemcials and Plastics Corporation*, 722 F. Supp.960, 967, 970 (W. D. N. Y. 1989) cited in Gifford (2013), *op. cit. supra* at n.2 chapter 3, at 149: A chemical company's sale of property which it had contaminated did not relinquish the company from its liability in creating public nuisance threating human health and the *State Department of Environmental Protection v. Exxon Corp.*, 151 N.J. Super. 464 (1977): A chemical company responsible for producing and emitting toxic waste – which was no longer in its control – was liable for having created a public health nuisance.

13   *In Re MTBE Prods. Liability Litig.*, 725 F. 3d 65, 96–100 (2d Cir. 2013).

injury and wrongful death caused by asbestos insulation which was added to the valves and pumps according to the Navy's specifications. The defendants Crane and Warren "never manufactured or sold any of the asbestos-containing materials" nor did their products require that asbestos be used.[14] Nevertheless, the plaintiffs applied the strict product liability theory alleging that the "defendants' products were defective because they included and were used in connection with asbestos-containing parts".[15] The Supreme Court disagreed finding that "any design defect in defendants' products was not a legal cause of (the plaintiff's) injury. More broadly, the Court held "that a product manufacturer may not be held liable in strict liability or negligence for harm caused by another manufacturer's product unless the defendant's own product contributed substantially to the harm, or the defendant participated substantially in creating a harmful combined use of the products".[16]

In coming to that conclusion, the court evaluated a number of factors. First, it assessed that the product which caused the plaintiff's injuries was asbestos and not the pumps and valves.[17] Second, it considered that another manufacturer had introduced asbestos into commerce, again not the pump and valve makers. Here, the Court stressed "that strict products liability should be imposed only on those entities responsible for placing a defective product into the stream of commerce".[18] Drawing on a New York decision in *Baughman v. General Motors Corp.* (1986), the Court restated:

> Where, as here, the defendant manufacturer did not incorporate the defective component part into its finished product and did not place the defective component into the stream of commerce, the rationale for imposing liability is no longer present. The manufacturer has not had an opportunity to test, evaluate, and inspect the component; it has derived no benefit from its sale; and it has not represented to the public that the component part is its own.[19]

---

14 *O'Neil v. Crane Co.*, 266 3d 987, 342–343 (Cal. 2012).

15 *Id.* at 343, 348.

16 *Id.* at 342. The question arose following a previous decision by the California Court of Appeals in the same case which found for the plaintiffs. The appeals court held broadly that "[A] manufacturer is liable in strict liability for the dangerous components of its products, and for dangerous products with which its product will necessarily be used".*Id.* at 346–347.

17 *Id.* at 350.

18 *Id.* at 349, quoting *Peterson v. Superior Court* (1995) 10 Cal. 4th 1185, at 1198–1990. Further, the rationale for this policy is that "those outside the marketing enterprise generally ha[ve] no 'continuing business relationship' with the manufacturer of the defective product", they "cannot exert pressure upon the manufacturer to make the product safe and cannot share with the manufacturer the costs of insuring the safety of the product's user". *Id.* at 1999.

19 *Baughman v. General Motors Corp.*, 780 F. 2d 1131, 1132–1133 (4th Cir. 1986).

Expanding on this opinion, in 2015, the California Court of Appeals concluded "that the supplier of a raw material used in the manufacture of another product can be held liable for a design defect under the consumer expectations test only if the raw material is itself inherently defective".[20] These findings would speak strongly in favour of the chemical producers' responsibility in the *ozone layer case*, since it was the introduction of ODCs into the stream of commerce which triggered and subsists as the source of harm. Moreover, the reflection on manufacturers' superior know-how of their products and ability to ensure their safety also supports that the defendant producers should bear primary responsibility.

However, in *O'Neil v. Crane Co.*, the Court further clarified that neither the valves nor pumps *required* that asbestos be used by their makers.[21] In that context, the court offered that:

> A stronger argument for liability might be made in the case of a product that required the use of a defective part in order to operate.... Similarly, if the product manufacturer specified or required the use of a defective replacement part, a stronger case could be made that the manufacturer's failure to warn was a proximate cause of resulting injury. In both contexts, however, the policy rationales against imposing liability on a manufacturer for a defective part it did not produce or supply would remain.

The Court's suggestion turns back to the notion that downstream users of ODCs equally could be liable in the *ozone layer case*, particularly regarding their failure to warn. This is because, as historical literature has reflected, the chemicals were required to make certain products work or produce different products to a particular performance standard. It is likely that user specifications also included the application of the chemicals. However, while this may be true, it is doubtful whether the users required chemicals which would run the risk of depleting the ozone layer. More likely, the users required chemicals or technologies that would be safe to consumers and that could achieve specific functions. Because they relied on the chemical producers for this know-how, their responsibility would not be primary but secondary. However, even if this were accepted, it is not certain that the downstream manufacturers should be relieved entirely of their ostensible failure to warn consumers about the presence and use of ODCs in products they marketed.

The *ozone layer case* does not limit that possibility. The defendant producers could implead companies which purchased and used their chemicals. For practical reasons such an approach would achieve greater efficiency

20 *Johnson v. United States Steel Corporation*, (Cal. Court of Appeal, 2015).
21 *O'Neil v. Crane Co.*, 266 3d 987 (Cal. 2012).

since the defendant producers would also be in the best position to assess the user class (their customers). It would also relieve much of the complexity of joining both producers and users in the *ozone layer case,* and potentially achieve a more equitable distribution of liability.

10 Open and obvious risks

The producers could also claim that the risk of ozone layer depletion was so **open** and **obvious** that they were under no obligation to warn about the chemical dangers. This notion relies on case law which asserts that product manufactures have no duty to warn when downstream purchasers know and are fully aware of the product dangers.[1] However, it is unlikely that this argument would be pursued given that the producers would be more inclined to claim that they were uncertain of the risk, hence others were as well. Still, if such a defence were raised, plaintiffs could rely on *Borel v. Fibreboard Paper Products Corp.* (1984). In that case, a former company employee sued asbestos manufacturers for his injuries (asbestosis and mesothelioma) as a result of his 33 years of working with asbestos insulation. He claimed, *inter alia*, that manufacturers were negligent for failing to warn of asbestos risks and for not providing safe handling instructions.[2] The defendant asbestos producers argued that they had no duty to warn because asbestos risks were obvious to the employer and to the plaintiff. The court disagreed assessing that the threat of cancer was foreseeable to the defendants but not sufficiently obvious enough "to asbestos installation workers to relieve the defendants of the duty to warn".[3]

Similarly, in the *ozone layer case*, given the multiple scientific complexities, conflicting information and sceptic responses regarding the risks at the time, it would be difficult to prove that the causes and effects of stratospheric loss were open and obvious. That is, even if people in American

1   *Hobart v. Sohio Petroleum Company*, 255 F. Supp.972, 974–97 (Dist. Ct. ND Miss. 1966): "An inherently dangerous substance is one burdened with a latent danger or dangers which derive from the very nature of the substance itself, and the duty arises only with respect to hidden or concealed dangers. Even though the danger may be hidden, the duty encompasses only dangers which are unknown, and there is no duty to warn when the user has actual knowledge of the danger. Knowledge of the danger is equivalent to prior notice, and a failure to warn of a fact of which the user is already fully aware is not a breach of duty". See also *Sprankle v. Bower Ammonia & Chemical Co.*, (5th Cir. 1987) 824 F. 2d 409, 412.
2   *Borel v. Fibreboard Paper Products Corp.*, 493 F. 2d 1076, 1086 (5th Cir. 1973).
3   *Id.* at 1103, 1093.

societies were aware of ozone layer depletion risks, they may not have been able to associate those risks with products absent of clear and understandable warnings. A vast majority of people would not be able to connect the dots when reading a product label that merely lists product ingredients e.g. "contains CCl_3F". Further, even if conclusive evidence did not prove the risks at the time, the aerosol warning label model could have been adopted i.e. by tagging the risks as "potentially harmful" as opposed to not addressing them at all.

10.1 Summary of conclusions to Part III

Based on the foregoing discussion on some key defences the chemical producers could raise to limit their liability in the *ozone layer case*, a few conclusions can be made. First, the federal pre-emption, regulatory compliance and open and obvious defences will not avail the defendants. Pending future court judgments, State common law actions are clearly not pre-empted by the Clean Air Act and the Act expressly does not pre-empt such actions in the context of stratospheric ozone protection. Further, case law supports that even if laws and regulations are wanting, common law duties to protect citizens from unreasonable risks of harm prevail. Also, the unlikely open and obvious defence must fail as it would assume a high level of scientific knowledge on the part of consumers.

However, State statutes of limitation could bar the *ozone layer case* given the long period which has passed since ODCs were produced and sold. Surpassing these time limits will require establishing that the producers created a public nuisance and that that nuisance continues but is not permanent. It further necessitates that the plaintiffs' discovery of injury is ripe today. This timely discovery can be facilitated by a peer reviewed technical report which qualifies the connection between ODC production and emissions and current skin cancer prevalence in the United States.

Finally, a veritable case can be made that companies which used ODCs to manufacture industrial and commercial products are also liable under product liability theories, in particular for their failures to warn about the potential chemical hazards to human health and the environment. However, those implicit responsibilities and duties must be viewed as secondary in relation to the chemical producers, who were in a superior position to know about and communicate the risks involved and who were relied on by the others to provide safe technologies. Thus to serve both efficiency and equity, it was suggested that the defendant chemical producers could implead downstream actors in further litigation.

Part IV

Rationale, relevance and objectives of the ozone layer case

11 The basis for assessing why the ozone layer case is relevant and important

One essential purpose of exploring the viability of the hypothetical *ozone layer case* is to assess whether a civil action can be pursued through the common law of torts. The aim is to assess whether it is legally possible to seek redress for latent environmental and health injuries and infringements on public rights which were caused by past allegedly negligent corporate conduct. By applying tort law, the case evokes both legal and policy questions. The previous chapters have focused on pertinent legal questions to gauge how common and statutory laws could be interpreted to support or refute a cause of action. The conclusion of that discussion was that the case could be theoretically viable if and only if sufficient evidence could be made available. However, it was also deliberated that in many instances, any court reviewing the case would be faced with policy judgments.

Such policy choices are linked with and guided by the overall purposes of the tort law. In compliment to public laws and policies, the law of torts exists to deter, correct and remedy wrongs and injustices within society.[1] Described as "a battle ground of social theory", "tort law has always been the contested legal terrain because of fundamental disagreements over who should bear the financial burden for an injury and what wrongs should be compensable".[2] This involves balancing competing claims over individual and social interests and freedoms.[3] These are essentially policy decisions taken by courts in determining "what society demands of an actor" or the "social desirability or undesirability of particular forms of conduct".[4] The political, social and economic impacts of such decisions

---

1   Prosser, W. L. (1971), *op. cit. supra* at n.4 chapter 4, at 3–4; Cooper-Stephenson, K. D. and Gibson, E. (1993). *Tort Theory.* North York: Captus University Publications, at 26 citing Jules Coleman; Koenig, T. and Rustad, M. (2003), *op. cit. supra* at n.5 chapter 7, at 1; Boston, G. and Madden, M. S., *The Law of Environmental and Toxic Torts,* 2nd ed., West Group, Minnesota, 2001.

2   Koenig, T. and Rustad, M. (2003), *op. cit. supra* at n.5 chapter 7, at 1.

3   Prosser (1971), *op. cit. supra* at n.4 chapter 4, at 6.

4   Goldberg, J. C. (2002). Twentieth Century Tort Theory. Vanderbilt University Law School. Published in *Georgetown Law Journal,* at 14, 16.

expand in tandem with the scope of rights and freedoms being contested such as in public nuisance cases.[5] However, the extent to which courts can and should take decisions affecting public policy is contested as the separation of powers delegates that Congress and not the judiciary is charged with and better placed to determine public policy i.e. Congress makes law and courts interpret and apply it as the rule of law demands.[6]

Nevertheless, when Congress has been silent on a particular issue or has refrained from passing legislation, judicial decision can set precedent in clarifying or interpreting existing laws. Inevitably, unclear boundaries of this divide between legislature and the judiciary as well as frustration over law making reticence have resulted in creating tension amongst federal branches of government.[7] Further, tort law's application remains vital in preventing negligent actors, in particular corporations from escaping liability, in redressing harm (**corrective justice function**),[8] in protecting the

---

5   Prosser (1971), *op. cit. supra* at n.4 chapter 4, at 602–606. For example, *People v. Atlantic Richfield Co.*, No. 1-00-CV-788657 (Cal. A 2014): Santa Clara Superior Court Case (2014). There the Court ordered the establishment of a publicly administered fund paid into by defendants to abate lead paint in pre-1978 homes in California.

6   Calabresi, S. G., Berghausen, M. E. and Albertson, S. (2012). The Rise and the Fall of the Separation of Powers. *Northwestern University Law Review*, 106(2), at 527–550. The issue is discussed in: *Milwaukee v. Illinois*, 451 US 304 S Ct. (1981); *Massachusetts v. EPA*, 127 S Ct. 1438 (2007); *Am. Electric Power Co. v. Connecticut*, 131 S Ct. 2527 (2011). Dewes, D., Duff, D., & Trebilcock, M. (1996). *Exploring the Domain of Accident Law: Taking the Facts Seriously*. New York, Oxford: Oxford University Press; Gifford, D. G. (2013), *op. cit. supra* at n.2 chapter 3; Koenig, T. and Rustad, M. (2003), *op. cit. supra* at n.5 chapter 7.

7   See e.g. *Coalition for Responsible Regulation v. EPA*, 684 F. 3d 102 (DC Cir. 2012), reversed in part in *Utility Air Regulatory Group v. EPA*, 134 S Ct. 2427 (2014): Regarding the issue of whether Congress would pass "'corrective legislation' to relieve the overwhelming permitting burdens on permitting authorities and sources" in relation to the government's greenhouse gas emissions reduction policy, the Court stated: "We have serious doubts as to whether, for standing purposes, it is ever 'likely' that Congress will enact legislation at all. After all, a proposed bill must make it through committees in both the House of Representatives and the Senate and garner a majority of votes in both chambers –overcoming, perhaps, a filibuster in the Senate. If passed, the bill must then be signed into law by the President, or go back to Congress so that it may attempt to override his veto. As a generation of schoolchildren knows, "by that time, it's very unlikely that [a bill will] become a law. It's not easy to become a law". Schoolhouse Rock, I'm just a Bill at 2:41, available at http://video.google.com/videoplay?docid=7266360872513258185#."

8   Goldberg, J. C. (2002), *op. cit. supra* at n.4, at 72–73, 80, citing both Aristotle and Perry, S. R. (1992). The Moral Foundations of Tort Law. *Iowa Law Review*, 77, 453, and citing Weinrib, E. J. (1995). *The Idea of Private Law*. Oxford: Oxford University Press, at 135: The corrective justice theory postulates that the main purpose of tort law is to rectify injustices by providing injured victims with a remedy. That remedy should achieve equilibrium by restoring a victim's condition to what it was before the injury. While in reality a victim's condition can never be restored fully, restitution is achieved functionally through monetary compensation. The tortfeasor is penalised by having to absorb that financial loss. Still, other forms of redress such as an apology or non-financial actions such as community service may also achieve the corrective justice goal. Given the theory's restorative purpose, punitive damages which go far beyond the compensation mark would not be feasible.

public and individuals from harm, and in promoting safety (**deterrence function**).[9] It enables that wrongs are punished (**social justice function**)[10] and that plaintiffs are not left without remedy when policy makers have opted out of providing for one (**compensation function**).[11]

Considering these parameters of tort law in the context of the *ozone layer case*, it is important to query:

1   Whether tort law is the correct forum for the alleged injustices to be addressed and if not, what other forums would be available?
2   What the policy implications would be should the case be tried and a decision favourable to the plaintiffs is reached?
3   What implications and learnings could be gleaned from the *ozone layer case* if it is never pursued?

All of these question speak to the relevance and importance of considering the *ozone layer case* today. The following chapters discuss these questions.

9   Goldberg, J. C. (2002), *op. cit. supra* at n.4, at 30, 41–45. The deterrence theory which posits that by imposing financial penalties on tortfeasors, tort law functions to deter future wrongful conduct or accidents. Such penalties create an incentive for tortfeasors and others to refrain from future negligence and take precautions necessary to avoid accidents. Deterrence through tort law can be socially economically efficient weighing precautionary costs against loss and damage costs to determine where liability rests.

10   Prosser, W. L. (1971), *op. cit. supra* at n.4 chapter 4, at 6, 9, 492. Goldberg, J. C. (2002), *op. cit. supra* at n.4, at 60–63 The social justice theory understands tort law as a way for citizens to protect individual and social interests and rights from "non-consensual invasions" and unreasonable interferences. Traditionally, tort law was used to remedy conflicts so as to preserve the peace by preventing individuals from taking revenge. Today, this means maintaining political power balances in society where public interests are often shadowed by corporate clout. Thus, "(b)y arming citizens with the power to sue corporations for misconduct outside of the legislative and regulatory process, tort corrects for this imbalance of power". Citizens can pursue punitive damages as a means to punish powerful actors for their intentional, deliberate or otherwise wilful, wanton or reckless conduct which harms individuals and significant segments of society.

11   Koenig, T. and Rustad, M. (2003), *op. cit. supra* at n.5 chapter 7, at 207; Dewes, D., Duff, D. and Trebilcock, M. (1996), *op. cit. supra* at n.6; Gifford, D. G. (2013), *op. cit. supra* at n.2 chapter 3; Ginsberg, W. and Weiss, L. (1981). Common Law Liability for Toxic Torts: A Phantom Remedy. *Hofstra Law Review*, 9(3), 860–941; Wright (1944). Introduction to the Law of Torts. *Cambridge Law Journal*, 8, 238 quoted in Prosser (1971), *op. cit. supra* at n.4 chapter 4, at 5; Goldberg, J. C. (2002), *op. cit. supra* at n.4, at 18; Fleming, F. (1956). Damages in Accident Cases. *Cornell Law Quarterly*, 41, 584–5; See Abraham, K. S. (1987). Individual Action and Collective Responsbility: The Dilemna of Mass Tort Reform. *Virginia Law Review*, 45–907; Huber, W. (1986). The Bhopalization of American Tort Law. In *Hazards: Technology and Fairness*. Washington, D.C.: National Academies Press: Compensation in itself is the end game where the victim receives a financial payment to redress injuries or harms he has suffered due to the wrongful or accidental conduct of another person. As such, compensation awards can insure damages in the absence of other means and achieve corrective compensation for accidents through out-of-court settlements. However, compensation may be more efficient and cost effective when it is administered through public funds or social insurance schemes. If such mechanisms are wanting, then tort claims are warranted.

11.1 Should tort law remedies be pursued in the ozone layer case?

The *ozone layer case* presents the critical social dilemma of people being compelled today to live with the burden of the unreciprocal harms of skin cancer which were brought on by alleged negligent conduct of chemical corporations: they produced and marketed defective products which have contributed to the destruction of the earth's ozone layer. The skin cancer epidemic in the United States[12] has caused and will cause individuals, households and US States significant economic and non-economic losses. The rights of individuals, in particular children, to recreation and enjoyment of the environment are infringed when they are forced to change their daytime behaviours to avoid sun exposure and skin cancer risks. The questions posed here are whether other administrative or legal remedies are or would be available to them to compensate their losses, and if not, whether those persons should pursue damage claims against those chemical companies through tort law.

11.2 Are administrative remedies available, and if not, is a tort remedy warranted?

In the US, the government provides for a range of public support and resources for skin cancer prevention and treatment. Public healthcare insurance is available which can help offset costs for individuals. In addition, public agencies administer several programmes and services including research, monitoring trends in disease prevalence and public awareness about skin cancer risks and avoidance methods.[13] These were described in Chapter 3.

However, there is no bespoke national or State level administrative fund which would provide compensation or even aid packages to citizens affected by skin cancer. The only possible but remote exception appears to be in California where the "Liability for Employers of State Employed Lifeguards" law has been enacted.[14] The policy allows active lifeguards who are employed by State public institutions for more than three consecutive months of a calendar year to be awarded compensation for skin cancer injuries which develop or become manifest during their employment. Compensation includes "full hospital, surgical, and medical treatment, disability indemnity, and death benefits".[15]

This is arguably an advanced form of public compensation policy.

---

12 Koenig, T. and Rustad, M. (2003), *op. cit. supra* at n.5 chapter 7, at 1.
13 Surgeon General's Report (2014), *op. cit. supra* at n.27 chapter 1, at 73–75.
14 Cal. Lab. Code § 3212.11; However, the State of New York has proposed similar legislation. See Skin Cancer: Prolonged Exposure to the Sun, H.R. Bill A4669-2009, New York State Assembly (2009).
15 *Id.*

However, it is unique in the United States as no other similar policy seems to exist which allows for skin cancer compensation to citizens engaged in other professions or trades which equally involve significant sun exposure.

Nevertheless, as skin cancer has become a major national health problem, the public costs required to prevent and remedy it are also soaring. In an attempt to sequester public resources to deal with the epidemic, Congress imposed a temporary federal commercial sales tax on indoor skin tanning services in 2010.[16] It is one of 12 different taxes imposed under the authority of the *Patient Protection and Affordable Care Act* to help fund national healthcare programmes.[17] The tax is estimated to generate federal revenue to the tune of US$2.7 billion by 2020.[18] While this money may help in addressing some of the skin cancer costs, it is not specifically designed to do so nor does it allow for a compensation type scheme.

Because there is no compensation fund at present, however, it does not mean that such a fund could not have been created in the past or could be formed in the future. In 1989, Congress passed the Omnibus Budget Reconciliation Act which imposed an excise tax on the sale of ODCs.[19] That tax could have been used as a financial source to invest and aid the plight of future skin cancers but was not. The purpose of the tax was twofold: (1) to deter production of the chemicals by making them more expensive and thereby encouraging the development of safer replacement chemicals, and (2) to take advantage of windfall profits achieved through the cap and trade scheme used to phase out the chemicals[20] and raise substantial public

16   Staff of the Joint Committee on Taxation (2011, January). *Present Law and Background Information on Federal Excise Taxes,* at 38. Although the link between suntan bed use and skin cancer has been researched and in some cases proven, as with other tax policies, the new levy does not attribute liability for skin cancer to indoor sun tanning services. That liability is being pursued by melanoma victims in tort litigation across the United States. See American Academy of Pediatrics (April 2014). Tanning Bed Restrictions. American Academy of Pediatrics. Retrieved from www.aap.org/en-us/advocacy-and-policy/state-advocacy/Documents/Tanning.pdf; Watson, M., Holman, D. M., Fox, K. A., Guy, G., Seidenberg, A. B., Sampson, B. and Lazovich, D. (2013). Preventing Skin Cancer Through Reduction of Indoor Tanning: Current Evidence. *American Journal of Preventative Medicine,* 682–689; Internal Revenue Service (2010, June 15). Indoor Tanning Services; Cosmetic Services; Excise Taxes. *Federal Register,* 75(114), 33683; Arentz Law Group (2014). Tanning Bed Skin Cancer Lawsuits. Retrieved from Defective Products: http://arentzlaw.com/defective-products/tanning-bed-skin-cancer-lawsuits/.
17   26 U.S.C. §5000B; Staff of the Joint Committee on Taxation (2011), *op. cit. supra* at n.16, at 38–51.
18   Ellis, B. (2010, March 24). Tanning Salons Burned by Healthcare Bill. CNNMoney.
19   House of Representatives (1989). *Bill Text 101st Congress (1989–1990) H. R. 3299.* Retrieved from The Library of Congress: http://thomas.loc.gov/cgi-bin/query/F?c101:1:./temp/~c101VghFLV:e228245: § 6505.
20   This enabled that chemical producers issued production allowances could ensure a monopoly on production while keeping prices high given that caps on production restricted quantities of the chemicals on the market. Barthold, T. A. (1994). Issues in the Design of Environmental Excise Taxes. *Journal of Economic Perspectives,* 8(1), at 136 at Note 4; Cook, E. (ed.) (1996, November), *op. cit. supra* at n.17 chapter 1.

revenue.[21] By 2012, the tax had generated US$4.4 billion. That money has been deposited in the General Fund of the US Treasury for untied government spending. Possibly with the exception of some of the revenue being spent on clean energy initiatives, the funds were not earmarked for any other specific purpose.[22] While Congress could have stipulated that the tax revenue be used to create a public fund to aid in compensating skin cancer losses, for future skin cancer, no documentation has been found that supports that such an idea was even floated.

This policy contrasts with government choices to allocate other excise tax revenue to compensatory trust funds. According to the Joint Committee on Taxation 2011 report, a total of 47 different excise taxes were imposed by the federal government, 24 of which were dedicated to specific trust funds. Of these, at least three serve to provide damage compensation:

- The Oil Spill Liability Trust Fund and excise tax was established under the same 1989 Omnibus Budget Reconciliation Act in 1989.[23] The oil tax[24] came in the aftermath of the Exxon Valdez incident[25] for the purpose of supporting oil spill prevention and clean-up costs as well as to compensate damaged parties – beyond what responsible parties are able to pay.[26] Individuals incurring property damage and economic losses (but not personal injury) as a result of oil spills can claim compensation directly from the Fund.[27] As of 2011, the Fund so far has accrued almost US$2 billion including tax payments, penalties and

21   Cook, E. (ed.) (1996, November), *op. cit. supra* at n.17 chapter 1, at 41; Barthold, T. A. (1994), *op. cit. supra* at n.20, at 137.

22   This has been suggested by a number of scholars, however, a clear policy statement on such budget allocation could not be found. See Barthold, T. A. (1994), *op. cit. supra* at n.20, at 133–151; Cook, E. (ed.) (1996, November), *op. cit. supra* at n.17 chapter 1; Gale, R. and Barg, S. (eds) (2013). *Green Budget Reform: An International Casebook of Leading Practices*. New York: Earthscan. In addition, a document by Friends of the Earth states that the revenue from increased taxes on the chemicals was earmarked to help pay for income tax credits for "clean-fuelled vehicles and the production of clean electricity" in line with the National Energy Policy Act of 1992, see Friends of the Earth (1997, June 17). Tax Bill Misses Green Mark: http://wgbis.ces.iisc.ernet.in/envis/doc97html/envenv618.html.

23   Boroshok, S. (1993). *Environmental Excise Taxes, Focusing on Ozone-Depleting Chemicals, 1993:* www.irs.gov/pub/irs-soi/93exenviro.pdf at 9.

24   Staff of the Joint Committee on Taxation (2011), *op. cit. supra* at n.16, at 19: Originally the tax was set at US$0.05 per barrel (42 gallons of crude oil). The tax has increased to US$0.08 per barrel and is expected to increase one cent in 2017.

25   Barthold, T. A. (1994), *op. cit. supra* at n.20, at 134.

26   Boroshok, S. (1993), *op. cit. supra* at n.23.

27   US Coast Guard National Pollution Funds Center (2012, April). A Compliance Guide for Submitting Claims Under the Oil Pollution Act of 1990. Retrieved from United States Coast Guard: www.uscg.mil/ccs/npfc/docs/PDFs/urg/Ch6/NPFCClaimantGuide.pdf, at 9.

interest over time and was projected to be valued at US$7.5 billion by 2020 if left untapped.[28]

* The Black Lung Disability Trust Fund taxes coal and provides resources to compensate coal miners for lung injuries and their survivors in case of death.[29]

* The Vaccine Injury Compensation Trust Fund was set up to pay compensation to individuals who suffered injury or death as a result of a defective vaccine administered after September 30, 1988.[30] It also supports the federal government in administering the compensation programme.[31]

These examples show that compensation oriented federal excise tax trust funds do exist and could have been applied as models for the use of ODC tax revenue. Given this and the current skin cancer plight in the US, it is fair to question whether Congress purposefully or inadvertently missed the opportunity to do so. Assuming the former, in light of Congresses' decision to expressly not pre-empt State common law tort actions which was taken at the same time the chemical excise tax was created, it may be inferred that Congress left open the door for future liability suits if and when a defensible cause of action could be brought. This conjecture would be supportive of the *ozone layer case*'s attempt to seek just remedies. However, if this was a missed opportunity then lessons may be drawn from this experience for the future. Had a trust fund been put in place, the plaintiffs in the *ozone layer case* would be greatly eased in accessing compensation as they could avoid litigation and litigation costs altogether.

In the future, Congress may establish a skin cancer compensation fund similar to the Radiation Exposure Compensation Program.[32] Courts have

---

28   Staff of the Joint Committee on Taxation (2011), *op. cit. supra* at n.16, at 66.

29   See *Federal Register. (2014, April 17). Workers Compensation Programs Office: www.federalregister.gov/agencies/workers-compensation-programs-office; United States Department of Labor. (2014). Division of Coal Mine Workers' Compensation (DCMWC): Important Notice Regarding Recent Changes in the Black Lung Benefits Act.*

30   Staff of the Joint Committee on Taxation (2011), *op. cit. supra* at n.16, at 26–27: Taxable vaccines include those containing polio virus, diphtheria toxoid, tetanus toxoid, pertussis bacteria, extracted or partial cell bacteria, or specific pertussis antigens, those against measles, mumps, or rubella, hepatitis A, hepatitis B, chicken pox, rotavirus gastroenteritis, streptococcus pneumonia, influenza and human papillomavirus and meningococcal vaccines.

31   *Id.* at 27.

32   Although upon reviewing the cases the Utah District Court found that the government had acted negligently and that some of the plaintiffs should be provided compensation as they had established causation, that decision was reversed when the United States Court of Appeals determined that the government was exempt from liability under the "discretionary function" provision of the Federal Tort Claims Act. The legal result left the plaintiffs without remedy until Congress enacted the Radiation Exposure Compensation Act in October 1990 which provides US$50,000 to victims suffering injuries from radiation exposure caused by governmental nuclear testing. (As of June 2014, compensation

recommended the same to streamline compensation for persons with asbestos related injuries.[33] However, unless Congress unilaterally decides to allocate public resources to that cause, the only possible way to trigger the development of a compensation scheme would be through litigating the *ozone layer case.*

11.3 Are other legal remedies available, and if not, is a tort remedy warranted?

Legal remedies other than the *ozone layer case* may be available to individual skin cancer victims. They could sue their employers or others responsible for their protection. Some such cases have been tried but with varying success. For example, a number of individuals have pursued redress through worker compensation schemes. In California, New York, Pennsylvania and Texas, appeal boards have determined that skin cancer is an occupational disease which has enabled injured petitioners to seek recovery.[34] Also, the Appellate Division of the New York Supreme Court has ruled similarly, recognising the causal link between skin cancer injury and occupational solar UV radiation exposure.[35] However, in other cases, the same success has not been witnessed.[36] One caveat may be the Occupational

to the tune of US$890 million had been authorized and a total of 22,615 claims had been received of which 17,799 had been approved, 4,202 were denied and 614 were pending.) Radiation Exposure Compensation Program (n.d.). *Radiation Exposure Compensation Act.* Retrieved from United States Department of Justice: www.justice.gov/civil/common/reca.html; *Allen v. United States*, 816 F. 2d 1417 (United States Court of Appeals, 10th Circuit April 20, 1987) at 1419, 1424; United States Department of Justice, Civil Division (2014, June 26). Radiation Exposure Compensation System, Claims to Date Summary of Claims Received by 06/26/2014 All Claims. Retrieved from United States Department of Justice: www.justice.gov/civil/omp/omi/Tre_SysClaimsToDateSum.pdf.

33   Gifford, D. G. (2013), *op. cit. supra* at n.2 chapter 3, at 72–76: However, examples of Congress establishing an individual compensation fund in reaction to court judgment are limited. In asbestos litigation, two attempts to establish funds as a part of a "global settlement agreement" were rejected by the Supreme Court for a number of reasons. One argument was that Congress, not the judiciary, should as a part of national policy set up a nationwide compensation fund to support asbestos victims.

34   Rocky Mountain Sunscreen (2005). Skin Cancer Caused by Sun Exposure Is A Work-Related Injury. Retrieved from www.rmsunscreen.com/pdf/UV_Law_Suit_Info.pdf.

35   *McKillop vs. McKillop Funeral Livery*, 188 AD 2d 996 (1992). However, the case appears unique as the plaintiff suffered from a rare form of skin cancer.

36   *Braden v. City of Hialeah*, 34146, 177 So. 2d 235 (Fla. 1965). In 1965, a woman who had been working as a lifeguard and swimming instructor for five years and later contracted skin cancer, claimed that her illness was an occupational disease and that she should be compensated for remedial treatment. In the case, the Florida Supreme Court examined the Florida Industrial Commission decision to award "certain compensation benefits". In its review, the Court found "debatable the issue of fact whether the petitioner's skin cancer was a direct result of exposure to the sun in her employment". On one hand the Court noted that her employment did subject her "to an unusual degree of exposure to the sun". It also noted that the victim's fair skinned physical make up may have made her more susceptible to skin cancer. Testimony provided however was not able to support the

Safety and Health Administration's (OSHA) reluctance to recognise skin cancer as an occupational disease and to demand that employers protect their employees from the sun's radiation. OSHA does impose the obligation to provide employees with a job and a place of work that is "free from recognized hazards that are causing or are likely to cause death or serious physical harm to his employees".[37] However, OSHA does not mandate employee exposure limits specific to UV radiation[38] or employee protection measures.[39]

Still, even if it would be possible to claim skin cancer as an occupational disease, plaintiffs invariably face challenges in proving that their injury was the result of sun exposure on and not off the job. Proving causation becomes even more complex if a plaintiff would have more than one employer during his or her lifetime prior to developing the disease. Further, such compensation schemes leave out unemployed persons, particularly young and elderly men and women. Overall, the approach to seek other legal remedies appears both daunting and uncertain to result in favourable outcomes to plaintiffs. Even if such remedies would be possible, they would not achieve the corrective purpose sought in the *ozone layer case*. The actors which allegedly caused the harm would not have been properly and fairly made to account for it. These considerations lead to the conclusion that a tort remedy pursued through the *ozone layer case* would be the most just way to remedy skin cancer damages and losses in America.

Apropos, the *ozone layer case* calls into question whether liability and compensation payment should be imposed on the companies, and their successors, for having contributed to a global harm which today has reverberating impacts on human health and the environment. It is both a legal and a policy question. On the policy side, the issues concern whether a legal judgment would achieve corrective justice, social justice and deterrence to which the purposes of tort law would aspire. Pertinently, what would be the effect of a legal judgment in favour of the plaintiffs or the defendants, and what would be the implications if the *ozone layer case* is never heard?

Court's conclusion that the resulting skin cancer could be construed as an occupational hazard. Accordingly, the Supreme Court affirmed the Commission's finding that skin cancer in this case could not constitute an occupational disease and reversed its decision to affirm some compensation on the grounds that the Commission had no legal basis to do so.

37 Surgeon General's Report (2014), *op. cit. supra* at n.27 chapter 1, at 78.
38 *Ibid.*
39 *Id.* at 42.

12 Tort law policy basis for the ozone layer case

12.1 Corrective justice

The contours of the *ozone layer case* would warrant a plea for corrective justice. It is fair to say that the increased skin cancer threat embodies an unreciprocal harm which vulnerable groups of people must now face as a result of the business behaviour of ODC producers between 1976 and 1992. Arguably, the injustices born by these victims should be rectified. That remedy should be afforded by the most direct harm causing actors by means of compensation, apologetic actions and/or abatement measures.

At present, the most plausible way that such a remedy could be achieved would be through tort litigation. However, for individual plaintiffs, seeking that remedy will not be easy. They will face an uphill battle in proving their health injuries and will bear significant legal costs in the process. If many persons seek compensation, the court system will become overstretched. Therefore, the best possibility for corrective justice to be achieved would be for State governments to bring claims on behalf of their citizens.[1] As discussed in Chapter 5, the plaintiffs could bring causes of action with best hope of victory on the public nuisance theory and the strict product liability failure to warn theory. Should liability be found or a settlement be reached,[2] States could then offer compensation through public healthcare programmes and funds. They could also remedy future skin cancer victims by investing in abatement measures such as education, early detection, medical research for skin cancer cures and building shaded play areas for children.

---

1   Although State governments are proposed as the primary litigants and recipients of compensation in the *ozone layer case*, this does not preclude the possibility of other public institutions, public interest groups, foundations, or other relevant organisations being party to and recipients of compensatory damages insofar as their purpose is to support present and future skin cancer victims and their families.
2   Percival, R. V. (2012, June 28). Testimony of Robert V. Percival before the House Committee on Oversight and Government Reform: Hearing on "Mandate Madness: When Sue and Settle Just isn't Enough". Retrieved from http://oversight.house.gov/wp-content/uploads/2012/06/6-28-12-TechIP-Percival.pdf. A settlement would "avoid the time and expense of protracted litigation, free up valuable judicial resources and enable both parties to reduce the risk of unfavourable litigation outcomes".

Another way corrective justice could be achieved is that the management of former and successor ODC producer companies voluntarily commit to apologetic actions. Such actions could be triggered through social pressure. Corporations concerned with reputation and adherence to their social responsibility policies may choose to independently provide redress. As a result, they may recognise their contribution to the current skin cancer malady in America and offer to contribute financially to alleviating some of the burden which individuals and US States must unduly bear. Conceivably, they could set up a skin cancer compensation fund which could be administered by US States or other third parties. They could also contribute to numerous abatement measures described above.

The advantage of such voluntary actions is that certain types of compensation could be afforded while litigation and reputational costs could be avoided. The remedies could suffice in correcting the skin cancer injustices. The downside is that the deterrence and social justice effect would be weakened. As discussed below, the former impact is sorely needed, arguably, to transform corporate behaviour in light of current global environmental challenges like climate change. Equally, the need for social justice is predicated by the loss of rights and freedoms of individuals which a legal judgement of fault may satisfy.

Both methods of achieving corrective justice will have economic impacts. Ideally, some of the financial burdens of the plaintiff class will be relieved through compensatory payments. However, soliciting compensation from the former ODC producers and their successor companies might set back their research and development of new chemicals and technologies that are of great value to society and possibly lifesaving. Further, the defendants would likely pass on those penalties in the price of their products (within competitive limits), thus adding to financial burdens of consumers. The valid concerns call into question whether Americans would be better off economically even with the increased skin cancer burden: is it more feasible that 245 million adults[3] pay higher prices for chemical products or that 5 million persons with skin cancer afford their disease related losses?

Further, it may be unfair to penalise the US companies alone and the other multinational chemical companies largely from Europe and Japan which also contributed to the depletion of the ozone layer during the 1970s and 1980s.[4] Although pursing the liability of such companies is possible, that effort requires taking into account a range of jurisdictional and other legal issues.[5] More research would be needed to investigate this option.

---

3   According to 2014 statistics collected by the US Census Bureau at http://quickfacts.census.gov/qfd/states/00000.html.
4   See Table 2.2 in Chapter 2 *supra*.
5   For example, the ability to pursue the liability of foreign companies in US courts has largely been extinguished following the Supreme Court ruling in *Daimler AG v. Bauman, et al.*, 134 S Ct. 746 (2014).

Nevertheless, the *ozone layer case* which is proposed as a first instance liability test would only join the US companies as defendants and assumes that they alone would be penalised. As a result, they may suffer competitive disadvantages.

This raises another related concern i.e. whether a plaintiff favourable decision in the *ozone layer case* would open the floodgates to hundreds of skin cancer cases filed by US and non-US citizens. However, as discussed above, this would probably not happen given the ordeal in providing causation in individual cases. Courts could foreclose on the possibility of individual claims for this reason. Foreigners would also likely face challenges in establishing jurisdiction as US courts often reject tort claims brought by aliens on the ground of *forum non conveniens*.[6] This is often because the wrongful behaviour which causes the injury takes place in another country. However, in the *ozone layer case*, the damage caused is global, having damaging effects in all countries. As such, foreign plaintiffs may have an advantage in establishing jurisdiction. This as well as whether US companies could be sued overseas requires further investigation. Further, whether the *ozone layer case* would have life outside the US also deserves further consideration. For example, Norway has the highest skin cancer incidence and death rates in Europe. Could Norwegian citizens or public agencies bring damage claims against European companies such as Solvay, Hoechst, and Arkema for their contributions to stratospheric ozone loss? These are relevant questions when contemplating the future of the *ozone layer case*.

12.2 Social justice

On its face, the *ozone layer case* is not imploring the cause of social justice. Today, there seems to be no observable public outrage which claims that skin cancer injustices against society have been perpetrated and which demands that the injuries of skin cancer victims be addressed.[7] Few people even recognise that the stratospheric ozone loss is still a problem let alone that its loss and cause of loss are connected with ODCs.[8] Some writers have

---

6   See e.g., Freedman, W. (1988). *Foreign Plaintiffs in Products Liability Actions The Defense of Forum Non Conveniens*. Quorum Books; Springer, B. J. (2015). An Inconvenient Truth: How Forum Non Conveniens Doctrine Allows Defendants to Escape State Court Jurisdiction. *University of Pennsylvania Law Review*, 163, 833.

7   News reports researched in preparing this publication did not reveal such public sentiment. This contrasts with media coverage on indoor tanning services which has stirred public outcry to enforce prohibitions on underage use. See e.g. Teich, M. (2010). Nations Unite Against Tanning: The Impact of the IARC Report. *The Melanoma Letter*, 28(2).

8   This statement is made based on personal interviews and conversations with individuals throughout the course of writing this study.

characterised this as form of social amnesia.[9] The ozone layer problem appears now not only physically and temporally distant but also cognitively removed. To the contrary, a number of former ODC companies have been awarded for their efforts to transition to safer technologies.[10] Further, in assessing the negligence of the defendant chemical companies, publicly available information regarding their conduct did not convey that it was socially reprehensible, reckless or wanton.

However, if chemical producers had concealed information or conspired to withhold information revealing that the risks of harm were unduly great or that chemical replacements were technically and commercially feasible much earlier, then grounds for gross or reckless negligence would exist. This would be the type of egregious behaviour which charged the tobacco industry with liability.[11] The companies' failure to take precautionary measures and to inflate the risk of harm by increasing production and growing domestic and global markets, would appear as an "entire want of care" and a display of conscious indifference to the welfare of people.[12] Still, the appearance and the existence of conscious indifference are two different matters. That indifference is conscious relates back to the certainty of what the companies knew about the harm which their products would cause rather than about who specifically would be hurt. The most telling analogy was made in *Atlas Chemical Industries, Inc. v. Anderson* (1974):

> It is certain that if one throws a live hand grenade into a crowd, and it explodes, it is bound to hurt some members of the crowd. No one would argue for a moment that the act was not malicious, and neither could it be successfully argued that, if the plaintiff were one of those hurt, the defendant did not intend to specifically hurt the plaintiff.[13]

In the *ozone layer case*, no circumstantial evidence reflects that the companies premeditated harm to the environment and skin cancer deaths. Such information could be disclosed at trial but that can only be assumed.

9   Singer, M. and Baer, H. A. (2009). *Killer Commodities: Public Health and the Corporate Production of Harm.* Lanham: AltaMira Press.
10 DuPont, Honeywell, AlliedSignal and Vulcan Materials were winners of the EPA Montreal Protocol Awards: www3.epa.gov/ozone/awards/winners.html; DuPont received the US National Medal of Technology for CFC Policy and Technology Leadership in 2003 (www.dupont.com/corporate-functions/our-company/insights/articles/position-statements/articles/montreal-protocol.html).
11 Gifford, D. G. (2013), *op. cit. supra* at n.2 chapter 3, at 108: "During the 1990s, the rising tide of antitobacco public sentiment was fueled by disclosure from several former tobacco company employees that tobacco companies had known for decades that nicotine was addictive and, in fact, that the companies had manipulated the nictine content to assure better delivery of the addictive substance".
12 *Missouri Pacific Railway Company v. Shuford,* 72 Tex. 165 (1888); *Stephens v. Dunn,* 417 SW 2d 608, 613 (Court of Civil Appeals of Texas 1967).
13 *Atlas Chemical Industries, Inc. v. Anderson,* 514 SW 2d 309, 320 (Tex: Court of Civil Appeals, 6th Dist. 1974).

Yet, unsettling issues remain. In his book *Moral Mazes*, Robert Jackall confronts directly the moral decisions which corporate managers of ODC companies were faced with in light of scientific uncertainty. Jackall bases his observations on research and interviews he conducted with those actors although he uses alias names in referring to those companies.[14] He argues essentially that corporate structures and decision-making frameworks are designed to predicate conscious indifference. An excerpt from his book reads:

> The sheer impersonality of the vast markets that corporations service also helps managers to achieve distance and abstractness appropriate to and necessary for their roles. A high-ranking official of Covenant Corporation muses about this problem, referring to the possible, though controverted, harm that one of Alchemy Inc.'s chemicals might produce:
>
>> It gets hard. Now, suppose that the ozone depletion theory were correct and you knew that these fifty people were going to get skin cancer because you produced chlorofluorocarbons (CFCs). Well, there would be no question. You would just stop production. But suppose that you didn't know the fifty people and it wasn't at all clear that CFCs were at fault, or entirely at fault. What do you do then?[15]
>
> An upper-middle official at the chemical company echoes the same sentiment talking about a different though similar problem:
>
>> Certainly no one wants to significantly damage the environment or the health of individuals. But it's a different thing to sit and say it's OK for twenty people out of one million to die because of chlorinated water in the drinking water supply when the cost of warding off those deaths is $25 million to remove the halogenated hydrocarbon from the water. Is it worth it to spend that much money? I don't know how to answer that question as long as I'm not one of those twenty people. As long as those people can't be *identified*, as long as they are not *specific* people, it's OK. Isn't that strange? So you put a filter on your own house and try to protect yourself.[16]
>
> Impersonality provides the psychological distance necessary to make what managers call "hard choices". The high-ranking Covenant official cited a moment ago extends his reflection on this issue by posing a hypothetical case:

14   Jackall, R. (2010). *Moral Mazes: The World of Corporate Managers*. Oxford University Press.
15   *Id.* at 134.
16   *Ibid.*

Suppose that you had a candy bar factory and you were touring the plant and you saw with your own eyes a worker slip a razor blade into a bar. And before you could stop the machine, there were a thousand bars more made and the one with the razor blade was mixed up. Well, there's no question that you would get rid of the thousand candy bars. But what if it were a million bars? Well, I don't know what I'd do.

The issues Jackall raises are critical because they help explain, partially, why corporate managers of ozone depleting companies could have avoided taking precautionary measures. The justification is important to reflect because it underscores the need for fundamental policy measures and incentives to direct ethical business decisions. The *ozone layer case* cuts to the heart and the chase of these dilemmas by urging a response on whether ODC producers had the technical capacity to take precautionary action and whether they chose not to use that technology at the expense of probable but not certain deaths of thousands of people. The case is highly unusual in that the fate of the ozone layer was in the hands of a handful of powerful companies which controlled both the problem and its solutions. They were relied on to stop and solve the threat of environmental catastrophe.[17] In such an extraordinary situation, a reasonable person should surmise that the companies had an exceptional obligation to take precautions. However, the companies rather contributed to amplifying the unreasonable risk of harm by increasing production. They achieved buy-in and complicity of downstream users and perhaps the public by maintaining that the risks were negligible – that CFCs were safe. Yet, they appear to have been as uncertain of the intensity of the risk as scientists and policy makers were – in being unable to provide conclusive evidence that the risk was certain. In light of such uncertainty, the corporations seem to have been gambling the probability of a risk which, one could argue, on moral and legal grounds, they should not have been permitted to do. Presumably, human reason should dictate that such behaviour should be deterred. Reasonable people in society might also conclude that the chemical producers' conduct at the time should be corrected even if they contributed to mitigating the risk they created afterwards and even if an irreversible environmental disaster was avoided. Demands for social justice, correction and deterrence could state the following rule:

> *When [a small] [limited] [number/group of] actors wield such considerable power over and substantially control or contribute to risks that can endanger a public good vital to life on earth and to safeguarding the environment and human wellbeing, and cause unreasonable interferences with public rights, those actors have an unconditional duty to prevent that risk even if full scientific certainty is not possible.*

17   Falkner, R. (2005), *op. cit. supra* at n.147 chapter 2.

The rule might beckon a liability finding which is more than negligence but less than gross negligence. On this basis, there would be a basis for tort litigation to be pursued to achieve social justice – even if the demand for social vengeance is not visible.

In the future if the public would become outraged by the moral issues the case evokes, or when skin cancer prevalence reaches an intolerable tipping point, then the tort litigation may not be alone in compelling the chemical producers to settle differences. Similar to the social pressure argument made in connection with the corrective justice goal, wide public pleas for damage payments and policy change may achieve something close to social justice. More effective corporate social responsibility programmes,[18] voluntary compensation schemes[19] and even regulatory reforms could evolve.[20]

One historic and most telling example of this is the Johnstown flood story. On May 31, 1889, one of the largest dams in the United States, covering 450 acres, burst and flooded Pennsylvania's Johnstown valley killing 2,000 people.[21] The dam supported Lake Conemaugh, a recreational area owned by the South Fork Fishing and Hunting Club, a group of wealthy Pittsburgh industrialists including Andrew Carnegie, Andrew Mellon and Henry Clay Frick.[22] Despite a decade of repeated warnings of the dam's engineering faults, the club owners failed to have it sufficiently repaired. As predicted, heavy waters brought on by a rainstorm exerted stress on the dam walls forcing it to give way and unleash 20,000,000 tons of water into the valley.[23] Although negligence was alleged, the historic catastrophe never resulted in a liability determination against the "club of the wealthy elite" due to the difficulty of establishing fault, the reluctance of courts to apply the no-fault doctrine and the stance of the judiciary to support industrial activities for the greater good of economic development.[24]

However, the death toll and alleged reckless conduct of the owners incited such public outrage and demand for justice across the country that

18   See Oliviero, M. B. and Simmons, A. (2002). Who's Minding the Store? Global Civil Society and Corporate Responsibility. In M. Glasius, M. Kaldor and H. Anheier (eds), *Global Civil Society 2002*. Oxford University Press.
19   See Roberts, R. C. (2005). *Injustice and Rectification*. New York: Peter Lang; Vinayagamoorthy, K. (2013). Apologies in the Marketplace. *Pace Law Review*, 33(3).
20   See generally, Glasius, M., Kaldor, M. and Anheier, H. (eds). (2005). *Global Civil Society 2005/6*. London: Sage.
21   Shugerman, J. H. (2000). The Floodgates of Strict Liability: Bursting Reservoirs and the Adoption of Fletcher v. Rylands in the Gilded Age. *The Yale Law Journal*, 110, 333, at 359; See also Commonwealth of Pennsylvania (2014). *The "Great Johnstown Flood" May 31, 1889*: www.portal.state.pa.us/portal/server.pt/community/documents_from_1865_-_1945/20425/johnstown_flood/998883; Johnstown Area Heritage Association; Johnstown Flood Museum (2014). *History of the Johnstown Flood*: www.jaha.org/FloodMuseum/history.html.
22   Shugerman, J. H. (2000), *op. cit. supra* at n.21, at 359.
23   *Ibid.*
24   *Id.* at 361.

social and legal change were inevitable. While the club never admitted responsibility for the disaster and never paid legal compensation, voluntary actions helped cover the flood damages. Some club members donated to relief and reconstruction efforts while national charity drives together with international assistance from 12 countries raised close to US$3.8 million to aid the victims.[25] Further, according to Jed Shugerman (2000), the blatant injustice of the tragedy exhorted courts in numerous jurisdictions to stand up to the challenge of preventing affluent business proprietors from escaping liability. This led to the adoption of strict liability rules in numerous jurisdictions. And, in ensuing cases, courts found industry liable for pollution and flooding.[26] This included at least one judgment against Carnegie Brothers & Co., Ltd. for property damage caused by pollution from the company's coal burning coke ovens.[27] In addition, the traumatic event also led to the adoption of local policies and projects to prevent future floods, assist the evacuation of people and ensure safe dam reconstruction.[28] So, while tort law did not prevail to achieve social justice in that case, public indignation largely fuelled by the media did spur subsequent social, judicial and legislative actions which, arguably, did rectify the imbalance of power previously weighted heavily on the side of industry.

Thus the same policy outcomes might also be possible in the *ozone layer case* – although they appear quite ambitious right now. Some realistic impacts could be that:

- The public's right to know is satisfied concerning the truth behind the corporate decisions taken in the last century which contributed to stratospheric ozone loss, increased skin cancer prevalence and also climate change.
- A legal duty of care is established for companies to uphold the precautionary principle, when they exert exclusive control over a risk of unreasonable harm which affects a public good.
- Judicial precedent is established that corporations can be held to account for not meeting that duty of care. As discussed next, such a precedent can act as a deterrent and incentive for companies to reduce their contribution to environmental harms, including global warming, which are injurious to public interests and goods.

---

25 Johnstown Area Heritage Association (2014). *History of the Johnstown Flood.* Retrieved May 2, 2014, from Johnstown Flood Museum: www.jaha.org/FloodMuseum/history.html.
26 Shugerman, J. H. (2000), *op. cit. supra* at n.21, at 366–72.
27 *Id.* citing Robb v. Carnegie Bros. & Co., Limited, 22 A. 649 (Supreme Court of Pennsylvania October 5, 1891).
28 Miller, A. (2010, March 30). *The Johnstown Flood of 1889:* www.academia.edu/1024972/The_Johnstown_Flood_of_1889#, at 8.

12.3 Deterrence

Tort law's deterrence function specific to the production, marketing and emission of ODCs is marginal since public laws and policies have clearly transformed those activities. The deterrence value is rather in curbing corporate behaviour which risks causing large scale, long term harm to the environment and ends up hurting people – individuals, vulnerable groups, even entire populations. As such, it would exhort such corporations to exercise precautionary care when making business decisions and conducting business activities.

A plaintiff favourable court judgment could:

- Establish a clear duty of precautionary care incumbent on actors in society whose activities could create unreasonable, long term and unreciprocal risks to the environment and human beings. Courts could adopt a rule which imposes a legal duty of care on actors who contribute substantially to non-reciprocal, unreasonable risk of harm of great magnitude, to take precautionary measures to prevent or control that risk *even if* the risk is uncertain. In doing so, that duty would apply irrespective of whether public policy, laws or regulations exist to impose that duty. This finding would establish a strong deterrence policy by sending a clear message to companies that regulatory signals alone are not needed for them to initiate precautionary actions to protect the environment and human health. In the absence of regulations, the threat of liability will exist. In light of policy constraints concerning climate change in the United States today, such a precedent could influence companies to proactively reduce greenhouse gas emissions while regulations are delayed. Chemical producers and downstream users would be encouraged to hasten innovation to curb HFC production, use and emissions.
- Reinforce the common law duty of companies to alert and inform their customers about the potential, latent dangers their products can cause even if those harms are remote. This can be achieved by a finding that the ODCs were defective products on the failure to warn theory. With respect to climate change, such a ruling, arguably, would have a significant deterrence impact on corporate conduct particularly regarding business activities which involve sizeable greenhouse gas emissions. Warnings and information attached to goods and services which contribute to global warming can influence consumer behaviour. Consumer choice can influence what products and services are placed on the market and can equally drive business innovation which reduces environmental and human harms.[29]

---

29 Benedick (1998), *op. cit. supra* at n.22 chapter 1, at 317: As recounted in this study, the US experience in requiring that warning labels be placed on aerosol products influenced consumer demands. This was the precise strategy which federal agencies pursued.

- Reduce the potential for negligent actors to escape liability in situations where proving causation is frustrated by the remoteness and latency of resulting injuries when factual causation exists. This requires giving preference and credibility to the substantial factor test and alternative, market share and "commingled product" market share liability theories. It also would need to be substantiated by imposing a financial penalty in the form of compensatory payments.
- Advance a "future-harm-sensitive" cost benefit analysis framework. Through litigating the *ozone layer case*, judges and juries would have to conduct a utility risk assessment to determine whether ODCs would have qualified as defective products in the 1970s and 1980s. That assessment could analyse costs and benefits with renewed attention to economic and non-economic damages. This would present an opportunity to advance correct economic models by weighing in the future costs of harm in a liability assessment. It would also push legal thinking on the valuation of non-economic losses in that equation. That exercise could be informed by a more sober accounting between what costs were projected (and the basis for those projections) and what the actual expenses have been. This is true for both damage and precautionary costs. The effort could flesh out the difference been real and inflated costs – which would be critical for an objective risk utility calculation. By working through these issues, the *ozone layer cases* provides an opportunity to reconsider and progress current costs benefit analysis frameworks which do not sufficiently capture the weight of long term injury. This can be useful for courts as well as policy makers.

Essentially, the policy goal which all of these possible deterrence effects could achieve through a tort remedy in the *ozone layer case*, is to fortify the recognition of a common duty on corporations to respect the precautionary principle. In this way, tort law can contribute to deterring socially undesirable conduct which causes harm in both near and far futures. The contribution can help address deeper concerns about inadequate public and private responses to long term catastrophes due to myopic political and economic interests. As Richard Benedick (1998) has reflected about the processes leading up to the adoption of the Montreal Protocol:

> Under current accounting standards, enterprises can avoid the "external" costs of environmental damage caused by their activities, but the bills, whether in terms of health or quality of life or depleted resources, must be paid somewhere or sometime by society. And the economist's prescription for coping with future monetary flows is inadequate for responding to large but distant damages: present-value discounting can reduce even huge long-term costs, in terms of harm to future generations, to insignificance, while predisposing managers to maximise short-run profits. Rather than rewarding environmental

protection efforts, our financial markets regard them as irksome charges against current profits. This, the application by policymakers and investors of the tools of conventional economics may result in precisely the wrong decisions from an ecological perspective."[30]

Benedick underscores a clear imperative that "politicians... resist a tendency to lend too much credence to self-serving economic interests that demand scientific certainty, maintain dangers are remote and unlikely, and insist that costs of changing their ways are astronomical."[31] In the face of uncertain knowledge concerning risks of high magnitude, ethics may drive ever difficult but responsible actions necessary to benefit future generations.[32]

Ultimately, the *ozone layer case* is an opportunity to revisit a near catastrophe and evaluate the behaviour of companies that were both part of the problem and the solution. It is chance to advance the legal and ethical obligations as well as the right incentives which corporations will ever need to embrace today in the face of serious climate change.

---

30   *Id.* at 309.
31   *Id.* at 314.
32   *Id.* at 332.

13 Lessons and benefits for climate change policy and litigation

Should the *ozone layer case* ever be tried and a favourable decision be delivered for the plaintiffs, it could establish some important legal rules which would benefit the development of common law and climate policy in the United States. Even if the case never sees its day in court, the conclusions reached in testing the case can nevertheless be useful in considering similar litigation or policy challenges involving potential or real long term environmental harm that causes latent injuries. These conclusions reflect the key legal determinations which a court would need to make for the *ozone layer case* to reach a successful outcome. These include:

- Establishing that a duty of care based on the precautionary principle exists for corporations which substantially control the source of harm which threatens to cause unreasonable risks of harm to the environment and human well-being, and unreasonable interferences with public rights. That duty of care can be used as a basis to hold those actors to account if they fail to thoroughly assess potential risks and take necessary precautions to avoid them even if full scientific uncertainty is wanting. Establishing this duty will create a cause of liability that functions as an incentive for such corporations to curb their emissions and transition to environmentally safe technology. This will aid in preventing an unnecessary escalation of future harms on account of delayed regulatory actions.
- Establishing that that duty of care extends to the duty to warn. Within acceptable limitations companies should be obliged to inform consumers of the carbon footprint of their products or services. Such information can influence consumer choices which can intern affect the market and either drive technological innovation or allow a pollution-heavy product to fall out (see below).
- Elaborating on the risk utility/cost benefit analysis frameworks employed to guide legal and policy decisions making. In assessing costs of precaution and costs of harm, it is important that long term economic and non-economic damage costs are fully accounted and weighed and that liberal discount rates are applied. Equally, cross-

checking the shorter term precautionary cost will help avoid gross overestimations. This can help steer courts, policy makers, and companies to err on the side of precaution.

The case might also support climate change litigation. As introduced in Chapter 2, given their high global warming potential (GWP), ODCs have also contributed to climate change. Moreover, HFCs and HCFCs, the gases chosen to replace ODCs, also have high GWPs. The case could be made that ODC and HFC producers have also contributed to climate change. It may be possible to isolate and show the overall impact these chemicals have had on the environment. However, given the causation challenges which plaintiffs would face, it is likely that this argument would be difficult to sustain and prevail in US courts.

Beyond this, the *ozone layer case* also provides important learning for citizens, governments and companies concerned with mitigating environmental risks and coping with latent environmental harms caused by those risks. Specific lessons can be applied for developing strategies to ensure and insure against global warming and climate change impacts.

- **Policy makers should heed the call to levy liabilities *ex ante* harm or establish adaptation oriented insurance schemes to cover costs of future damage.** Drawing from lessons learned in the *ozone layer case*, policy makers should expedite such measures to cope with climate change impacts in the United States.[1] By imposing a carbon tax,[2] in particular for large emissions sources, public revenue could be sequestered. It would be important that a sufficient portion of that money is invested to serve as future aid source for e.g. relief and recovery efforts in cases of drought, flooding, sea level rise and extreme weather events. If such a safety net is not created and sustained, then the government will find itself in a predicament similar to what it is now experiencing with regard to funding skin cancer prevention and treatment programmes. As the scale and costs of climate change impacts will be astronomically higher,[3] it will be critical that funds are ring fenced starting yesterday.

- **Policy makers should also be aware that if such a tax is not imposed on the source of emissions, then future scenarios will arise where the liability for climate-induced loss and damage and related adaptation costs will be displaced to other actors in society.** As in the *ozone layer*

1   US EPA (2015). Clean Power Plan for Existing Power Plants, at www.epa.gov/cleanpowerplan/clean-power-plan-existing-power-plants#federal-plan.

2   Carbon Tax Center (2015). What's a Carbon Tax?: www.carbontax.org/whats-a-carbon-tax/

3   Ackerman, F. and Stanton, E. (2008). *The Cost of Climate Change*. NRDC; United States Global Change Research Program (USGCRP) (2014). Third National Climate Assessment.

case, that responsibility to compensate injured parties may shift from the harm causing agents (chemical producers) to the actors charged with protection duties (lifeguards). This may be the inevitable reality in a future climate changed world since establishing the liability of the harm causing agents (heavy greenhouse gas emitters) will face the overwhelming challenge of proving causation. As discussed in Chapter 4, a number of US courts have pronounced that given the global nature of global warming and the sheer multitude of greenhouse gas emission sources, it is impossible to connect the concentrated emissions of power plants in one State with climatic damages experienced in that same State.[4] Further, the main demand in climate litigation has been for abatement measures, a personal injury or even a case brought by a US State would be more complex and not likely to succeed. These considerations underscore the need for an *ex ante* liability regime through a carbon or other environmental tax.

- **Consumers and citizens should be aware that their actions do have an impact on injuries and damages which they or future generations will face.** By using their purchasing power, consumers can drive technological change toward sustainable economic growth that avoids risking environmental and human harms.[5] Citizens can likewise influence public polices to insure against future damages. This should include accepting and supporting the levy of an *ex ante* environmental liability programme. As per the previous point, regarding climate change this would be a critical undertaking given predicted vulnerabilities of the United States to climate change impacts.[6]
- **Policy makers and citizens should be aware that the costs of transitioning to safer technologies will likely be inflated at the outset of policy change but in the long term may actually prove to be more affordable and sustainable.** Adequate information disclosure will be key in this regard. This was demonstrated in in the 1970s and 1990s when the production and use of ozone depleting chemicals was curbed. Ex-poste economic analyses revealed that switch costs were much less than the industry had projected. While the technology changes required to mitigate global warming are much more extensive, this experience can urge governments and citizens to demand accurate short and long term cost analyses. These estimates should be weighed against longer term projected damage costs to inform decisions and hasten actions to enable sustainable economic growth and environmental protection.

---

4   *Environmental Council v. Bellon*, 732 F.3d 1131 (9th Cir. 2013); *Native Village of Kivalina v. Exxon Mobile et al.*, No. 09-17490 (9th Cir. 2012).
5   Business Decisions Limited (2003). *The Power of Customers to Drive Innovation*. European Commission.
6   Lynn, K., MacKendrick, K. and Donoghue, E. (2011, August). *Social Vulnerability and Climate Change: Synthesis of Literature*. United States Department of Agriculture.

14 Conclusion

The *ozone layer case* may be a genuine possibility and an opportunity to remedy the stratospheric ozone damage and to deter human activities which pose unreasonable risks and threaten long term consequences. The best route for a plaintiff favourable outcome to be achieved would be for US States to bring product liability failure to warn and public nuisance actions on behalf of their residents. Their burden of proof to establish causation will be much less daunting than for individual plaintiffs. However, to prove negligence, more credible evidence will be needed to confirm what the defendants knew about their products' risks and about the feasibility of marketing alternative technologies. Such information which is not publicly disclosed could come to light through discovery procedures in litigation. Statutes of limitation and repose may be the most significant legal obstacles which will need to be overcome. A scientific, peer-reviewed report which clearly states the link between ozone depleting chemical production and the increased prevalence of skin cancers can help prove that the injuries are ripe for discovery.

Should the *ozone layer case* achieve a favourable decision, the judicial precedent could establish a duty of care on corporations to demonstrate the precautionary principle. It could deter future harms by sending a clear message to corporations that they will not escape liability when they contribute substantially to non-reciprocal, unreasonable risks of harm of great magnitude, even if the risks are uncertain. This is ultimately a policy question for courts to consider also in light of predictable climate change harms. The Paris Agreement reached in December 2015 may accelerate regulatory actions to limit greenhouse gas emissions at national levels. However, notwithstanding American leadership that made the Agreement possible, global warming regulation in the United States as elsewhere has been critically delayed. A court decision which adopts this precautionary rule, could incentivise companies to make the switch to environmentally sustainable technologies sooner rather than later.

A plaintiff favourable decision could also correct injustices and provide compensation to support skin cancer victims today and prevent future incidences and deaths. The financial contribution to cover additional costs due to increased skin cancer risks based on a 1975 year baseline is estimated at US$60 billion cumulatively between 2015 and 2030. This amount excludes non-economic losses. However, it includes appropriate liability discounts and represents approximately 13 percent of all costs during that period.

However, should a favourable outcome not be achieved, or should the *ozone layer case* never be attempted, a critical moral dilemma remains: *should a small group of corporations, which wield concentrated technical capacities and control over products or activities on which society relies and which pose potentially serious and irreversibly environmental risks, be allowed to gamble on the certainty of and increase those risks? Should such corporate actors be permitted to escape liability for the consequences of delaying precautionary actions to mitigate those risks, and for actually increasing the risks through market expansion?* These question may inspire public debate and action for social justice that leads to a non-legal solution for the *ozone layer case*. The question may also contribute to wider social environmental and human rights concerns which are at the heart of the struggle towards achieving sustainable development across the planet.

Appendix

Annual production of ozone depleting substance globally and by US companies in the United States, 1931–2012

Table A.1 Annual production of ozone depleting substance globally and by US companies in the United States, 1931–2012, in ODP metric tonnes, based on available data

Source/Year	Chlorofluorocarbons (CFC 11, 12, 113, 114 and 115)		Halon gases 1201 and 1302		Methyl chloroform		HCFCs		Methyl bromide		All chemicals	
	Global	US	Global	US	Global	US	Global	USA	Global	USA	Global	US
1931	544	280									544	280
1932	136	70									136	70
1933	318	164									318	164
1934	3,325	373									3,325	373
1935	3,743	537									3,743	537
1936	4,714	935									4,714	935
1937	6,120	1,658									6,120	1,658
1938	5,903	1,495									5,903	1,495
1939	7,137	2,079									7,137	2,079
1940	8,017	2,429									8,017	2,429
1941	9,932	3,364									9,932	3,364
1942	9,760	3,224									9,760	3,224
1943	12,318	4,438									12,318	4,438
1944	20,901	8,807									20,901	8,807
1945	24,457	10,535									24,457	10,535
1946	21,473	8,947									21,473	8,947
1947	25,755	11,049									25,755	11,049
1948	32,360	14,296									32,360	14,296
1949	35,418	15,768									35,418	15,768
1950	46,187	21,211									46,187	21,211
1951	50,514	23,337									50,514	23,337
1952	56,202	26,163									56,202	26,163
1953	69,175	32,844									69,175	32,844
1954	75,635	36,068									75,635	36,068
1955	89,869	43,193					100	100			89,969	43,293
1956	107,451	52,093					500	500			107,951	52,593
1957	114,592	55,667					1,000	1,000			115,592	56,667
1958	109,666	53,027					1,200	1,200			110,866	54,227

Table A.1 continued

Source/Year	Chlorofluorocarbons (CFC 11, 12, 113, 114 and 115)		Halon gases 1201 and 1302		Methyl chloroform		HCFCs		Methyl bromide		All chemicals	
	Global	US	Global	US	Global	US	Global	USA	Global	USA	Global	US
1959	130,151	63,423					1,500	1,500			131,651	64,923
1960	156,442	76,808					1,847	1,386			158,289	78,194
1961	176,563	87,016					1,945	1,458			178,508	88,474
1962	214,004	106,195					2,047	1,535			216,051	107,730
1963	247,824	123,458	250	93			2,155	1,616			250,229	125,166
1964	290,122	144,809	500	185			2,268	1,701			292,890	146,695
1965	322,349	170,452	900	333			2,388	1,552			325,637	172,337
1966	367,024	193,275	1,300	481			2,513	1,634			370,837	195,389
1967	412,859	216,612	2,000	740			2,645	1,720			417,504	219,071
1968	461,520	241,373	2,700	999			2,785	1,810			467,005	244,183
1969	525,956	275,434	3,700	1,369			2,931	1,905			532,587	278,708
1970	571,215	298,444	5,780	2,139			3,086	1,851			580,081	302,434
1971	617,391	321,874	10,600	3,922	17,500	9,625	3,333	2,000			648,824	337,421
1972	686,740	353,671	14,990	5,546	22,700	12,485	3,482	2,089			727,912	373,791
1973	786,483	408,236	21,170	7,833	27,900	15,345	4,087	2,452			839,640	433,865
1974	827,442	428,886	24,510	9,069	31,400	17,270	4,587	2,752			887,939	457,977
1975	758,021	392,234	31,590	11,688	30,700	16,885	4,125	2,475			824,436	423,283
Subtotal 1931–1975	8,503,728	4,336,254	119,990	44,396	130,200	71,610	50,522	34,236			8,804,440	4,486,496
1976	822,217	423,442	44,788	16,572	40,700	22,385	4,989	2,993	26,713	11,708	939,407	477,099
1977	781,953	308,444	50,500	18,685	48,000	26,400	5,638	3,343	27,258	11,947	913,349	368,818
1978	770,087	287,595	57,100	21,127	52,400	28,820	6,287	3,892	27,815	12,190	913,688	353,625
1979	742,711	263,657	66,020	24,427	50,600	27,830	7,210	3,817	28,382	12,439	894,923	332,171
1980	743,371	332,621	69,500	25,715	55,100	27,630	6,947	3,612	28,962	12,693	903,879	402,271
1981	745,064	335,279	77,007	28,493	54,800	26,230	7,194	3,741	29,553	12,952	913,617	406,694
1982	709,671	319,352	98,105	36,299	51,200	22,810	6,798	3,535	30,156	13,216	895,930	395,212
1983	775,008	348,754	98,637	36,496	54,000	23,460	7,915	4,116	30,771	13,486	966,331	426,311
1984	853,665	384,149	118,624	43,713	60,000	26,690	8,382	4,359	31,399	13,761	1,072,070	472,673

Table A.1 continued

Source/Year	Chlorofluorocarbons (CFC 11, 12, 113, 114 and 115)		Halon gases 1201 and 1302		Methyl chloroform		HCFCs		Methyl bromide		All chemicals	
	Global	US	Global	US	Global	US	Global	USA	Global	USA	Global	US
1985	875,874	394,143	136,018	50,055	58,700	24,550	8,437	4,387	33,609	14,043	1,112,639	487,179
1986	1,072,296	311,021	197,458	58,756	60,800	24,870	9,075	5,473	34,128	14,287	1,373,757	414,407
1987	1,142,205	339,829	168,729	64,632	62,700	25,110	9,532	5,473	39,357	16,103	1,422,522	443,146
1988	1,165,071	339,129	188,683	72,387	67,900	27,150	11,193	5,473	43,082	17,394	1,475,929	461,533
1989	1,045,998	320,436	185,252	61,229	69,400	31,517	46,029	6,559	45,240	18,244	1,391,918	437,985
1990	764,284	199,697	172,854	51,401	72,600	30,000	42,478	6,059	43,207	19,671	1,095,422	306,828
1991	664,310	172,164	150,289	41,565	60,500	28,000	44,354	6,059	39,857	18,151	959,311	265,940
1992	590,809	152,730	104,995	25,843	60,883	25,723	40,648	5,560	42,058	18,926	839,393	228,781
Subtotal 1976–1992	14,264,594	5,224,442	1,984,559	677,394	980,283	449,175	273,102	78,450	581,547	251,211	18,084,085	6,680,672
1993	506,031	127,712	71,189	18,915	39,532	20,637	40,329	7,127	43,895	19,753	700,975	194,144
1994	338,462	78,208	26,466		14,862	5,795	32,526	12,317	34,683	17,890	446,999	114,210
1995	253,768	34,728	42,241		11,505	4,599	38,055	14,810	36,243	18,331	381,812	72,467
1996	151,617	676	45,167		1,504	448	29,811	12,508	36,825	18,878	264,924	32,510
1997	158,755	739	50,559		1,856	437	30,551	12,488	37,047	16,424	278,768	30,088
1998	146,832	191	30,660		1,489	262	33,766	15,298	29,147	12,602	241,894	28,353
1999	146,780	436	25,192		1,695	246	36,762	14,451	27,569	10,360	237,998	25,493
2000	133,029	461	20,345		1,406	300	38,050	14,291	20,640	8,345	213,469	23,398
2001	100,934	495	13,660		1,042	197	34,831	12,280	17,014	5,901	167,480	18,873
2002	93824.5	593	9,368		1,373	2	35,755	12,399	15,323	7,727	155,644	20,722
2003	89854.3	570	4,695		728	2	30,725	5,503	14,782	7,718	183,958	13,793
2004	70925.8	453	1,318		329	125	31,894	6,151	10,883	6,589	145,358	13,318
2005	49558	211	5,780		641	125	32,536	6,009	11,777	6,502	144,559	12,846
2006	31761.6	1,088	1,147		616	172	36,627	5,716	7,726	4,689	128,970	11,664
2007	10388.4	576	1,003		509	13	41,507	5,645	6,471	3,771	120,415	10,004
2008	2746	32	895		423	99	39,150	4,865	6,700	3,563	96,725	8,559
2009	-3765.5	-76	1,703		263	-8	37,996	2,799	4,496	2,277	76,220	4,991
2010	-51.2	-888					38,283	2,348	2,733	1,662	51,405	3,122

Table A.1 continued

Source/Year	Chlorofluorocarbons (CFC 11, 12, 113, 114 and 115)		Halon gases 1201 and 1302		Methyl chloroform		HCFCs		Methyl bromide		All chemicals	
	Global	US	Global	US	Global	US	Global	USA	Global	USA	Global	US
2011	−2182.7	−1,272					38,627	2,089	2,403		43,777	1,425
2012	−1431.9	−1,015					39,721	1,498		608	35,955	483
Subtotal												
1992–2012	2,270,834	243,917	351,388	18,915	79,772	33,450	717,501	170,592	366,357	173,591	4,117,303	640,465
Total												
1930–2012	25,039,155	9,804,613	2,455,937	740,705	1,190,255	554,234	1,041,125	283,278	947,903	424,801	31,005,828	11,807,632

Sources include:

- United Nations Environment Programme Ozone Secretariat (2012). *Data Access Centre*. Retrieved from Publications: http://ozone.unep.org/new_site/en/ozone_data_tools_access.php. Chemical Manufacturers Association (1980). *UNEP/CCOL/5/9: 1980 WORLD PRODUCTION AND SALES OF FLUOROCARBONS*. Copenhagen: UNEP.
- Annual Fluorocarbon Production Reported (metric tons) (2009, June 2). Retrieved from Alternative Fluorocarbons Environmental Acceptability Study: www.afeas.org/data.php?page=prod_table.
- Alternative Fluorocarbons Environmental Acceptability Study (2007). Production and Sales of Fluorocarbons. Retrieved from Alternative Fluorocarbons Environmental Acceptability Study: www.afeas.org/overview.php.
- *Historical US Methyl Bromide Sales* (n.d.). Retrieved from Methyl Bromide Alternatives Outreach: http://mbao.org/methyl_back/sales.pdf; United Nations Environment Programme. Methyl Bromide Technical Options Committee (1998). Report of the Methyl Bromide Technical Options Committee. UNEP/Earthprint at 22.
- Gamlen, H., Lane, B. C., Midgley, M. and Steed, J. M. (1986). The production and release to the atmosphere of CCl3F and CCl2F2 (chlorofluorocarbons CFC 11 and CFC 12). *Atmospheric Environment*, 1077–1085.

Bibliography

Abraham, K. S. (1987). Individual Action and Collective Responsibility: The Dilemma of Mass Tort Reform. *Virginia Law Review.*

Ackerman, F. (2008, January). Critique of Cost–Benefit Analysis, and Alternative Approaches to Decision-making. Retrieved from Global Development and Environment Institute, Tufts University: www.ase.tufts.edu/gdae/Pubs/rp/Ack_UK_CBAcritique.pdf.

Ackerman, F. and Stanton, E. (2008). *The Cost of Climate Change.* NRDC.

Airgas (2005, July 1). Airgas Completes Acquisition of LaRoche Industries Ammonia Distribution Business. Retrieved from: www.airgas.com/content/pressReleases.aspx?PressRelease_ID=1164.

Airgas (2013). Refrigerant Gases. Retrieved from Airgas Products: www.airgas.com/browse/product_list.aspx?catID=316&WT.svl=316.

Akzo Nobel NV (2014). Carbon Tetrachloride. Retrieved May 12, 2014, from AkzoNobel Industrial Chemicals: www.akzonobel.com/ic/products/carbon_tetrachloride/.

Akzo Nobel NV (2014). History. How did we get where we are today? Retrieved May 5, 2014, from AkzoNobel Corporate: www.akzonobel.com/aboutus/history/.

Albemarle Corporation. (1997, March 31). Retrieved May 2, 2014, from Corpwatch: www.corpwatch.org/article.php?id=901.

Albemarle Corporation (2011, April 7). History. Retrieved May 2, 2014, from Albemarle: www.albemarle.com/about/history-10.html.

Albemarle Corporation (2014, April 16). Agricultural Actives and Intermediates. Retrieved May 2, 2014, from Albemarle: www.albemarle.com/products—markets/performance-chemicals/fine-chemistry-services/agricultural-actives—intermediates-673.html.

Alliance for Responsible Atmospheric Policy, The (n.d.). Alliance Fact Sheet. Retrieved from The Alliance for Responsible Atmospheric Policy: www.alliance-policy.org/downloads/documents/Alliance_Fact_Sheet.pdf.

Alliance for a Responsible CFC Policy (n.d.). Q&A Chlorofluorocarbons and Ozone. Retrieved May 21, 2014, from Legacy Tobacco Documents Library: http://legacy.library.ucsf.edu/tid/ema84c00/pdf.

Alliance for a Responsible CFC Policy (n.d.). The Alliance is an Industry Coalition. Retrieved from Alliance for Responsible Atmospheric Policy: www.alliancepolicy.org/about.php.

Alliance for a Responsible CFC Policy (1980, September). Alliance for Responsible CFC Policy Charter. Alliance for Responsible CFC Policy News.

Alliance for a Responsible CFC Policy (1986, October). Policy Statement. CFC Alliance Newsletter.

Alternative Fluorocarbons Environmental Acceptability Study (1993, August). Production, Sales and Atmospheric Release of Fluorocarbons Through 1992. Retrieved January 3, 2014, from Center for International Earth Science Information Network, Earth Institute, Colombia University: www.ciesin.columbia.edu/docs/011-423/011-423.html.

Alternative Fluorocarbons Environmental Acceptability Study (2006, June 2). AFEAS Research and Assessment Program. Retrieved from AFEAS: www.afeas.org/about.html.

Alternative Fluorocarbons Environmental Acceptability Study (2007). Production and Sales of Fluorocarbons. Retrieved from Alternative Fluorocarbons Environmental Acceptability Study: www.afeas.org/overview.php.

Alternative Fluorocarbons Environmental Acceptability Study (2009, June 2). Annual Fluorocarbon Production Reported (metric tons). Retrieved January 12, 2014, from Alternative Fluorocarbons Environmental Acceptability Study: www.afeas.org/data.php?page=prod_table.

Amber, K. T., Bloom, R., Staropoli, P., Dhimam, S. and Hu, S. (2014). Assessing the Current Market of Sunscreen: A Cross-sectional Study of Sunscreen Availability in Three Metropolitan Counties in the United States. *Journal of Skin Cancer*, 7.

American Academy of Pediatrics (2014, April). Tanning Bed Restrictions. American Academy of Paediatrics.

American Bar Association (2004). *Chapter Thirteen: Personal Injury*. Random House. New York.

American Cancer Society (2013). Cancer Facts and Figures 2013. Atlanta, Georgia, USA.

American Cancer Society (2014). Cancer Facts and Figures 2014. Atlanta, Georgia, USA.

American Cancer Society (2014). Economic Impacts of Cancer. Retrieved January 13, 2014, from American Cancer Society: www.cancer.org/cancer/cancerbasics/economic-impact-of-cancer.

American Hospital of Paris (n.d.). The Sun and Skin Cancer: Interview with Dr Louis Zylberberg: www.american-hospital.org/en/health-information/diseases-et-conditions/the-sun-and-skin-cancer.html

American Law Institute (1942). Restatement (First) of the Law Records.

American Law Institute (1965). Restatement (Second) of Torts.

American Law Institute (1998). Restatement (Third) of Torts: Products Liability.

American Law Institute (2010). Restatement (Third) of Torts: Liability for Physical and Emotional Harm.

American Society of Refrigerating Engineers (1934). Index to Refrigerating Engineering 1905–1934. Retrieved from American Society of Heating, Refrigerating and Air-Conditioning Engineers: www.ashrae.org/.../docLib/.../ASRE-Index_1905-1934.pdf .

American Society of Refrigerating Engineers (1940). Index to Refrigerating Engineering 1935–1940. Retrieved from American Society of Heating, Refrigerating and Air-Conditioning Engineers: www.ashrae.org/.../docLib/.../ASRE_Indexes_1935-1940.pdf

American Society of Refrigerating Engineers (1945). Index to Refrigerating Engineering, Five Year Index 1941–1945. Retrieved from American Society of

Heating, Refrigerating and Air-Conditioning Engineers: www.ashrae.org/.../ docLib/.../ASRE_Indexes_1941-1945.pdf.

Anand, R. (2004). *International Environmental Justice: A North–South Dimension.* Ashgate Publishing Ltd.

Andersen, S. O., Halberstadt, M. L. and Borgford-Parnella, N. (2013). Stratospheric Ozone, Global Warming, and the Principle of Unintended Consequences: An Ongoing Science and Policy Success Story. *Journal of the Air & Waste Management Association,* 63(6), 607–647.

Andersen, S. O. and Sarma, K. M. (2002). Protecting the Ozone Layer: The United Nations History. Earthscan, Ltd., United Nations Environment Programme.

Andersen, S. O., Sarma, K. M. and Taddonio, K. N. (2007). Technology Transfer for the Ozone Layer: Lessons for Climate Change. London: Earthscan.

Ando, M. (1990). Risk Evaluation of Stratospheric Ozone Depletion Resulting from Chlorofluorocarbons (CFCs) on Human Health. *Nihon Eiseigaku Zasshi,* 45(5), 947–953.

Annual Records (2013, May 31). Retrieved from Ozone Hole Watch: http://ozonewatch.gsfc.nasa.gov/meteorology/annual_data.html.

Ansul Incorporated (2004). Ansulex R-102 Material Safety Data Sheet. Retrieved May 3, 2014, from www.wellsbloomfield.com/oldsite/new-bloomfield-ind/~WELLS/WELLS%20LIBRARY/Wells%20Agency%20Docs/Ansulex%20R-102%20MSDS.pdf.

Arentz Law Group (2014). Tanning Bed Skin Cancer Lawsuits. Retrieved from Defective Products: http://arentzlaw.com/defective-products/tanning-bed-skin-cancer-lawsuits/.

Arkema (2014). Forane. Retrieved from Products: www.arkema-americas.com/en/ products/product-portal/range-viewer/Forane/?back=true.

Arkema (n.d.). The Creation and Growth of the Arkema Group. Retrieved January 2, 2014, from Arkema History: www.arkema.com/en/arkema-group/history/ index.html.

Australian Government, Department of the Environment (n.d.). *The Ozone Layer.*

Balic, V. and Human, S. (2002). Contribution to Skin Cancer Prevention in South Africa: Modeling the UV Index Utilizing Imprecise Data. *Austrian Journal of Statistics,* 31, 169–175.

Banks, R. E., Smart, B. E. and Tatlow, J. C. (1994). *Organofluorine Chemistry: Principles and Commercial Applications.* Plenum Press.

Barkin, J. S. *et al.* (1999). *Anarchy and the Environment: The International Relations of Common Pool Resources.* SUNY Press pp. 101–102.

Barnes, E. A., Barnes, N. W. and Polvani, L. M. (2014, January). Delayed Southern Hemisphere Climate Change Induced by Stratospheric Ozone Recovery, as Projected by the CMIP5 Models. *Journal of Climate,* 27(2), 852–867.

Barrett, S. (2007). *Why Cooperate? The Incentive to Supply Global Public Goods.* Oxford University Press.

Barthold, T. A. (1994). Issues in the Design of Environmental Excise Taxes. *Journal of Economic Perspectives,* 8(1), 133–151.

Bastuji-Garin, S. and Diepgen, T. (2002, April 30). Cutaneous Malignant Melanoma, Sun Exposure, and Sunscreen Use: Epidemiological Evidence. *British Journal of Dermatology,* 146(s61), 24–30.

Bearden, D. M. (2012). Comprehensive Environmental Response, Compensation, and Liability Act: A Summary of Superfund Clean-up Authorities and Related

Provisions of the Act. Congressional Research Service.

Bekki, S., Rap, A., Poulain, V., Dhomse, S., Marchand, M., Lefevre, F. *et al.* (2013, June). Climate Impact of Stratospheric Ozone Recovery. *Geophysical Research Letters*, 40(11), 2796–2800.

Benedick, R. E. (1998). *Ozone Diplomacy: New Directions in Safeguarding the Planet.* Cambridge, Massachusetts: Harvard University Press.

Beyer, J. (2005). Left holding the bag? Understanding the Successor Liability Defense. *In-House Defense Quaterly*, 20.

Bishop, F. S. (1979). *Report on the Progress of Regulations to Protect Stratospheric Ozone: Report to Congress.* US Environmental Protection Agency, Office of Toxic Substances.

Blackden, C. M. (2009). *Gender Equality and Global Public Goods: Some Reflections on Shared Priorities.* OECD.

Bloomberg BusinessWeek. (2014, January 29). Chemicals: Company Overview of Solvay Solexis, Inc.: http://investing.businessweek.com/research/stocks/private/snapshot.asp?privcapId=4319716.

Bodinus, W. S. (1999, April). The Rise and Fall of Carbon Dioxide Systems. *ASHRAE Journal*, 37–42.

Boroshok, S. (1993). Environmental Excise Taxes, Focusing on Ozone-Depleting Chemicals, 1993: www.irs.gov/pub/irs-soi/93exenviro.pdf.

Bosserhoff, A.-K. (ed.) (2011). *Melanoma Development: Molecular Biology, Genetics and Clinical Application.* Vienna: Springer.

Boston, G. W. and Madden, M. S. (2001). *Law of Environmental and Toxic Torts: Cases, Materials and Problems* (Second edn). St. Paul, Minnesota: West Group.

Boyd, J. E. (n.d.). Thanks to Chemistry: A Burning Desire. Retrieved from Chemical Heritage Foundation: www.chemheritage.org/discover/online-resources/thanks-to-chemistry/ttc-health-suntan_lotion.aspx.

Boyle, Dore, J. F., Autier and Ringborg, U. (2004). Cancer of the Skin: A Forgotten Problem in Europe. *Annals of Oncology*, 15(1), 5–6.

Browne, M. W. (1990, July 17). Grappling With the Cost of Saving Earth's Ozone. *The New York Times.*

Buckley, W. R. and Okrent, C. J. (2004). *Torts and Personal Injury Law.* Clifton Park, NY.

Business Decisions Limited (2003). *The Power of Customers to Drive Innovation.* European Commission.

Butler, J., Montzka, S., Clarke, A., Lobert, J. and Elkins, J. (1998, January 20). Growth and Distribution of Halons in the Atmosphere. *Journal of Geophysical Research*, 103, 1503–1511.

Byrd, E. H. (1988, July). Reflections on Wilful, Wanton, Reckless and Gross Negligence. *Louisiana Law Review*, 48(6).

Cagin, S. and Dray, P. (1993). *Between Earth and Sky: How CFCs Changed our World and Endangered the Ozone Layer.* New York: Pantheon Books.

Calabresi, S. G., Berghausen, M. E. and Albertson, S. (2012). The Rise and the Fall of the Separation of Powers. *Northwestern University Law Review*, 106(2).

Caldwell, M., Ballare, C., Bornman, Flint, L., Broern, L., Teramura, A. *et al.* (2003, January). Terrestrial Ecosystems, Increased Solar Ultraviolet Radiation and Interactions with other Climatic Change Factors. *Photochemical and Photobiological Science*, 2(1), 29–38.

Campbell, H. and Corley E. (2015). *Urban Environmental Policy Analysis.* London,

New York: Routledge p. 28.

Cancer Council SA (n.d.) What is skin cancer?. Retrieved December 7, 2013, from: www.cancersa.org.au/information/a-z-index/what-is-skin-cancer#How common is skin cancer.

Cancer Research UK (2014). Skin Cancer Incidence Statistics. Retrieved May 5, 2014, from Cancer Research UK: www.cancerresearchuk.org/cancer-info/cancerstats/types/skin/incidence/uk-skin-cancer-incidence-statistics.

Carbon Tax Center (2015). What's a Carbon Tax?: www.carbontax.org/whats-a-carbon-tax/

Carlisle, R. (2005). *Scientific American Inventions and Discoveries: All the Milestones in Ingenuity From the Discovery of Fire to the Invention of the Microwave Oven.* Hoboken, USA: John Wiley & Sons.

Carlowicz, M. (n.d.). New Simulation Shows Consequences of a World Without Earth's Natural Sunscreen. Retrieved May 15, 2014, from National Aeronautics and Space Administration Goddard Space Flight Center: www.nasa.gov/topics/earth/features/world_avoided.html.

Center for International Earth Science Information Network, E. I. (n.d.). Production and Use of Chlorofluorocarbons. Retrieved from CIESIN Thematic Guide on Ozone Depletion Issues: www.ciesin.org/TG/OZ/prodcfcs.html.

Centers for Disease Control and Prevention (1992, January 17). *Death Rates of Malignant Melanoma Among White Men — United States, 1973–1988.* Retrieved January 17, 2014, from Morbidity and Mortality Weekly Report: www.cdc.gov/mmwr/preview/mmwrhtml/00015916.htm.

Centers for Disease Control and Prevention (2001, June 11). Investigation of Human Health Effects Associated with Potential Exposure to Genetically Modified Corn. Retrieved from US Department of Health & Human Services: www.cdc.gov/nceh/ehhe/Cry9CReport/pdfs/cry9creport.pdf.

Centers for Disease Control and Prevention (2011, November 11). Melanoma Surveillance in the United States. Retrieved November 30, 2013, from Cancer Prevention and Control: www.cdc.gov/cancer/dcpc/research/articles/melanoma_supplement.htm.

Cercato, M. *et al.* (2013, March). Improving Sun-safe Knowledge, Attitude and Behaviour in Parents of Primary School Children: A Pilot Study. *Journal of Cancer Education,* 28(1), 151–157.

Chapman, B. (1983). Ethical Issues in the Law of Tort. In M. D. Bayles and B. Chapman (eds), *Justice, Rights and Tort Law.* Dordrecht/Boston: D. Reidel Publishing Company pp. 13–43.

Chemical Manufacturers Association (1980). UNEP/CCOL/5/9: 1980 World Production and Sales of Fluorocarbons. Copenhagen: UNEP.

Chemical Manufacturers Association (1981, October 12–16). Summary of Recent Results. Coordinating Committee on the Ozone Layer, Fifth Session, UNEP/CCOL/54/4.

Chemical Manufacturers Association (1983, April 5–8). Assessment of Ozone Depletion and its Impact Revised Text for Effects. Coordinating Committee on the Ozone Layer, Sixth Session, UNEP/CCOL/6/5Add.1.

(Chemical Manufacturers Association 1986, February 24–28). Assessment of Ozone Depletion and its Coordinating Committee on the Ozone Layer, Eighth Session, UNEP/CCOL/8/3.

Chemtura Corporation (2014). About Chemtura: Historical Timeline. Retrieved from Chemtura: www.chemtura.com/corporatev2/v/index.jsp?vgnextoid= cfa9708b7507d210VgnVCM1000000753810aRCRD&vgnextchannel=cfa9708b75 07d210VgnVCM1000000753810aRCRD&vgnextfmt=default.

Choi, E. K. and Hartigan, J. C. (2008). *Handbook of International Trade: Economic and Legal Analyses of Trade Policy*. John Wiley & Sons.

Cicerone, R. J. and Stolarski, R. (June 1973). Assessment of Possible Environmental Effects of Space Shuttle Operations (NASA CR-129003). National Aeronautics and Space Administration.

Clark, R. P. (2000). *Global Life Systems: Population, Food, and Disease in the Process of Globalization*. Rowman & Littlefield.

Collins, C. (2010). *Toxic Loopholes: Failures and Future Prospects for Environmental Law*. New York: Cambridge University Press.

Committee on Environmental Health (1999). Ultraviolet Light: A Hazard to Children. *Pediatrics*, 328–333.

Commonwealth of Pennsylvania (2014). The "Great Johnstown Flood" May 31, 1889. Retrieved May 2, 2014, from Pennsylvania Historic and Museum Commission: www.portal.state.pa.us/portal/server.pt/community/documents_ from_1865_-_1945/20425/johnstown_flood/998883.

Contracting Business (2009, January 1). The 1940s: War and Amazing Prosperity. Retrieved May 12, 2014, from Contracting Business.com: http://contracting-business.com/feature/1940s_war_prosperity.

Cook, E. (1990). Global Environmental Advocacy: Citizen Activism in Protecting the Ozone Layer. Ambio, 19(6/7), 334–338.

Cook, E. (ed.) (1996, November). *Ozone Protection in the United States: Elements of Success*. Washington, D.C.: World Resources Institute.

Cooper-Stephenson, K. D. and Gibson, E. (1993). *Tort Theory*. North York: Captus University Publications.

Copenhagen Post, The (2010, June 10). Skin Cancer Rate Highest in Europe.

Corporate Europe Observatory (2012). Climate Bombs Called HFCs: How the Industry Lobby is Trying to Block a Phase-out of Super Greenhouse Gases in Europe's Refrigeration and Air Conditioning Systems.

CPSC/FDA/EPA Announce Phase Out Of Chlorofluorocarbons (1977, May 11). Retrieved from US Consumer Product Safety Commission: www.cpsc.gov/en/ Newsroom/News-Releases/1977/CPSCFDAEPA-Announce-Phase-Out-Of-Chlorofluorocarbons/.

Cronin, J. and Kennedy, R. J. (1999). *The Riverkeepers*. New York: Touchstone.

Dauvergne, P. (2008). *The Shadows of Consumption: Consequences for the Global Environment*. Cambridge, Massachusetts: Massachusetts Institute of Technology.

DeCanio, S. (2003). Economic Analysis, Environmental Policy and Intergenerational Justice in the Reagan Administration. In *International Environmental Agreements: Politics, Law and Economics*. Netherlands: Kluwer Academic Publishers pp. 299–321.

Dell'Amore, C. (2011, March 22). First North Pole Ozone Hole Forming? "Put On Your Sunscreen": Damaging Air Mass Could Drift Far South. *National Geographic News*.

DeSombre, E. R. (2000). The Experience of the Montreal Protocol: Particularly Remarkable, and Remarkably Particular. *UCLA Journal of Environmental Law and Policy*, 19(1), 49–81.

Deutsch, C. H. (1999, June 7). Allied Signal and Honeywell to Announce Merger

Today. *New York Times.*

Dewes, D., Duff, D. and Trebilcock, M. (1996). *Exploring the Domain of Accident Law: Taking the Facts Seriously.* New York, Oxford: Oxford University Press.

Diamond, J. (2008). Lessons from Environmental Collapses of Past Societies. Fourth Annual John H. Chafee Memorial Lecture on Science and the Environment. Washington, D.C.

Dickinson and Cicerone (1986). Future Global Warming from Atmospheric Trace Gases, 319 *Nature* 109.

Doniger, D. and Quibell, M. (2007). *Back from the Brink: How NRDC Helped Save the Ozone Layer.* New York: Natural Resources Defence Council.

Dotto, L. and Schiff, H. (1978). The Ozone War. Garden City, New York: Doubleday.

Dow Chemical Company, The (1995–2014) (n.d.). Dow Chlorinated Organics. Retrieved May 12, 2014, from Dow: www.dow.com/gco/prod/c_tetra.htm.

E. I. DuPont Nemours & Company (Inc.) (1981). Ozone Depleting Chlorofluorocarbons: Proposed Production Restriction. Wilmington, Delaware: US Environmental Protection Agency.

E. I. DuPont Nemours & Company (Inc.) (2001, April). *DuPont DATABOOK 2000,* at 33.

E. I. DuPont Nemours & Company (Inc.) (2007). DuPont Advocates Accelerated Phaseout of Ozone-Depleting Substances, http://investors.dupont.com/phoenix.zhtml?c=73320&p=irol-newsArticle&ID=1050654&highlight=.

E. I. DuPont Nemours & Company (Inc.) (2011, April 20). Position Statement: 20 Years of Progress: Implementing the Montreal Protocol. Retrieved from DuPont: www2.dupont.com/Media_Center/en_US/position_statements/montreal_protocol.html?src=position_statements_index.

E. I. DuPont Nemours & Company (Inc.) (2014). Product Stewardship. Retrieved from DuPont: www.dupont.com/corporate-functions/our-approach/ sustainability/commitments/product-stewardship-regulator/articles/product-stewardship.html.

Ekwueme, D., Guy, G., Li, C., Rim, S., Parelkar, P. and Chen, S. (2011). The Health Burden and Economic Costs of Cutaneous Melanoma Mortality by Race/Ethnicity – United States, 2000 to 2006. *J Am Acad Dermatol,* 133–143.

Ellis, B. (2010, March 24). Tanning Salons Burned by Healthcare Bill. CNNMoney.

Elrifi, I. (1990). Protection of the Ozone Layer: A Comment on the Montreal Protocol. *McGill Law Journal,* 387–423.

Emmett, E. A. (1986). Health Effects of Ultraviolet Radiation. In Effects of Changes in Stratospheric Ozone and Global Climate, Vol. 1, US EPA, Washington.

End, J. (2000). The Open and Obvious Danger Doctrine: Where Does it Belong in our Comparative Negligence Regime? *Marquette Law Review,* 84.

English, D., Armstrong, B. K., Kricker, A. and Fleming, C. (1997). Sunlight and Cancer. *Cancer Causes Control,* 8, 271–283.

Environmental Working Group. (2014). The Trouble With Sunscreen Chemicals. Retrieved from EWG's 2014 Guide to Sunscreens: www.ewg.org/2014sunscreen/the-trouble-with-sunscreen-chemicals/.

Euromonitor International (2014). *Sun Care in the US.* Euromonitor International.

Evans, J. E. (2013). See Repose Run: Setting the Boundaries of the Rule of Repose in Environmental Trespass and Nuisance Cases. *Wm. & Mary Envtl. L. & Pol'y Rev.,* 119, 119–167.

Evonik Industries (n.d.). Evonik Industries: More than 150 years competence in chemicals. Retrieved May 2, 2014, from Evonik Industries: http://history.evonik.com/sites/geschichte/en/Timeline/Pages/default.aspx.

Executive Committee of the Multilateral Fund for the Implementation of the Montreal Protocol. (2011). Status of Contributions and Disbursements (as of June 2011) UNEP/OzL.Pro/ExCom/64/3. Montreal: United Nations Environment Programme.

Fabian, P. and Onkar, S. N. (1999). *Reactive Halogen Compounds in the Atmosphere.* Germany: Springer-Verlag Berlin Heidelberg.

Fahey, D. W. and Heggin, M. I. (2010). Twenty Questions and Answers about the Ozone Layer: 2010 Update. In W. M. Organisation, *Report of the 2010 Assessment of the Scientific Assessment Panel.* Geneva: World Metrological Organisation.

Falkner, R. (2005). The Business of Ozone Layer Protection: Corporate Power in Regime Evolution. In D. L. Levy and P. Newell (eds), *The Business of Global Environmental Governance.* Cambridge: MIT Press.

Farman, J. (2002). Halocarbons, the Ozone Layer and the Precautionary Principle. In Harremoes, D., Gee, M., MacGarvin, Stirling, A., Keys, J., Wynne, B. *et al.* (eds), *The Precautionary Principle in the 20th Century: Late lessons for Early Warnings.* Earthscan.

Farman, J., Gardiner, B. G. and Shanklin, J. D. (1985). Large Losses of Total Ozone in Antarctica Reveal Seasonal ClOx/NOx interaction. *Nature,* 315, 207–10.

Farmer, R. and Nelson, T. (1988, March). *Control Technology Overview Report: CFC-11 Emissions from Flexible Polyurethane Foam Manufacturing.* Research Triangle Park, NC: United States Environmental Protection Agency.

Faure, M. (ed.). (2009). *Tort Law and Economics.* Cheltenham: Edward Elgar Publishing Ltd.

FDA and CPSC Announce Fluorocarbon Labelling Plan. (1977, April 26). Retrieved from United States Consumer Product Safety Commission: www.cpsc.gov/en/Newsroom/News-Releases/1977/FDA-And-CPSC-Announce-Fluorocarbon-Labeling-Plan/.

Federal Register (2014, April 17). Workers Compensation Programs Office. Retrieved from Federal Register: www.federalregister.gov/agencies/workers-compensation-programs-office.

Federal Register (1978, March 17). No. 43(53).

Fergusson, A. (2010). The Arctic Ozone Layer: How the Arctic Ozone Layer is Responding to Ozone-Depleting Chemicals and Climate Change. Toronto: Canadian Ministry of the Environment.

Fergusson, I. F. (2014). The US Export Control System and the President's Reform Initiative. Congressional Research Service.

Ferlay, J., Steliarova-Foucher, E., Lortet-Tieulent, J., Rosso, S., Coebergh, J. W., Comber, H. *et al.* (2013). Cancer Incidence and Mortality Patterns in Europe: Estimates for 40 Countries in 2012. *European Journal of Cancer,* 49, 1374–1403.

Ferrer, A. A. (2006). Excuses, Excuses: The Application of Statutes of Repose to Environmentally-Related Injuries. *B. C. Envtl. Aff. L. Rev,* 33, 345–381.

Ferroni, M. and Mody, A. (2002). *International Public Goods: Incentives, Measurement, and Financing.* Washington, D.C.

Fischer, S. K., Hughes, P. and Fairchild, P. (1991, December). Energy and Global Warming Impacts of CFC Alternative Technologies. Retrieved from www.ciesin.org/docs/011-459/011-459.html.

Fitzka, M., Simic, S. and Hadzimustafic, J. (2012, December). Trends in Spectral UV

Radiation from Long-term Measurements at Hoher Sonnblick, Austria. Theoretical and Applied Climatology, 110(4), 585–593.

Fleming, F. (1956). Damages in Accident Cases. *Cornell Law Quarterly*, 41, 584–585.

Ford, C. L. (1975). An Overview of Halon 1301 Systems. American Chemical Society Symposium Series. Washington, D.C.: American Chemical Society.

Freedman, W. (1988). Foreign Plaintiffs in Products Liability Actions: The Defense of Forum Non Conveniens. Quorum Books.

Friends of the Earth (1997, June 17). Tax Bill Misses Green Mark. Retrieved from Indian Institute of Science: http://wgbis.ces.iisc.ernet.in/envis/doc97html/envenv618.html.

G. Bernhard, G. M.-U. (2013, November 26). Ozone. Retrieved April 25, 2014, from Arctic Report Card: Update for 2013: Tracking recent environmental changes: www.arctic.noaa.gov/reportcard/ozone.html.

Gale, R. and Barg, S. (eds) (2013). *Green Budget Reform: An International Casebook of Leading Practices*. New York: Earthscan.

Galyen, J. (2009, September 9). Hydrocarbons Charge Up Refrigeration Innovations: Industry Likely to See Propane and Isobutane Products. Retrieved from Danfoss North America: www.danfoss.com/North_America/EnVisioneering/EnVisioneering/Hydrocarbons+charge+up+refrigeration+innovations.htm.

Gifford, D. G. (2013). *Suing the Tobacco and Lead Pigment Industries: Government Litigation as Public Health Prescription*. Ann Arbor: The University of Michigan Press.

Ginsberg, W. and Weiss, L. (1981). Common Law Liability for Toxic Torts: A Phantom Remedy. *Hofstra Law Review*, 9(3), 860–941.

Glasius, M., Kaldor, M. and Anheier, H. (eds). (2005). *Global Civil Society 2005/6*. London: Sage.

Maroto-Valer, M. M. (2010). Developments and Innovation in Carbon Dioxide (CO2) Capture and Storage Technology. Cambridge, UK: Woodhead Publishing.

Godar, D., Urbach, F., Gasparro, F. and Van der Leun, J. (2003). UV Doses of Young Adults. *Photochem Photobiol*, 77(4), 453–457.

Goldberg, J. C. (2002). Twentieth Century Tort Theory. Vanderbilt University Law School. Published in *Georgetown Law Journal*.

Goldberg, J. C. and Zipursky, B. C. (2014). Tort Law and Responsibility. In J. Oberdiek (ed.), *Philosophical Foundations of the Law of Torts*. Oxford University Press p. 464.

Gostin, L. O. (2008). *Public Health Law: Power, Duty, Restraint*. Berkeley: University of California Press.

Greenpeace International (n.d.). HFCs and other F-gases: The Worst Greenhouse Gases You've Never Heard Of. Amsterdam.

Greenstone, M., List, J. A. and Syverson, C. (2012). The Effects of Environmental Regulation on the Competitiveness of US Manufacturing. NBER Working Paper No. 18392.

Grundmann, R. (1998). The Protection of the Ozone Layer. UN Vision Project on Global Policy Networks.

Gruntfest, I. (1976, February). *Chemical Technology and Economics in Environmental Perspectives, Task 1: Technical Alternatives to Selected Chlorofluorocarbons Uses*. Midwest Research Institute. Washington, D.C.: United States Environmental Protection Agency.

Guy, G. P., Machlin, S., Ekwueme, D. and Yabroff, K. (2014, November 9). Prevalence and Costs of Skin Cancer Treatment in the US, 2002–2006 and 2007–2011. Retrieved from www.ajpmonline.org/article/S0749-3797(14)00510-8/fulltext#tbl2fna.

Haas, P. M. (1992). Banning Chlorofluorocarbons: Epistemic Community Efforts to Protect Stratospheric Ozone. *International Organization*, 46(1), 187–224.

Harper, F. V. and James, F. (1956). The Law of Torts. Boston: Little Brown.

Harrington, W., Morgenstern, R. D. and Sterner, T. (eds). (2004). Choosing Environmental Policy: Comparing Instruments and Outcomes in the United States and Europe. Washington, D.C.: Resources for the Future.

Harris, O. F. (1986). Toxic Tort Litigation and the Causation Element. *Southwestern Law Journal*, 909.

Harvey, F. (2005, April 12). Ozone-friendly Gases "Cause Global Warming". *Financial Times*.

Herman, J. R. (2010, February). Global Increase in UV Irradiance During the Past 30 Years (1979–2008) Estimated from Satellite Data. *Journal of Geophysical Research: Atmospheres (1984–2012)*, 115.

Hollingsworth (n.d.). Framework for Toxic Tort Litigation. Washington, D.C.: Washington Legal Foundation.

Holmes, O. W. (1881). *The Common Law*. Boston: Little, Brown and Company.

Honeywell International Inc. (2012, August 15). Whirlpool Corporation and Honeywell Introduce Most Environmentally Responsible and Energy Efficient Insulation Available into US Made Refrigerators. Retrieved from Honeywell Press Releases: http://honeywell.com/News/Pages/Whirlpool-Corp-and-Honeywell-Introduce-Most-Environmentally-Responsible-and-Energy-Efficient-Insulation-Available-Refridge.aspx.

Honeywell International Inc. (2014). Chemicals, Specialty Materials & Fertilizers. Retrieved January 29, 2014, from Honeywell: http://honeywell.com/Products-Services/Pages/chemicals.aspx#Solvents, Reagents and Aerosols.

Honeywell International Inc. (2014). Honeywell History. Retrieved January 29, 2014, from Honeywell: http://honeywell.com/About/Pages/our-history.aspx.

House of Representatives (1989). Bill Text 101st Congress (1989–1990) H. R. 3299. P. P. Retrieved from The Library of Congress: http://thomas.loc.gov/cgi-bin/query/F?c101:1:./temp/~c101VghFLV:e228245.

Huber, W. (1986). The Bhopalization of American Tort Law. In *Hazards: Technology and Fairness*. Washington, D.C.: National Academies Press.

Hunt, Y., Augustson, E., Rutten, L., Moser, R. and Yaroch, A. (2012). History and Culture of Tanning in the United States. In C. J. Heckman and S. L. Manne, *Shedding Light on Indoor Tanning*. Dordrecht, New York: Springer.

IARC Working Group on the Evaluation of Carcinogenic Risks to Humans (2012). Solar and Ultraviolet Radiation. In *Radiation, Volume 100D: A Review of Human Carcinogens*. Lyon: International Agency for Research on Cancer, p. 362.

Iliades, C. (2010). Skin Cancer Diagnosis on the Rise. Retrieved from Everyday Health: www.everydayhealth.com/skin-cancer/diagnosis-on-the-rise.aspx.

Internal Revenue Service (2010, June 15). Indoor Tanning Services; Cosmetic Services; Excise Taxes. *Federal Register*, 75(114), 33683.

International Commission on Non-Ionizing Radiation Protection (2010). ICNIRP Statement on Protection of Workers against Ultraviolet Radiation. *Health Physics*, 99(1), 66–87.

International Law Commission (2001). Draft articles on Prevention of Transboundary Harm from Hazardous Activities, with commentaries. In I. L. Commission, Yearbook of the International Law Commission (Vol. 2).

Jackall, R. (2010). *Moral Mazes: The World of Corporate Managers.* Oxford University Press.

Johansen, B. E. (2009). *The Encyclopaedia of Global Warming Science and Technology.* Santa Barbara, California: Greenwood Press.

Johnstown Area Heritage Association (2014). History of the Johnstown Flood. Retrieved May 2, 2014, from Johnstown Flood Museum: www.jaha.org/FloodMuseum/history.html.

Jones, R. J. (2002). *Routledge Encyclopaedia of International Political.* Routledge, p. 573.

Kaniaru, D., Shende, R., Stone, S. and Durwood, Z. (2007). Strengthening the Montreal Protocol: Insurance against Abrupt Climate Change. *Sustainable Development Law & Policy*, 7(2), 3–9.

Kanner, A. (2005). The Public Trust Doctrine, Parens Patriae, and the Attorney General as the Guardian of the State's Natural Resources. *Duke Environmental Law & Policy Forum*, 16, 57–115.

Kauffman, J. (1997). A Case Study of the Montreal Protocol. In M. A. Schreurs and E. C. Economy (eds), The Internationalization of Environmental Protection. Cambridge: Cambridge University Press pp. 74–96.

Kerr, J. and McElroy, C. (1993). Evidence for Large Upward Trends of Ultraviolet-B Radiation Linked to Ozone Depletion, *Science*, 262, 1032.

Knibbe, J., van der A, R., and de Laat, A. (2014). Spatial Regression Analysis on 32 Years Total Column Ozone Data. *Atmospheric Chemistry and Physics Discussion* (14), 5323–5373.

Knopeck, G., Zwolinski, L. and Selznick, R. (1989). An Evaluation of Carbon Absorption for Emissions Control and CFC-11 Recovery in Polyurethane Foam Processes. *Journal of Cellular Plastics*, 164–172.

Koenig, T. and Rustad, M. (2003). *In Defence of Tort Law.* New York: New York University Press.

Kowalok, M. E. (1993). Common Threads: Research Lessons from Acid Rain, Ozone Depletion, and Global Warming. *Environment*, 35(6), 12–20, 35–38.

Kroll, E. M. and Westerlind, J. M. (2011). Arent Fox LLP Survey of Damage Laws of the 50 States Including the District of Columbia and Puerto Rico. Washington, D.C.: Arent Fox LLP.

Kumar, K. K. (n.d.). Montreal Protocol. Retrieved June 16, 2013, from www.mse.ac.in/trade/pdf/Compendium%20Part%20B/4.%20Kavi-MP.pdf.

La Fave, D. J. (2005). Remedying the Confusion between Statutes of Limitations and Statutes of Repose in Wisconsin: A Conceptual Guide. *Marquette Law Review*, 88, 927–945.

Liberman, S. (2011). *American Food by the Decades.* Santa Barbara, California: Greenwood.

Liftin, K. T. (1995). *Ozone Discourses: Science and Politics in Global Environmental Cooperation.* New York: Colombia University Press.

Lovelock, J. (1971, April). Atmospheric Fluorine Compounds as Indicators of Air Movements. *Nature*, 230(5293).

Lowe, G. C., *et al.* (2014). Increasing Incidence of Melanoma among Middle-Aged Adults: An Epidemiologic Study in Olmsted County, Minnesota. *Mayo Clinic Proceedings*, 89(1), 52.

Lynn, K., MacKendrick, K. and Donoghue, E. (2011, August). *Social Vulnerability and Climate Change: Synthesis of Literature*. United States Department of Agriculture.

McCarthy, R., Bower, F. A. and Jesson, J. P. (1977). The Fluorocarbon-Ozone Theory—I. Production and Release—World Production and Release of CCl$_3$F and CCl$_2$F$_2$ (fluorocarbons 11 and 12) through 1975. *Atmospheric Environment*, 11(6), 491–497.

McCulloch, A., and Midgley, P. M. (2001). The History of Methyl Chloroform Emissions: 1951–2000. *Atmospheric Environment*, 5311–5319.

McDaid, C. F. (2010). Sun Protection Resources and Environmental Changes To Prevent Skin Cancer: A Systematic Review. University of York.

Mack, J. (2006, April). Nullum Tempus: Governmental Immunity to Statutes of Limitation, Laches, and Statutes of Repose. *Defence Counsel Journal*.

MacKie, R. M. (1996). *Skin Cancer: An Illustrated Guide to the Aetiology, Clinical Features, Pathology and Management of Benign and Malignant Cutaneous Tumours*. London: Martin Dunitz Ltd.

Maclaine-Cross, I. L. (2003). Usage and Risk of Hydrocarbon Refrigerants in Motor Cars for Australia and the United States. *International Journal of Refrigeration*, 12.

Manney, G. L. *et al.* (2011). Unprecedented Arctic Ozone Loss in 2011. *Nature*.

March, D. and Meyer, E. (eds) (2014, April 22). Earth Day 2014 Planetary Health is Public Health. (Mialman School of Public Health, Columbia University) Retrieved May 5, 2014, from The 2x2 Project–Health beyond the headlines: http://the2x2project.org/earthday2014/.

Markandya, A. (1991). Economics and the Ozone Layer. In D. Pearce, *Blueprint 2: Greening the World Economy*. London: Earthscan.

Martens, W. (1998, February). Health Impacts of Climate Change and Ozone Depletion: An Ecoepidemiologic Modeling Approach. *Environmental Health Perspectives*, 106(Supplement 1).

Maxwell, J. and Briscoe, F. (1997). There's Money in the Air: The CFC Ban and DuPont's Regulatory Strategy. *Business Strategy and the Environment*, 6, 276–286.

MBAO (n.d.). Historical US Methyl Bromide Sales. Retrieved from Methyl Bromide Alternatives Outreach: http://mbao.org/methyl_back/sales.pdf.

Meadows, D. H., Meadows, D. L. and Randers, J. (1992). Beyond the Limits: Confronting Global Collapse, Envisioning a Sustainable Future. Chelsea Green Pub.

Megie, G. (2006). From Stratospheric Ozone to Climate Change: Historical Perspective on Precaution and Scientific Responsibility. *Science and Engineering Ethics*, 12(4), 596–606.

Merrill, T. W. (1997). Agency Capture Theory and the Courts: 1967– 1983. Chicago-Kent Law Review, 72, 1039–1053.

Metra Consulting Group Ltd (1981). Aspects of Effecting Further Reductions in Chlorofluorocarbon Usage in the EEC: Final Report. Commission of the European Communities, Environment and Consumer Protection Service. London: European Economic Community.

Metz, B. E. (n.d.). Reconstitutionalizing Parens Patriae: How Federal Parens Patriae Doctrine Appropriately Permits State Damages Suits Aggregating Private Tort Claims. Retrieved from Columbia Law School: http://web.law.columbia.edu/sites/default/files/microsites/career-services/Reconstitutionalizing%20 Parens%20Patriae.pdf

Midgley, T. and Henne, A. (1930, May). Organic Fluorides as Refrigerants. Industrial and Engineering Chemistry, 5420545.

Miller, A. (2010, March 30). The Johnstown Flood of 1889. Retrieved May 2, 2014, from Academia.edu: www.academia.edu/1024972/The_Johnstown_Flood_of_1889#.

Miller, A. (1990, October). The Development of Substitutes for Chlorofluorocarbons: Public–Private Cooperation and Environmental Policy, *Ambio* 19(6/7).

Molina, M. J. and Rowland, F. S. (1974, June 28). Stratospheric Sink for Chlorofluoromethanes: Chlorine Atom-catalyzed Destruction of Ozone. *Nature*, 810–812.

Mooz, W. E., Wolf, K. A. and Camm, F. (1986). Potential Constraints on Cumulative Global production of Chlorofluorocarbons. Santa Monica, California: Rand Corporation.

Mooz, W., Dole, S., Jaquette, D., Krase, W., Morrison, P., Salem, S. *et al.* (1982, March). Technical Options for Reducing Chlorofluorocarbon Emissions. Retrieved from Rand Corporation: www.rand.org/content/dam/rand/pubs/reports/2008/R2879.pdf.

Morgenstern, R. D. (1997). Economic Analyses at EPA: Assessing Regulatory Impact. Washington, D.C.: Resources for the Future.

Morone, J. G. *et al.* (1986). Chapter 5: Threats to the Ozone Layer. In *Averting Catastrophe: Strategies for Regulating Risky Technologies*. Berkley: University of California Press.

Morris, S., Cox, B. and Bosanquet, N. (2008). Cost of Skin Cancer in England. *European Journal of Health and Economics*.

Morrisette, P. (1989). The Evolution of Policy Responses to Stratospheric Ozone Depletion. *Natural Resources Journal*, 793–820.

Morrison, R., Murphy, B. L. and Mudge, S. (2013). Chlorinated Solvents: A Forensic Evaluation. Cambridge: Royal Society of Chemistry.

Mueller, D. B. and Metcalf, B. A. (2013). Adoption of the Risk-Utility Rule in Negligent Design Cases: Jablonski v. Ford Motor Co. *IDC Quarterly*, 23(4).

Nagengast, B. A. (2006, May). Air Conditioning and Refrigeration Chronology. Retrieved from American Society of Heating, Refrigerating and Air Conditioning Engineers.

National Academy of Sciences (1982). Causes and Effects of Stratospheric Ozone Reduction: An Update. Washington, D.C.: National Academy Press.

National Aeronautics and Space Administration (2005, August 24). Basics on Ozone. Retrieved November 3, 2013, from National Aeronautics and Space Administration: www.nasa.gov/vision/earth/environment/ozone_hole101.html.

National Aeronautics and Space Administration (2013, September 25). History of the Ozone Hole. Retrieved from NASA Ozone Watch: http://ozonewatch.gsfc.nasa.gov/facts/history_SH.html.

National Aeronautics and Space Administration (2016). Goddard Space Flight Center, Ozone Hole Watch website: http://ozonewatch.gsfc.nasa.gov/meteorology/SH.html.

National Aeronautics and Space Administration (n.d.). The Ozone Resource Page. Retrieved November 6, 2013, from NASA website: www.nasa.gov/vision/earth/environment/ozone_resource_page.html.

NASA Jet Propulsion Laboratory (2014, May 12). West Antarctic Glacier Loss

Appears Unstoppable. Retrieved May 22, 2014, from: www.jpl.nasa.gov/news/news.php?release=2014-148.

National Cancer Institute (2014). SEER Cancer Statistics Review 1975–2011. Retrieved May 5, 2014, from Surveillance, Epidemiology, and End Results Program: http://seer.cancer.gov/csr/1975_2011/browse_csr.php?sectionSEL=16&pageSEL=sect_16_table.01.html.

National Cancer Institute (2014, February 27). Skin Cancer Prevention. Retrieved from National Cancer Institute: www.cancer.gov/cancertopics/pdq/prevention/skin/HealthProfessional/page4#Section_129.

National Center for Atmospheric Research (1975, August 18). NCAR Scientists add Support to Ozone Destruction Theory. Yorktown Saskatchewan.

National Center for Atmospheric Research (1975, June 11). Two Record Set at the Scientific Balloon Facility. Information Release. Palestine, Texas.

Oberth, S. (1997). *Production and Consumption of Ozone-Depleting Substances, 1986–1995*. Bonn, Germany: Deutsche Gesellschaft für Technische Zusammenarbeit (GTZ) GmbH.

Occidental Chemical Corporation (2010, July 13). Carbon Tetrachloride Safety Data Sheet. Retrieved May 12, 2014, from OxyChem: http://sds.oxy.com/private/document.aspx?prd=M47013~~PDF~~MTR~~ANSI~~EN~~2010-12-17%2011:35:15.0~~Carbon%20Tetrachloride,%20Technical %20Grade.

Occidental Chemical Corporation (n.d.). Chlorine and Derivatives. Retrieved May 12, 2014, from Our Business: www.oxy.com/ourbusinesses/chemicals/products/pages/chlorineandderivatives.aspx.

Occidental Chemical Corporation (n.d.). Historical Highlights. Retrieved May 12, 2014, from Oxy: www.oxy.com/AboutOxy/WhoWeAre/Pages/Historical Highlights.aspx.

O'Dea, D. (2009). The Costs of Skin Cancer to New Zealand. Retrieved January 22, 2014, from Cancer Society of New Zealand: www.cancernz.org.nz/: www.cancernz.org.nz/assets/files/info/SunSmart/CostsofSkinCancer_NZ_22 October2009.pdf.

Office of the Attorney General (2014). Master Settlement Agreement. Retrieved from State of California Department of Justice: http://oag.ca.gov/tobacco/msa.

Oliveria, S., Saraiya, M., Geller, A. C., Heneghan, M. K. and Jorgensen, C. (2006, February). Sun Exposure and Risk of Melanoma. *Archives of Disease in Childhood*, 91(2), 131–138.

Oliviero, M. B. and Simmons, A. (2002). Who's Minding the Store? Global Civil Society and Corporate Responsibility. In M. Glasius, M. Kaldor and H. Anheier (eds), *Global Civil Society 2002*. Oxford University Press.

Organic Consumers Association (n.d.). US Farmers to Get $112 Million for GE Starlink Corn Contamination. Retrieved from www.organicconsumers.org/Corn/starlink.cfm.

Ozone Secretariat (1987, September 16). *The Montreal Protocol on Substances that Deplete the Ozone Layer.*

Palmer, A., Mooz, W., Quinn, T. and Wolf, K. (1980). Economic Implications of Regulating Chlorofluorocarbon Emissions from Nonaerosol applications Prepared from the United States Environmental Protection Agency. Santa Monica: The RAND Corporation.

Palmer, A. and Quinn, T. (1981). Economic Impact Assessment of a Chlorofluorocarbon Production Cap. US EPA.

Parson, E. A. (1993). Protecting the Ozone Layer. In P. M. Haas, R. O. Keohane and M. A. Levy (eds), Institutions for the Earth: Sources of Effective International Environmental Protection. Cambridge, Massachusetts: MIT Press.

Parson, E. A. (2003). Protecting the Ozone Layer: Science and Strategy. New York: Oxford University Press.

Patel, R. V. and Goldenberg, F. A. (2011). An Update on Nonmelanoma Skin Cancer. *J. Clin. Aesthet. Dermatol.*, 4(2), 29–27.

Pennello, G., Devesa, S. and Gail, M. (2000, March). Association of Surface Ultraviolet B Radiation Levels with Melanoma and Nonmelanoma Skin Cancer in United States Blacks. *Cancer Epidemiology*, Biomarkers and Prevention, 9, 291.

Percival, R. *(1997). Responding to Environmental Risk: A Pluralistic Perspective. *Pace Environmental Law Review*, 14(2), 513–529.

Percival, R. (2005). Who's Afraid of the Precautionary Principle? Legal Studies Research Paper No. 2005 – 62. University of Maryland School of Law.

Percival, R. (2012, June 28). Testimony of Robert V. Percival Before the House Committee on Oversight and Government Reform: Hearing on "Mandate Madness: When Sue and Settle Just isn't Enough". Retrieved from http://oversight.house.gov/wp-content/uploads/2012/06/6-28-12-TechIP-Percival.pdf.

Percival, R. (2014). Argument Preview: Law School Clinic Seeks to Preserve Day in Court for Victims of Polluted Well Water. Supreme Court of the United States blog.

Percival, R. (2014, June 10). Opinion Analysis: Court's Narrow Reading of Superfund's Preemption Provision Leaves Victims of Toxic Exposure Without Legal Recourse. Retrieved from Supreme Court of the United States blog: www.scotusblog.com/2014/06/opinion-analysis-courts-narrow-reading-of-superfunds-preemption-provision-leaves-victims-of-toxic-exposure-without-legal-recourse/.

Perry, S. R. (1992). The Moral Foundations of Tort Law. *Iowa Law Review*, 77.

Pew Environment Group (2010). Industry Opposition to Government Regulation. The Pew Environmental Group.

Pool, R. (1989). The Elusive Replacements for CFCs. *Science*, 242, 666–68.

Portney, R. (ed.) (1990). *Public Policies for Environmental Protection*. Washington, D.C.: Resources for the Future.

Prevenslik, T. (2009). DNA Damage and Cancer by Nanoparticles. Retrieved from nanoqed 2014: www.nanoqed.org/resources/DNA.pdf.

Previdi, M. and Polvani, L. M. (2014). Climate System Response to Stratospheric Ozone Depletion and Recovery. *Quarterly Journal of the Royal Meteorological Society*.

Priest, G. L. (1985, December). The Invention of Enterprise Liability: A Critical History of the Intellectual Foundations of Modern Tort law. *The Journal of Legal Studies*, 14(3).

Prosser, W. L. (1971). *Handbook of the Law of Torts*. St Paul, Minnesota: West Publishing Co.

Radiation Exposure Compensation Program (n.d.). Radiation Exposure Compensation Act. Retrieved from United States Department of Justice: www.justice.gov/civil/common/reca.html.

Razman, M. R., Hadi, A., Jamaluddin, M., Shah, A., Sani, S. and Yusoff, G. (2009). Negotiations of the Montreal Protocol to Protect Global Ozone Layer (O3) from Chlorofluorocarbons (CFCS) by Using UNEP as Global Forum in Promoting the Precautionary Principle Based on Global Environmental Governance and Law Perspectives. *Research Journal of Biological Sciences*, 765–772.

Rees, J. (2013). *Refrigeration Nation: A History of Ice, Appliances, and Enterprise in America*. Baltimore: The Johns Hopkins University Press.

Reitze, A. W. (2001). Air Pollution Control Law: Compliance and Enforcement. Washington, D.C.: Environmental Law Institute.

Restatement (First) of Torts. (1934). American Law Institute.

Rigel, D. S. (2010). Epidemiology of Melanoma. *Seminars in Cutaneous Medicine and Surgery*, 29, 204–209.

Roan, S. (1990). *Ozone Crisis: The 15-Year Evolution of a Sudden Global Emergency*. New York: Wiley.

Roberts, R. C. (2005). *Injustice and Rectification*. New York: Peter Lang.

Robin, M. L. (n.d.). Halon Alternatives: Recent Technical Progress. Retrieved March 22, 2014, from National Institute of Standards Safety: www.nist.gov/el/fire_research/upload/R9400569.pdf.

Rocky Mountain Sunscreen (2005). Skin Cancer Caused by Sun Exposure Is A Work-Related Injury. Retrieved from www.rmsunscreen.com/pdf/UV_Law_Suit_Info.pdf.

Rogers, H. W., Weinstock, M. A., Harris, A. R., Hinkley, M. R., Feldman, S. R., Fleischer, A. B. *et al.* (2010). Incidence Estimate of Nonmelanoma Skin Cancer in the United States, 2006. *Archives of Dermatology*, 146(3), 283–287.

Romey, M. G., Potash, A. and Fuoco, G. (2014, June 17). US Supreme Court Allows to Stand Ruling That Sources of Air Pollutants are Subject to State Common Law Tort Claims. Retrieved from Clean Energy Law Report: www.cleanenergylawreport.com/energy-regulatory/us-supreme-court-allows-to-stand-ruling-that-sources-of-air-pollutants-are-subject-to-state-common-l/.

Rosencranz, A., Milligan, R. (1990, October). CFC Abatement: The Needs of Developing Countries. Ambio, CFCs and stratospheric Ozone, 19(6/7), 312–316.

Rothenberg, S. and Maxwell, J. (1997). Industrial Response to the Banning of CFCs: Mapping the Paths of Technical Change. *Technology Studies*, 213–236.

Rowlands, I. H. (1995). *The Politics of Atmospheric Change*. Manchester: Manchester University Press.

Rustad, M. L. and Koenig, M. H. (2011). Reforming Public Interest Tort Law to Redress Public Health Epidemics. *Journal of Health Care Law and Policy*, 14(2), 331–373.

Sargent Shriver National Center on Poverty Law (2013). 9.1 Damages. In Sleasman, *Federa Practice Manual for Legal Aid Attorneys*

Schreurs, M. (2004). Environmental Politics in Japan, Germany, and the United States. Cambridge University Press.

Schuck, H. (1988). *Agent Orange on Trial: Mass Toxic Disasters in the Courts*. Cambridge: Harvard University Press.

Schultz, G. (2012). Economic Strength and American Leadership. In L. E. Ohanian, J. B. Taylor and I. J. Wright (eds), *Government Policies and the Delayed Economic Recovery*. Stanford, California, Hoover Institution Press, Stanford University.

Schwartz, V. E. and Silverman, C. (2010). Preemption of State Common Law by Federal Agency Action: Striking the Appropriate Balance that Protects Public Safety. *Tulane Law Review*, 84, 1204.

Seckmeyer, G., Mayer, B., Erb, R. and Bernhard, G. (1994). UV-B in Germany Higher in 1993 than in 1992, *Geophys. Res. Lett.*, 21, 577–580.

Shepherd, T. G. *et al.* (2014). Reconciliation of Halogen-induced Ozone Loss with the Total-Column Ozone Record. *Nature Geoscience*.

Shindell, D. T., Rind, D. and Lonergan, P. (1998, April). Increased Polar Stratospheric Ozone Losses and Delayed Eventual Recovery Owing to Increasing Greenhouse Gas Concentrations. *Nature*, 392, 589–592.

Showalter, J. (2014). Supreme Court Decides CTS Corp. v. Waldburger Evaluating Whether CERCLA Precludes State-Law Statutes of Repose. *The National Law Review*.

Shugerman, J. H. (2000). The Floodgates of Strict Liability: Bursting Reservoirs and the Adoption of Fletcher v. Rylands in the Gilded Age. *The Yale Law Journal*, 110, 333.

Singer, M. and Baer, H. A. (2009). *Killer Commodities: Public Health and the Corporate Production of Harm*. Lanham: AltaMira Press.

Sivasakthivel, T. and Siva Kumar Reddy, K. K. (2011, February). Ozone Layer Depletion and Its Effects: A Review. *International Journal of Environmental Science and Development*, 2(1).

Skin Cancer Foundation, The (2014). Basal Cell Carcinoma (BCC). Retrieved May 3, 2014, from The Skin Cancer Foundation: www.skincancer.org/skin-cancer-information/basal-cell-carcinoma.

Skin Cancer Foundation, The (2014). Melanoma. Retrieved May 5, 2014, from Skin Cancer Information: www.skincancer.org/skin-cancer-information/melanoma.

Skin Cancer Foundation, The (2014). *Ozone and UV: Where Are We Now?* Retrieved from www.skincancer.org/prevention/uva-and-uvb/ozone-and-uv-where-are-we-now.

Skin Cancer Foundation, The (2014). Skin Cancer Facts. Retrieved from www.skin-cancer.org/skin-cancer-information/skin-cancer-facts.

Skin Cancer Foundation, The (2014). Squamous Cell Carcinoma (SCC). Retrieved May 2, 2014, from The Skin Cancer Foundation: www.skincancer.org/skin-cancer-information/squamous-cell-carcinoma.

Slaper, H., den Elzen, M., de Woerd, H. and de Greef, J. (1992). *Ozone Depletion and Skin Cancer Incidence: An Integrated Modelling Approach*. Rijksinstituut voor Volksgezondheid en Milieu RIVM.

Slaper, H., Velders, G. J., Daniel, J. S., de Gruijl, F. F. and van der Leun, J. C. (1996). Estimates of Ozone Depletion and Skin Cancer Incidence to Examine the Vienna Convention achievements. *Nature*, 256–8.

Slaughter, J. B. and Auslander, J. M. (2008). Preemption Litigation Strategies Under Environmental Law. *Natural Resources & Environment*, 22(4).

Smith, B. (1998, April). Ethics of DuPont's CFC strategy 1975–1995. *Journal of Business Ethics*.

Solvay (2013, October 12). Welcome to SOLKANE® A brand by Solvay Fluor. Retrieved from Solvay Products: www.solvaychemicals.com/EN/products/Fluor/solkane.aspx.

Solvay (2014, January 15). History. Retrieved from About Solvay: www.solvay.com/en/about-solvay/history/index.html.

Soman, K. (2011). *Thermal Engineering*. New Delhi: PHI Learning.

Spadafora, R. R. (n.d.). Halon Replacement: Water Mist Fire Extinguishing Systems. Retrieved January 3, 2014, from Fire Engineering University: www.fireengineeringuniversity.com/courses/7/PDF/Spadafora-Jan08.pdf.

Springer, B. J. (2015). An Inconvenient Truth: How Forum Non Conveniens Doctrine Allows Defendants to Escape State Court Jurisdiction. *University of Pennsylvania Law Review*, 163, 833.

Sprinz, D. and Vaahtoranta, T. (1994, Winter). The Interest-based Explanation of International Environmental Policy. *International Organization*, 48(1), 77–105.

Staff of the Joint Committee on Taxation (2011, January). Present Law and Background Information on Federal Excise Taxes. Retrieved from US Government Printing Office: www.gpo.gov/fdsys/pkg/CPRT-112JPRT63427/html/CPRT-112JPRT63427.htm.

Steiner, J. M. (1983). Putting Fault Back into Products Liability. In M. D. Bayles and B. Chapman (eds), *Justice, Rights and Tort Law*. Dordrecht/Boston: D. Reidel Publishing Company pp. 179–209.

Stevenson, A. (1925). Report on Domestic Refrigerating Machines 1923–1925. Retrieved from American Society of Heating, Refrigerating and Air-Conditioning Engineers: www.ashrae.org/File%20Library/docLib/.../200611215455_347.pdf .

Stevenson, M. K. (2011). Minnesota Negligence Law and the Restatement (Third) of Torts: Liability for Physical and Emotional Harms. *William Mitchell Law Review*, 37(3).

Stockholm Environment Institute (1999). Costs and Strategies presented by Industry during the Negotiation of Environmental Regulations. Stockholm, Sweden: Stockholm Environment Institute.

Stoel, T., Miller, A. S. and Milroy, B. (1980). Fluorocarbon Regulation: An International Comparison. Lexington, Massachusetts: Lexington Books.

Stolarski, R. and Cicerone, R. J. (1974, January 18). Stratospheric Chlorine: A Possible Sink for Ozone. *Canadian Journal of Chemistry*, 52, 1610.

Sunstein, C. R. (2007). *Worst-case Scenarios*. Cambridge: Harvard University Press.

Suntan (2014). The History of the Suntan. Retrieved from suntan.com: www.suntan.com/?factshistory.

Syngenta (2013). Company History. Retrieved May 2014, from Syngenta: www.syngenta.com/global/corporate/en/about-syngenta/Pages/company-history.aspx.

Teich, M. (2010). Nations Unite Against Tanning: The Impact of the IARC Report. *The Melanoma Letter*, 28(2).

Teramura, A. (1986). Overview of Our Current State of Knowledge of UV Effects on Plants. In *Stratospheric Ozone and Climate*.

Thomas, H. (1978). Some Non-Essential Aerosol Propellant Uses Finally Banned. Retrieved June 3, 2012, from University of New Mexico School of Law Library: http://lawlibrary.unm.edu/nrj/19/1/16_thomas_some.pdf.

Thomas Reuters (2014). Wrongful Death Overview. Retrieved from FindLaw: http://injury.findlaw.com/torts-and-personal-injuries/wrongful-death-overview.html.

Tobacco Settlement Proceeds (1988). Retrieved from Texas Department of State Health Services: www.dshs.state.tx.us/tobaccosettlement/tobsett.shtm.

Tol, R. S. (2002). Estimates of the Damage Costs of Climate Change. Part 1: Benchmark Estimates. *Environmental and Resource Economics*, 47–73.

Tran, A. D., Aalborg, J., Asdigian, N. L., Morelli, J. G., Mokrohisky, S. T., Dellavalle, R. P. *et al.* (2012). Parents' Perceptions of Skin Cancer Threat and Children's Physical Activity. *Preventing Chronic Disease*, DOI: http://dx.doi.org/10.5888/pcd9.110345.

Twerski, A. and Henderson, J. A. (2009). Manufacturer's Liability for Defective Product Designs: The Triumph of Risk-Utility. Cornell Law Faculty Publications. Paper 794.

Tyco (2013). ANSUL History. Retrieved May 27, 2014, from ANSUL: www.ansul.com/en/us/Pages/OurHistory.aspx?value=Our History.

Underwriters Laboratories (2011). White Paper: Revisiting Flammable Refrigerants. Retrieved from http://ul.com/global/documents/library/white_papers/UL_WhitePaper_FlammableRefrigerants.pdf.

Unilever (2014). Climate Friendly Refrigeration. Retrieved from www.unilever.com/sustainable-living-2014/reducing-environmental-impact/greenhouse-gases/climate-friendly-refrigeration/.

United Nations Environment Programme (n.d.). Key Achievements of the Montreal Protocol to date 1987–2012. Retrieved December 22, 2013, from United Nations Environment Programme: https://ozone.unep.org/new_site/en/Information/Information_Kit/Key_achievements_of_the_Montreal_Protocol_2012.pdf

United Nations Environment Programme (1996). Plan for Halon Phase-out in China, Working paper submitted to the Executive Committee of the Multilateral Fund for the Implementation of the Montreal Protocol 20th meeting. Montreal, Canada: UNEP.

United Nations Environment Programme (1998). Methyl Bromide Technical Options Committee (1998). Report of the Methyl Bromide Technical Options Committee. UNEP/Earthprint.

United Nations Environment Programme (2002). Information Paper: The Montreal Protocol Control Schedule and its Evolution. Retrieved from www.unep.fr/ozonaction/information/mmcfiles/3326-e.pdf.

United Nations Environment Programme (2007). A Success in the Making: The Montreal Protocol on Substances that Deplete the Ozone Layer. Kenya: United Nations Environment Programme.

United Nations Environment Programme (2012). Data Access Centre. Retrieved from Publications: http://ozone.unep.org/new_site/en/ozone_data_tools_access.php.

United Nations General Assembly (12 August 1992). Report of the United Nations Conference on Environment and Development, Annex 1: Rio Declaration on Environment and Development. A/CONF.151/26 (Vol. I).

United States Coast Guard National Pollution Funds Center (2012, April). A Compliance Guide for Submitting Claims Under the Oil Pollution Act of 1990. Retrieved from United States Coast Guard: www.uscg.mil/ccs/npfc/docs/PDFs/urg/Ch6/NPFCClaimantGuide.pdf.

United States Consumer Product Safety Commission (1977, April 26). FDA and CPSC Announce Fluorocarbon Labelling Plan. Retrieved January 15, 2014, from US Consumer Product Safety Commission: www.cpsc.gov/en/Newsroom/News-Releases/1977/FDA-And-CPSC-Announce-Fluorocarbon-Labeling-Plan/.

United States Department of Health and Human Services (2014). *The Surgeon General's Call to Action to Prevent Skin Cancer.* Washington, D.C.: US Dept of Health and Human Services, Office of the Surgeon General.

United States Department of Justice, Civil Division (2014, June 26). Radiation Exposure Compensation System, Claims to Date Summary of Claims Received by 26/06/2014. Retrieved from United States Department of Justice: www.justice.gov/civil/omp/omi/Tre_SysClaimsToDateSum.pdf.

United States Department of Labor (2014). Division of Coal Mine Workers' Compensation (DCMWC): Important Notice Regarding Recent Changes in the

Black Lung Benefits Act. Retrieved from United States Department of Labor: www.dol.gov/owcp/dcmwc/ImportantNotice.htm.

United States Environmental Protection Agency (1987). Regulatory Impact Analysis: Protection of Stratospheric Ozone. Washington, D.C.: United States Environmental Protection Agency.

United States Environmental Protection Agency (2006). Human Health Benefits of Stratospheric Ozone Protection. Washington, D.C.

United States Environmental Protection Agency (2008, April). Starlink™ Corn Regulatory Information. Retrieved from United States Environmental Protection Agency: www.epa.gov/opp00001/biopesticides/pips/starlink_corn.htm.

United States Environmental Protection Agency (2010, October). Transitioning to Low-Gwp Alternatives in Commercial Refrigeration. Retrieved from www3.epa.gov/ozone/downloads/EPA_HFC_ComRef.pdf

United States Environmental Protection Agency (2010, August 19). Environmental Indicators: Ozone Depletion. Retrieved May 15, 2014, from Ozone Layer Protection – Science: www.epa.gov/Ozone/science/indicat/.

United States Environmental Protection Agency (2010, August 19). Ozone. Retrieved November 4, 2013, from United States Environmental Protection Agency: www.epa.gov/ozone/.

United States Environmental Protection Agency (2010). Ozone Layer Protection – Science. www.epa.gov/spdpublc/science/ods/index.html

United States Environmental Protection Agency (2011, May). Benefits of the CFC Phaseout, www.epa.gov/ozone/geninfo/benefits.html;

United States Environmental Protection Agency (2011). Health and Environmental Effects of Ozone Layer Depletion. Retrieved from Ozone Layer Protection: www.epa.gov/ozone/science/effects/index.html.

United States Environmental Protection Agency (2012). Halon Substitutes Under SNAP as of December 14, 2012: www2.epa.gov/sites/production/files/2014-11/documents/halons_as_of_12-14-12-final.pdf

United States Environmental Protection Agency (2012). Substitute Aerosol Solvents and Propellants Under SNAP as of August 10, 2012 www2.epa.gov/sites/production/files/2014-11/documents/aerosol.pdf.

United States Environmental Protection Agency (2013, June 21). Class I Ozone-depleting Substances. Retrieved March 2, 2014, from Ozone Layer Protection – Science: www.epa.gov/ozone/science/ods/classone.html.

United States Environmental Protection Agency (2013). Substitute Refrigerants Under SNAP as of May 17, 2013: www2.epa.gov/sites/production/files/2014-11/documents/reflist.pdf.

United States Environmental Protection Agency (2014). Foam Sector Substitutes under SNAP as of October 21, 2014: www2.epa.gov/sites/production/files/2014-11/documents/foams.pdf.

United States Environmental Protection Agency (2014). Skin Cancer Facts for Your State. Retrieved from SunWise: www2.epa.gov/sunwise/skin-cancer-facts-your-state.

United States Environmental Protection Agency (2014, April 29). SunWise. Retrieved June 17, 2014, from United States Environmental Protection Agency: www2.epa.gov/sunwise.

United States Environmental Protection Agency (2014). 2014 North American

Amendment Proposal to Address HFCs under the Montreal Protocol. Retrieved from Ozone Layer Protection – Recent International Developments Under the Montreal Protocol: www.epa.gov/ozone/intpol/mpagreement.html.

United States Environmental Protection Agency (2015). Substitutes in Tobacco Expansion: www2.epa.gov/snap/substitutes-tobacco-expansion.

United States Environmental Protection Agency (2015). Clean Power Plan for Existing Power Plants: www.epa.gov/cleanpowerplan/clean-power-plan-existing-power-plants#federal-plan.

United States Global Change Research Program (USGCRP) (2014). Third National Climate Assessment.

United States Preventive Services Task Force (2003). *Counseling to Prevent Skin Cancer: Recommendations and Rationale of the US Preventive Services Task Force.* Atlanta: Centers for Disease Control and Prevention.

University of California, San Francisco, School of Medicine, Department of Dermatology (2007, May 4). Sun Avoidance. Retrieved from Skin Cancer: www.dermatology.ucsf.edu/skincancer/General/prevention/Sun_Avoidance.aspx.

Vanderheiden, S. (2008). *Atmospheric Justice: A Political Theory of Climate Change.* Oxford University Press.

Van der Linde, C. (1994). Competitive Implications of Environmental Regulation in the Refrigerator Industry. Management Institute for Environment and Business.

Vanner, R. (June 2006). Ex-post Estimates of Costs to Business of EU Environmental Policies: A Case Study Looking at Ozone Depleting Substances. Policy Studies Institute.

Vinayagamoorthy, K. (2013). Apologies in the Marketplace. *Pace Law Review*, 33(3).

Volle, Seiler and Bolin (1986). Other Greenhouse Gases and Aerosols: Assessing Their Role for Atmospheric Radiative Transfer. *The Greenhouse Effect, Climatic Change, and Ecosystems*, 157.

Vulcan Materials Company. (2013). Company History. Retrieved May 2, 2014, from About Vulcan: www.vulcanmaterials.com/about-vulcan/history.

Walker, S. J., Weiss, R. and Salameh, P. (2000). Reconstructed Histories of the Annual Mean Atmospheric Mole Fractions for the Halocarbons CFC-11, CFC-12, CFC-113, and Carbon Tetrachloride. *Journal of Geophysical Research*, 14285–14296.

Wallach, J. (1992, April). Removing CFCs from old appliances. Popular Science.

Watson, M., Holman, D. M., Fox, K. A., Guy, G. P., Seidenberg, A. B., Sampson, B. P. *et al.* (2013). Preventing Skin Cancer Through Reduction of Indoor Tanning: Current Evidence. *American Journal of Preventative Medicine*, 682–689.

Weinrib, E. J. (1995). *The Idea of Private Law.* Oxford: Oxford University Press.

Weisenberg, H. (2014). Legislation to Require Expiration Date Labels for Sunscreen Awaits Governor's Action. Retrieved from New York State Assembly: http://assembly.state.ny.us/mem/Harvey-Weisenberg/story/58994/.

White House Office of the Press Secretary, The (2013, September 6). United States, China, and Leaders of G-20 Countries Announce Historic Progress Toward a Global Phase Down of HFCs. Retrieved from United States Environmental Protection Agency, Ozone Layer Protection: www.epa.gov/ozone/intpol/mpagreement.html.

White House Office of the Press Secretary, The (2013, June 8). United States and China Agree to Work Together on Phase Down of HFCs. Retrieved from same.

Whiteman, D. and Green, A. (2011). Epidemiology of Malignant Melanoma. In R. Dummer, M. Pittelkow, K. Iwatsuki, A. Green and N. Elwan (eds), *Skin Cancer: A*

World-wide Perspective. Springer-Verlag Berlin Heidelberg.

Wijmans, J. and Hans, G. (1993). Treatment of CFC and HCFC Emissions. http://cfpub.epa.gov/ncer_abstracts/index.cfm/fuseaction/display.abstractDet ail/abstract/1675/report/0.

Winer, K. (1999). Doing it Right – Overseas: Compliance Programs Take on New Importance in a Global Economy. *ABA Section of Business Law, Business Law Today.*

Worcester Polytechnic Institute, Eastern Kentucky University (2012). Ordinary People and Effective Operation of Fire. Fire Equipment Manufacturers' Association.

World Health Organisation (1990). Environmental Health Criteria for Fully Halogenated Chlorofluorocarbons. Geneva: World Health Organisation.

World Health Organisation (1998). Global Solar UV Index: Fact Sheet No. 133. Retrieved August 23, 2012, from www.who.int/inf-fs/en/fact133.html.

World Health Organisation (2002). *Global Solar UV Index: A Practical Guide.* Geneva: World Health Organisation.

World Health Organisation (2003). *Climate Change and Human Health: Risks and Responses.* In A. J. McMichael, D. H. Campbell-Lendrum, C. F. Corvalán, K. L. Ebi *et al.* (eds) Geneva: World Health Organisation.

World Health Organisation (2014). How Common is Skin Cancer? Retrieved from Ultraviolet Radiation and the INTERSUN Programme: www.who.int/uv/faq/ skincancer/en/index1.html

World Meteorological Organization (1986), Report of the International Conference on the Assessment of the Role of Carbon Dioxide and of Other Greenhouse Gases in Climate Variations and Associated Impacts Pub. No. 661.

World Meteorological Organization (2007). Scientific Assessment of Ozone Depletion: 2006, Global Ozone Research and Monitoring Project – Report No. 50. Geneva: World Meteorological Organization.

World Meteorological Organization (2010). Scientific Assessment of Ozone Depletion: 2010, Global Ozone Research and Monitoring Project-Report.

(World Meteorological Organization 2011). What are the Chlorine and Bromine Reactions that Destroy Stratospheric Ozone? In Scientific Assessment of Ozone Depletion: 2010, Global Ozone Research and Monitoring Project-Report (Vol. 52). Geneva.

World Resources Institute (n.d.). Black Market CFCs. Retrieved from World Resources Institute: http://d5.wri-main.atendesigngroup.com/publication/ content/8360.

Worley, L. L. (2006). The Iceberg Emerged: Wisconsin's Extension of Risk Contribution Theory Beyond DES. *Marquette Law Review,* 90.

Worrest (1986). The Effect of Solar UV-B Radiation on Aquatic Systems: An Overview. In *Stratospheric Ozone and Climate,* 175.

Wright (1944). Introduction to the Law of Torts. *Cambridge Law Journal,* 8, 238.

Young, C. (2009). Solar Ultraviolet Radiation and Skin Cancer. *Occupational Medicine,* 59, 82–89.

Zerefos, C. S., Bais, A. F., Meleti, C. and Ziomas, I. C. (1995). A Note on the Recent Increase of Solar UV-B Radiation over Northern Middle Latitudes. *Geophys. Res. Lett.,* 22, 1245–1247.

Ziegler, O. (2013). *EU Regulatory Decision Making and the Role of the United States: Transatlantic Regulatory Cooperation as a Gateway for US Economic Interests?* Wiesbaden: Springer.

Index